War, Culture and Society, 1750–1850

Series Editors

Rafe Blaufarb
Tallahassee, USA

Alan Forrest
York, UK

Karen Hagemann
Chapel Hill, USA

Richard Hall

Atlantic Politics, Military Strategy and the French and Indian War

palgrave
macmillan

Richard Hall
Department of History and Classics
University of Swansea
Swansea, United Kingdom

War, Culture and Society, 1750–1850
ISBN 978-3-319-80864-2   ISBN 978-3-319-30665-0   (eBook)
DOI 10.1007/978-3-319-30665-0

© The Editor(s) (if applicable) and The Author(s) 2016
Softcover reprint of the hardcover 1st edition 2016
This work is subject to copyright. All rights are solely and exclusively licensed by the Publisher, whether the whole or part of the material is concerned, specifically the rights of translation, reprinting, reuse of illustrations, recitation, broadcasting, reproduction on microfilms or in any other physical way, and transmission or information storage and retrieval, electronic adaptation, computer software, or by similar or dissimilar methodology now known or hereafter developed.
The use of general descriptive names, registered names, trademarks, service marks, etc. in this publication does not imply, even in the absence of a specific statement, that such names are exempt from the relevant protective laws and regulations and therefore free for general use.
The publisher, the authors and the editors are safe to assume that the advice and information in this book are believed to be true and accurate at the date of publication. Neither the publisher nor the authors or the editors give a warranty, express or implied, with respect to the material contained herein or for any errors or omissions that may have been made.

Cover Image © North Wind Picture Archive / Alamy Stock Photo

Printed on acid-free paper

This Palgrave Macmillan imprint is published by Springer Nature
The registered company is Springer International Publishing AG Switzerland

Preface

Atlantic Politics, Military Strategy and the French and Indian War

Summary

It was the year of 1755 that truly marked the point at which events in America ceased to be considered subsidiary affairs in the great international rivalry between two of the foremost colonial powers of the eighteenth century, Great Britain and France. Events prior to 1755, centered around the Ohio Valley (a strategically vital region of North America), had seen Britain's sovereign claims in this region truncated, as the French built a series of forts designed to hem in its rival's colonies along the Atlantic seaboard, preventing any future expansion into North America's lucrative interior.

This book is dedicated to an examination of Braddock Campaign of 1755, a component segment of the grand "Braddock Plan" devised in London and guided principally by the aggressive predispositions of the Duke of Cumberland. It was a strategy aimed at driving the French from all of the contested regions they occupied in North America. Rather than being an archetypal military-historical analysis of the defeat of General Edward Braddock on the banks of the Monongahela, this work will argue that the failure of that ill-starred officer and the wider "Braddock Plan" should be viewed as one that embodied military, political and diplomatic divergences and weaknesses within the British Atlantic World of the eighteenth century. These, ultimately, were factors that hinted at the growing schisms which would see the American colonies break from the motherland in the 1770s. Such an interpretation is to move away from the conclusion so often suggested that Braddock's defeat was a distinctly, almost uniquely, "British catastrophe." Essentially, it is my belief that the application of British Atlantic studies—and indeed "New Military" historiography—to an interpretation of the failure of Edward Braddock (and the Braddock Plan) allows this strategy, and its overall outcome, to be interpreted in a different vein than has hitherto been possible.

Acknowledgements

No book or scholarly article is written in isolation and I, like so many of my peers before me, have had considerable help and guidance at various stages during the compilation of this work. First, I owe an enormous debt of gratitude to Dr. Steven Sarson, now of the Université de Lyon, whose advice has been so incredibly useful in the formulation of the major premise of this work. Dr. Sarson's assistance has, in reality, been instrumental in improving this book on instances too numerous to count and his prompt, thoughtful deliberations are greatly appreciated.

My sincere thanks also extend to Dr. Leighton James, Associate Professor of History at Swansea University, who, sharing a passion for eighteenth-century military history, has provided many an interesting conversation concerning the direction this work has taken. His knowledge of the field has also been a source of some very useful material and for that I am, once again, extremely grateful.

Research assistance has also been gratefully received from Hugh Alexander at the National Archives (UK); Catherine T. Wood at the Norman B. Leventhal Map Center, Boston Public Library and staff at the William L. Clements Library Michigan.

There are, of course, many other debts of appreciation that I would also like to express, but these are too numerous to mention here. Finally, therefore, I must extend my deepest gratitude to my parents, whose encouragement and support has always been so profoundly appreciated over the course of the composition of this book.

Contents

1 Introduction, Book Structure and the Context of Historiography   1

2 The Causes of the French and Indian War and the Origins of the "Braddock Plan": Rival Colonies and Their Claims to the Disputed Ohio   21

3 Metropolitan Intervention: Britain's Strategy for a New Colonial War   51

4 "Stupid Brutes Led by an Eighteenth-Century Colonel Blimp?" The British Army of the Eighteenth Century   97

5 Edward Braddock in America: Provincial Politics, Indian Alliances and the Prolonged and Arduous March to the Monongahela   145

6 The Battle of the Monongahela: A Clash of Military Cultures   185

Conclusion: Braddock's Defeat and Its Legacy   227

Bibliography   237

Index   259

LIST OF FIGURES AND MAPS

Fig. 1.1 Benjamin Franklin's 1754 political cartoon 'Join, or Die'. 5

Maps:

Colonies during the French and Indian War, 1754–1760 (Accessed, 23 July 2013)
'Plan of Fort Le Quesne [sic]. Built by the French, at the Fork of the Ohio and Monongahela in 1754' (Courtesy William Clements Library, University of Michigan)
Braddock's March: 'A Plan of the Line of March with the whole Baggage' (Map reproduction courtesy of the Norman B. Leventhal Map Center at the Boston Public Library)
'A Plan of the Line of March of the Detachment from the little Meadows' (Map reproduction courtesy of the Norman B. Leventhal Map Center at the Boston Public Library)
'Map of the Battle of the Monongahela, July 9th, 1755, from a contemporary plan by Patrick Mackellar, Engineer' CO 5/46, f.135 (Courtesy National Archives (UK))

Maps and Plans

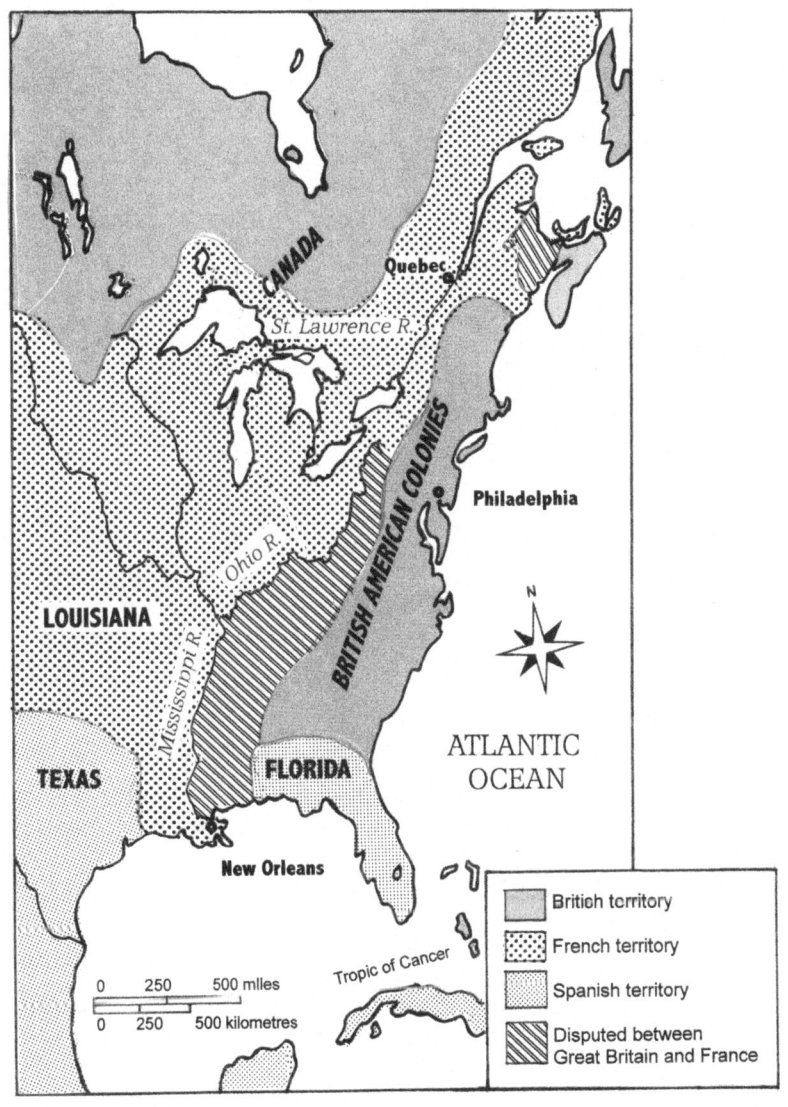

Colonies during the French and Indian War, 1754–1760 (Accessed, 23 July 2013)

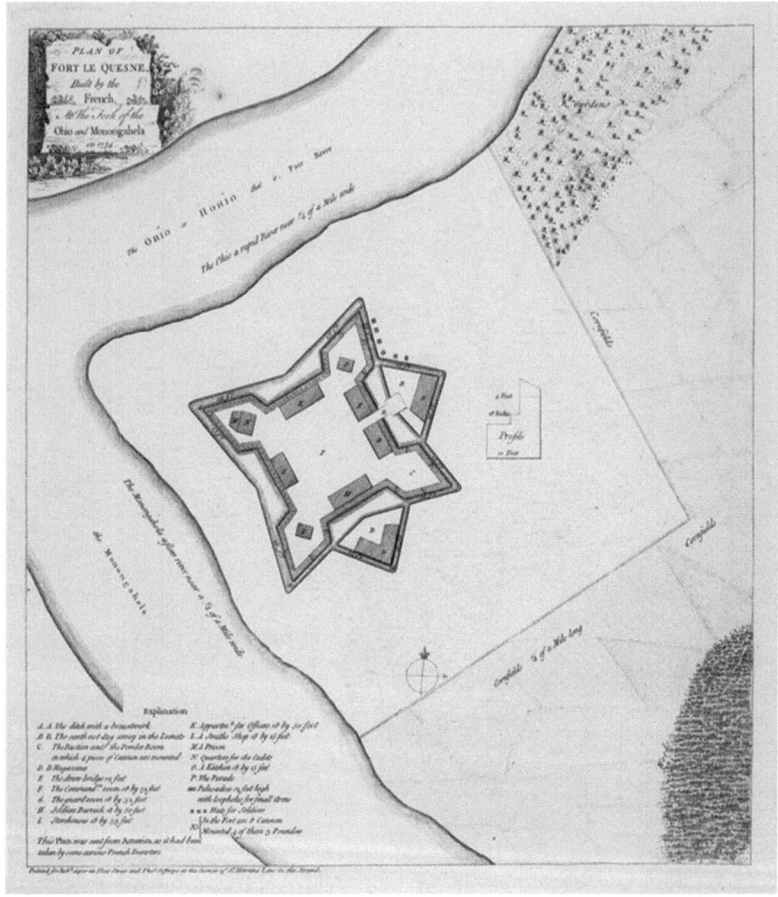

'Plan of Fort Le Quesne [sic]. Built by the French, at the Fork of the Ohio and Monongahela in 1754' (Courtesy William Clements Library, University of Michigan)

MAPS AND PLANS xv

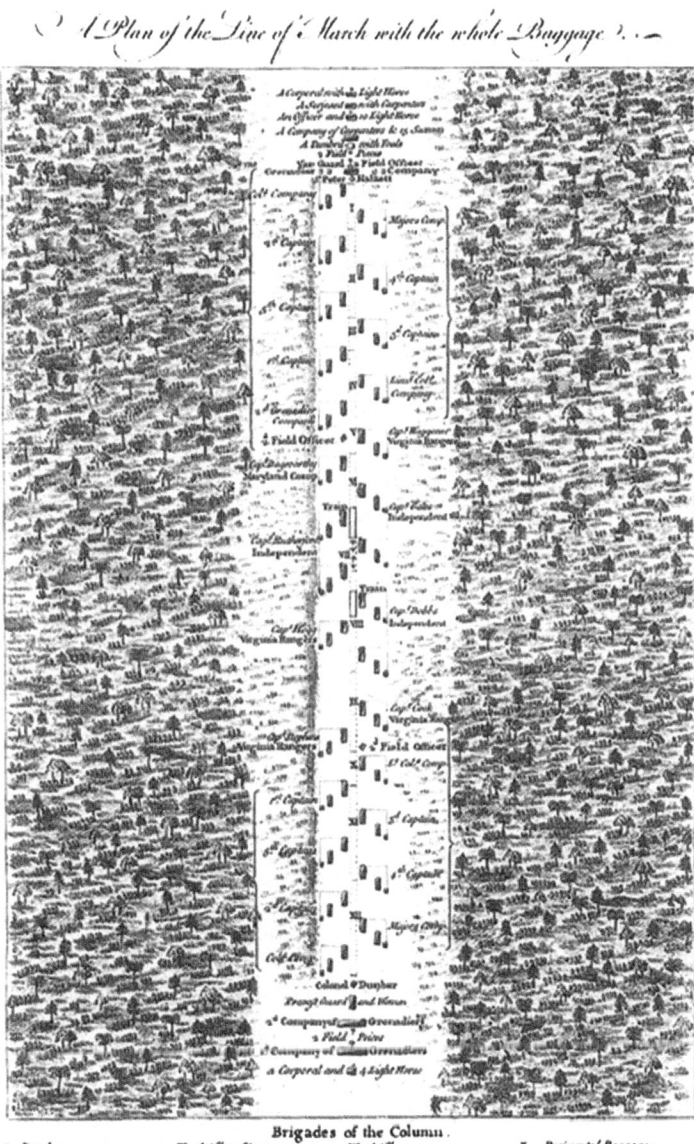

Braddock's March: 'A Plan of the Line of March with the whole Baggage' (Map reproduction courtesy of the Norman B. Leventhal Map Center at the Boston Public Library)

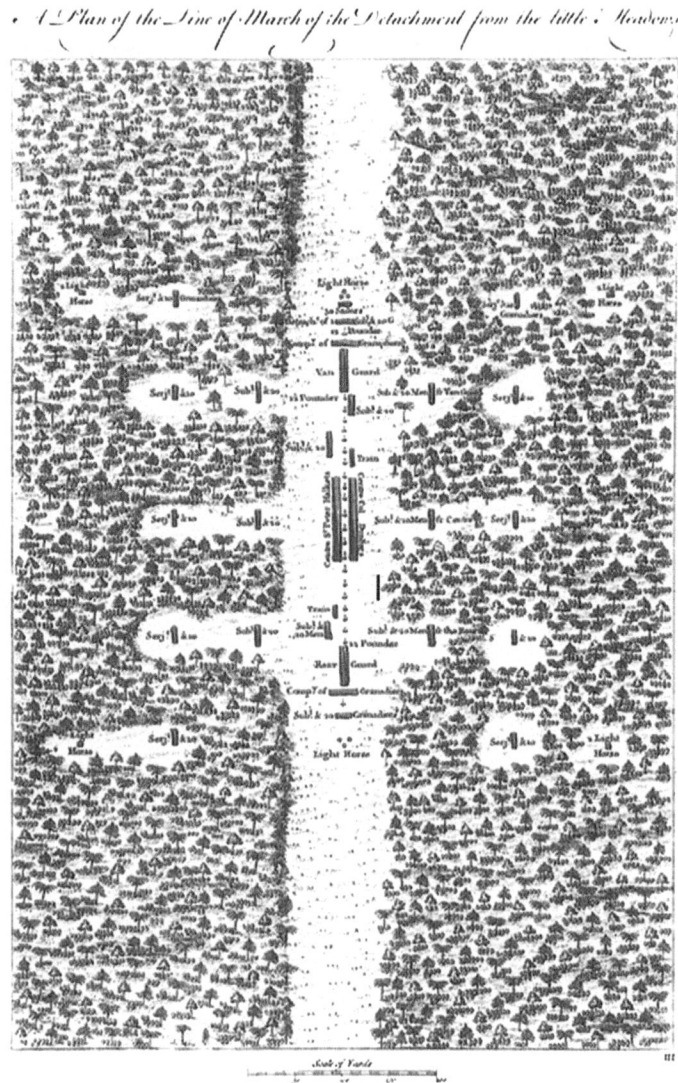

'A Plan of the Line of March of the Detachment from the little Meadows' (Map reproduction courtesy of the Norman B. Leventhal Map Center at the Boston Public Library)

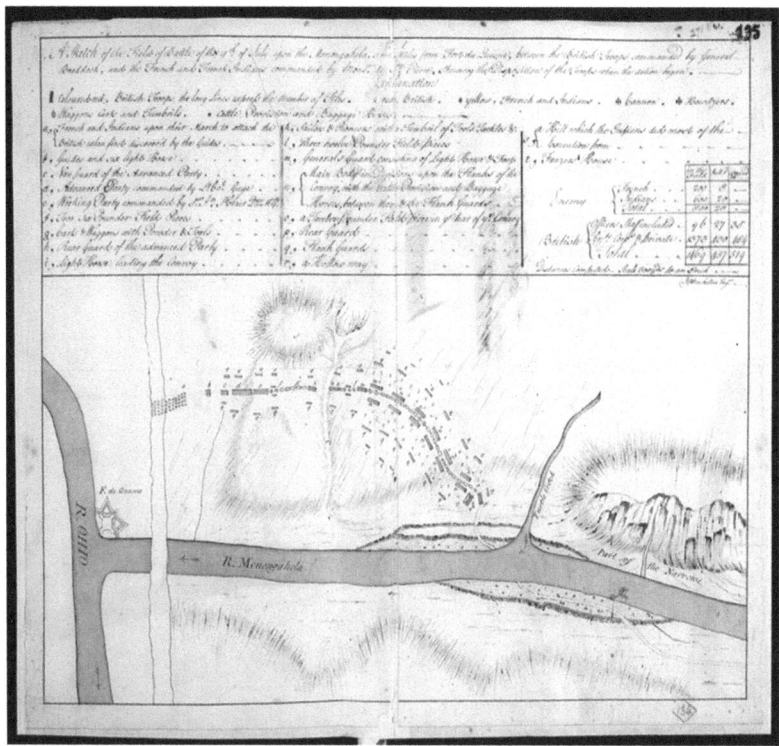

'Map of the Battle of the Monongahela, July 9th, 1755, from a contemporary plan by Patrick Mackellar, Engineer' CO 5/46, f.135 (Courtesy National Archives (UK))

CHAPTER 1

Introduction, Book Structure and the Context of Historiography

Francis Parkman, one of nineteenth-century America's most recognized early scholars of the French and Indian War, once commented that "great events obscure the great events that came before them," as he reflected on the Seven Years War and its declining relevance in the eyes of his contemporaries.[1] In this statement of undoubted lamentation, Parkman was alluding to the unfortunate reality that the Seven Years War was increasingly slipping into the haze of historical obscurity as subsequent events, such as the American War of Independence and Napoleonic conflicts, overshadowed what had been one of the world's major conflagrations. Even to this day, Parkman's reflection carries some weight and, as a consequence, legendary names such as James Wolfe, Edward Braddock, Louis-Joseph de Montcalm and Tanaghrisson (the "Half King") do not have the same iconic impact they once possessed in the eighteenth and even nineteenth centuries. Perhaps, however, it always was inevitable that the passage of time and the influence of subsequent history would push these fundamental characters and events to the back of national consciousness.[2] Certainly, unless one were to place the chronology of the French and Indian War in the context of fiction, such as James Fennimore Cooper's iconic *Last of the Mohicans* and subsequent associated twentieth-century films, then widespread familiarity with this most pivotal of conflicts is very unlikely indeed. Alas, as time progresses and as new historic epochs are written, it is probable that this great war for imperial preeminence will fade yet further into the distance of national memory.

© The Editor(s) (if applicable) and The Author(s) 2016
R. Hall, *Atlantic Politics, Military Strategy and the French and Indian War*, War, Culture and Society, 1750-1850,
DOI 10.1007/978-3-319-30665-0_1

Nevertheless, the French and Indian War and the wider Seven Years War it spawned *are* decisive conflicts in global history. The latter was a conflagration that would be fought on all of the world's major continents; from Europe to Asia, the Americas and Africa. Its immediate legacies included the bankrupting of nations, the wanton sacrifice of countless lives and the devastation of whole communities. In Europe, the Seven Years War led to the emergence of Russia and Prussia as great continental powers, while in North America, the French and Indian War was instrumental in laying the political foundations of the American Revolution; which in turn led to the birth of the United States of America.

What was an undoubtedly global war should, therefore, be proclaimed the true First World War and, indeed, this is how many historians now view this momentous event. That such a transformative conflict began in the sparsely settled and unfamiliar terrain of the Ohio Valley, a region in the then backwoods of North America, is testimony to that continent's increasing strategic importance to the courts and governments of eighteenth-century Europe.[3] From being a region completely devoid of any major European influence prior to 1492, North America, settled by the French, British (and Dutch) in the early seventeenth century, became a theater that by 1754, the eve of conflict, played a pivotal role in the great dynastic game that was European diplomacy in the eighteenth century. Consequently, as the frontiers of British and French America began to merge as they expanded inexorably, the jealousies and rivalries of the "Old World" became violently transposed upon the New.

Book Structure

The purpose of the preliminary chapters will be to outline the central premise of this project and examine the causes of the French and Indian War. Concurrently, this will provide an opportunity to highlight several features of the early skirmishes between the British and French which clearly portended some of the reasons for Britain's failure to successfully prosecute the grand designs of the "Braddock Plan" of 1755. Therefore, by assessing the rival colonies and their claims to the disputed lands of the Ohio, the territory that was truly the catalyst of the French and Indian War, it will be shown that while both sides had very real strengths and failings—politically, militarily and economically—the fractured political traditions of the British colonies, manifested in the intense rivalries that had developed between them, severely offset the vast numeric and economic supremacy they enjoyed over New France. In 1755, such divisions made the prosecution of the ambitious Braddock Plan, in particular Edward Braddock's Fort Duquesne campaign, that much more arduous, as assumptions made about the essential provisos of the strategy—recruiting colonists into the British Army, raising a colonial central fund to support the war effort, and appointing a commander-in-chief with sweeping prerogative powers (at least by American standards)—were policies that bore little appreciation of the political culture that existed within Britain's North American Empire. Further into this work, a more detailed examination of such issues will be used to demonstrate that the quasi-pluralism the colonies had enjoyed, exacerbated by the *laissez faire* attitude the British ministry had historically adopted towards the governance of its American possessions, made a hugely ambitious military strategy, devised in London, principally by the authoritarian hand of the Duke of Cumberland, and reliant upon the centralisation of authority among the various colonial *bodies politic*, flawed from its very outset.

Interestingly, the historiography of this period, specifically as it relates to the French and Indian War's final outcome, has not always shared this assumption. In the nineteenth century, the popular consensus among many American historians (those who ostensibly represented the "Whig" interpretation of the Revolutionary and pre-Revolutionary period) was that the greater individual autonomy enjoyed by the British colonies, when compared to the autocratic government of New France (and its pervasive corruption), made British victory in the French and Indian War virtually inevitable.[4] According to this theory, Braddock's defeat, for example, was a wholly military disaster that he, and his army, brought about through their contempt for their American allies and a mode of war that was unique to the New World. As an examination of that unfortunate officer's campaign proves, this was always a specious argument failing, as it does, to properly account for the impact a fractured political base can have upon a distinctly centralised military campaign. Indeed, the British colonies' inability to independently drive the French from the Ohio Valley (and other contested regions) prior to 1755 had already provided ample evidence of the divided nature of that segment of Britain's empire; and the effect such separation had upon a concerted approach to what were considered serious French encroachments in the Ohio and beyond.

Most contemporary provincial statesmen would have been familiar with the dichotomies emergent from the parochial political structure of British North America. Benjamin Franklin, commenting on provincial jealousies after news reached him of Ensign Ward's surrender of Fort Prince George at the Forks of the Ohio in 1754, would summarise the effect of British-American particularism when he lamented that,

> The Confidence of the French in this Undertaking [the capture of Fort Prince George] seems well-grounded on the present disunited State of the British Colonies, and the extreme Difficulty of bringing so many different Governments and Assemblies to agree in any speedy and effectual Measures for our common defense and Security; while our Enemies have the very great Advantage of being under one Direction, with one Council, and one Purse.[5]

Compounding this "extreme difficulty" was the fact that, within the bodies politic of individual British colonies, matters were hardly less tumultuous than the wider field of inter-colonial diplomacy. Fundamentally, internal politics in British America was a minefield of inherent mistrust between governor and assembly that was often epitomised by the struggle over prerogative powers and the respective rights of lower houses. This constitutional reality had also frequently hamstrung efforts to meet the challenges the French posed to British territorial claims in the American interior, as attempts to raise money and soldiers for military campaigns became enmeshed in disputes over who had the right to raise taxes or appropriate funds (Fig. 1.1).[6]

Edward Braddock, commander-in-chief of the British war effort in America for 1755, would very quickly learn of these tribulations as they encumbered his pivotal campaign against Fort Duquesne.

This political fragmentation within British America and its divisive consequences also hampered efforts in the crucial field of American-Indian affairs—a factor that significantly contributed to the failure of the Braddock Plan (the Acadia expedition of Robert Monkton notwithstanding) in 1755. Instead of forging a united and coordinated approach towards Indian diplomacy, the British colonies often pursued individualistic policies that protected vested local interests as opposed to any common good (including the "good" of Britain's indigenous allies).

The establishment of a Covenant Chain with the Iroquois from 1677 was one of the more successful avenues through which the British colonies had attempted to improve security and defend their sovereign rights along their borders, using Indian alliances as the guarantor of these various territorial claims. However, by the 1750s, the traditional conventions of

Fig. 1.1 Benjamin Franklin's 1754 political cartoon 'Join, or Die'.

American-Indian diplomacy had shifted considerably from what they had been in 1677. The Covenant Chain, and its subsequent evolutions, rested on the diplomatic and, to a certain extent, military primacy of Six Nations who had traditionally dominated regional politics. This provided a convenient syllogism to justify British sovereignty over the Iroquois and, by extension, their vassals in the Ohio Valley and beyond. As Francis Jennings suggested, British dominion over distant western lands became tied to a belief that,

> …if the Iroquois had conquered the western tribes who held "natural right," and had thus set up a "savage empire," Britain would have the Iroquois rights of conquest because Iroquois dependency meant that what belonged to the Iroquois belonged to Britain.[7]

The problem with this interpretation was that, by the outbreak of the French and Indian War, Iroquois power, undermined by years of near-incessant war with the French and their native allies (frequently on behalf of the English), was beginning to wane and those tribes who had once formed the vassals of "Greater Iroquoia" gradually demanded greater autonomy over their own affairs. Further corrosive to the Chain's initial premise was the fact that, over time, the Iroquois became closely linked to New York, seeking military supplies and even direct intervention in their wars against the French and their affiliated Indian tribes. When their aspirations for control of areas governed by the English led to difficulties, the Six Nations used their New York allies to resolve matters. Likewise, New York officials used their relationship with the Iroquois to promote their trading and territorial ambitions at the expense of their fellow colonies. Needless to say, this rather convenient (some feared exclusive) arrangement had for some time caused a degree of discontent among New York's equally ambitious neighbors.[8]

The issue of British-Native American relations is important because it directly affected the prosecution of Britain's strategy for 1755. Specifically, the loss of many western groups to the French by the eve of conflict requires explanation, as it was a factor that had a demonstrable effect on the Fort Duquesne prong of the Cumberland strategy (or "Braddock Plan") of 1755; in addition, of course, to the two other campaigns of this grand strategy—those of William Johnson and William Shirley in New York. Edward Braddock himself has been, perhaps rightly, criticized for his failure to retain his native allies. He, however, was merely the apex of an array of Anglo-American officials that simply did not grasp the evolving nature of Indian affairs and the implications of this among the tribes of the Ohio.

The concluding section of the following chapter will be dedicated to a brief examination of the events that would lead directly to the deployment of Braddock and two British regiments to America in 1755. The infamous Great Meadows defeat, for example, exemplifies the difficulties of merging two very different military traditions (British regulars and locally raised American units) under one unified command. This was most obviously reflected by George Washington's bitter disputes over seniority with Captain James Mackay of the Independent South Carolina Regiment, which resulted in a rather awkward (and eventually failed) joint command.[9] Unsurprisingly, this issue of precedence between British and American officers would become a notorious source of resentment between Anglo-American units raised to fight the wider French and Indian War. These divergent military traditions would also be exemplified by the conflicting approaches to warfare adopted by the British army and many of their colonial allies on July 9, 1755 at the Battle of the Monongahela; an engagement which in part demonstrated the dangers of fusing the two styles of war in a force that was mainly geared to fight in a distinctly "European" manner.

Chapter 3, "Britain's Strategy for a New Colonial War", will include an analysis of the principal men involved in drawing up the Braddock Plan and the reasons why they adopted the conservative approach that they did. This will include an examination of the foreign policy concerns of the British government in the mid-eighteenth-century which, in 1754, were challenged by the increasing economic, political and strategic importance of the American empire; a reality intensified by the perceived encroachments of the French into areas such as the Ohio Valley, upper New York and, of course, Acadia (Nova Scotia). Also to be covered towards the end of this third chapter is a brief biography of Edward Braddock himself. Here it will be shown that Braddock, as a commissioned and experienced officer, possessed many qualities often overlooked by traditional histories of the Monongahela catastrophe.[10]

For historians such as Douglas Edward Leach, Guy Fregalt and J. H. Parry (in addition to the many others who share their interpretation of Braddock's defeat), the Anglo-American catastrophe on the banks of the Monongahela is in significant part attributable to the inherent flaws (and inevitable outcome of these) in sending regular soldiers to fight on the geographic fringes of British America.[11] Therefore, in Chapter 4, "The British Army of the Eighteenth Century", the oversights of this assessment of the eighteenth-century British Army are examined by explaining its context within Whiggish, and later non-military, analyses of this institution. Essentially, in the later battle for American Independence, the British were the antagonists of the story and were thus vilified in order stoke the "manifest," or "exceptionalist," theory many Americans once applied to their nation's foundation. The experiences of the numerous colonial soldiers that served alongside the British Army during the French and Indian War—who were often so abhorred by its seemingly barbaric martial traditions—significantly helped to shape this ideal.[12] Ultimately, the aim of this fourth chapter will be to provide a more balanced review of the eighteenth-century British Army, using modern military historiography to dispel the many deep rooted myths that surround the service and, consequently, Edward Braddock and his British soldiers.

Naturally, Braddock's defeat on the banks of the Monongahela is the central act of this book and several chapters will be dedicated to understanding the context, causes and consequences of this monumental event. Such a study follows logically from the outlined examination of the British Army of the eighteenth century and will highlight how, for example, though the regiments Braddock took with him to America were British in name (or numerical denomination following a royal warrant of 1751), their constitution hardly qualified them as being the best the army had to offer. In short, they were woefully under-manned, poorly trained and had to be brought up to full-strength by draftees from other regiments, in addition to raw American recruits. The drafting of soldiers and "green" provincial enlistees, would have had a distinct impact on the caliber of men assigned to Braddock's army.[13] The fact that his force was a profoundly hybrid one makes the assertion that the Anglo-American defeat of July 9, 1755 was at root a wholly British disaster that much more difficult to sustain.

"BRADDOCK'S FAILURE" WITHIN THE CONTEXT OF HISTORIOGRAPHY

Braddock's defeat (and indeed the failure of the wider Braddock Plan), though the center of much debate within the context of wider analyses of the French and Indian War, generally has its disappointment attributed to the strategic ignorance of the British ministry, the unpreparedness of the British Army to engage Native American forces along the European frontiers of North America, and the failure (even personal inability) of General Edward Braddock, commander-in-chief of the American war effort, to adapt to the harsh realities of warfare on a continent so alien to him and his regular regiments. As Dallas Irvine (and later Ian McCulloch) have identified, in many American nationalist histories Braddock and the British Army he led thus fare very poorly, quite often appearing as the root cause of the plan's eventual disappointment.[14] Contemporarily, as one observer, in a rather stereotypical analysis of the Monongahela debacle (and one that forms something of a progenitor for so much of the battle's subsequent historiography) decried, the common colonial belief was that,

> This [Braddock's defeat] is, and always will be the consequence of Old England Officers and Soldiers being sent to America; they have neither Skill nor Courage for this method of Fighting, for the Indians will kill them as fast as Pigeons, and they stand no Chance, either offensive or defensive: 300 New England Men would have routed this Party of Indians...This is our Country Fighting.[15]

For many American scholars such as the afore-cited Douglas Edward Leach, Braddock himself was, therefore, a deeply flawed officer and—despite the failings of colonial assemblies—represented a blunt, obstinate and overbearing commander, totally out of his depth as he struggled with, and failed to conquer, the political, diplomatic and indeed military realities of a campaign in the American colonies.[16] His regular army, ill-at-ease outside of the European campaigning environment, is also likewise derided and together they are held significantly accountable for the Monongahela catastrophe.

Of course, there are truths in the assertions of this school of thought that view the Braddock's failure as a profoundly *British* setback (and for which Edward Braddock himself *can* be apportioned blame). For instance, it would be futile to argue against the contention that Braddock could never quite grasp the importance of consensus and compromise within provincial politics. This was apparent, for example, at the Conference of Alexandria, where he first conveyed the financial and supply demands of his army only to be met with the distinctly indifferent (though perfectly honest) pleas of the assembled governors that such appropriations were impossible to make without the expressed consent of their assemblies.[17] Such concerns undoubtedly irked the impatient Braddock who was schooled in martial command, not negotiation. Quite often during the campaign, the irritable general would publicly express his ire at his American allies' seeming intransigencies; frequently alienating those colonists he served alongside.[18]

Nonetheless, the political machinations Braddock encountered in America were symptomatic of much wider constitutional issues within the Atlantic World at this time; and their impact upon the Braddock Plan requires a far more thorough explanation than a simple condemnation of the commander-in-chief's so-called irascible personality, automaton tendencies and an intolerable distaste for any kind of dissent allows. Indeed, if one were to examine the works of British Atlantic historians such as Jack P. Greene and James Henretta (and their corresponding schools of thought), then it is soon evident that Edward Braddock was entering a complex political fray that he, like the British government in general, simply did not understand.[19] In America, political power had over some time been significantly devolved so that the lower houses of the various colonial legislatures were the true governing powers of their respective colonies. This was a consequence of the growing power of secretaries of state and other senior ministers (leading to bureaucratic chaos); parochial local politics and the selfish interests of domestic lobbyists—all of which was compounded by incoherent metropolitan policies. Though this "neglect" had ironically been conducive to the demographic and economic strength of the British provinces (at least when compared to their French rivals in Canada and Louisiana), such indifference to direct governance had led to politically quasi-autonomous states emerging in British America by the mid-eighteenth century. This was something Edward Braddock, who took command of a campaign that was supposedly denoted by the centralization of the colonies' war efforts (and one in which he, in theory, wielded substantial executive power), was not fully prepared for.[20]

Braddock could not, therefore, expect much in the way of assistance from colonial governors in executing his orders. These, in the absence of any real patronage (the possibility of which had been significantly truncated by the Duke of Newcastle in particular as he staunchly retained control of such appointments), had to negotiate for influence with the very assemblies they were expected to command.[21] Essentially, the North American Empire had never been one dominated by the "center." Rather, it was synonymous with the necessity of "negotiation" in which the peripheries (in this instance the various American assemblies) exerted authority over local affairs as a consequence of the historic weakness of metropolitan coercive and fiscal resources—something which had been caused by years of aforementioned British "neglect." Braddock was entering a political climate of diffused sovereignty that he, like the British government, did not understand.

Fred Anderson's much celebrated narrative, *Crucible of War* is one relatively recent work which explores the implications of this colonial paradigm in the context of a wide-ranging survey of the Seven Years War. In essence, Anderson ties what he defines as "competing visions of Empire" to the constitutional dilemmas of the 1760s that eventually led to the American Revolution and the colonies' final breach with Great Britain.[22] This work, however, contends that the "competing visions" Anderson describes and associates with the 1760s in fact became evident when the ministry's appointed viceroy for America (or *generalissimo* as the Duke of Cumberland seems to have intended), Major General Edward Braddock, brought to a head, through his attempts to wield the authority he was granted by his orders, the emerging, and increasingly divergent, British Atlantic vision of the place and extent of central authority within the empire; and the notion of British/English "liberties" that the colonists clung to, and would defend so tenaciously (and violently), in the 1760s and 1770s. Upon closer contemplation and reflection it becomes apparent that Braddock was, in essence, to be engaged in one of the first battles of two increasingly differing political cultures. These, when driven together by America's first truly large-scale "Europeanized" war began, as Stephen Conway has argued, to sense that the ideal of "Britishness" might mean different things to colonies and mother country.[23] If, as Eric Hinderaker has argued in his summary of the concept of the British Atlantic, empires were indeed "processes" rather than "structures" created by the exchanges of peoples who "could shape, challenge or resist colonialism in many ways," then the tendency of historians of Braddock's expedition to focus on his immediate leadership decisions in the field is an even greater oversight. Such analyses fail to truly acknowledge the impact the complexities of the political environment he operated within had on his mission; marginalizing a crucial factor in the failure of the 1755 campaign (and, it must be added, those simultaneous expeditions conducted by William Shirley and William Johnson in New York).[24]

Of course, it would be impossible to study the failure of the Braddock's campaign without examining the associated martial occurrences and aspects that formed the background and narrative of the campaign itself. As has been outlined in this work, within the historiography of the French and Indian War the failure of the wider Braddock Plan has, most notably in America, been categorized as a stereotypical *British* defeat that stemmed from core failures within the British Army and its commander-in-chief, Edward Braddock. In more extreme cases, as represented by neo-progressive historians such as Francis Jennings, we are also led to believe that Braddock's defeat was one of brutalized, oppressed and dehumanized automatons blundering their way to inevitable destruction at the hands of their equally fatuous, though vastly more socially privileged, officers, whose idea of leadership extended no further than the length of a cat o' nine tales or, indeed, the hangman's noose.[25]

Attitudes such as this can, and have, been challenged. Beginning with works such as Michael Roberts's "The Military Revolution 1560–1660" and later John Shy's *Toward Lexington: the Role of the British Army in the American Revolution*, military history has, over the past 50 years or so, undergone something of a much-needed revolution. Historians in the field have, and are, increasingly moving away from the "nuts-and-bolts" approach to great battles and generalship and into more focused approaches towards the social, legal and, of course, martial elements of the army.[26] Consequently, a new understanding of the British Army has emerged and it is now widely accepted that the service was an institution that fundamentally reflected the social construct of eighteenth-century Britain itself.[27] This was notably outlined in John Brewer's *Sinews of Power: War, Money, and the British State, 1688–1783*.[28]

Furthermore, with approaches to military history also moving away, albeit gradually, from a top-down examination of the relationships between officers and their men, there has also emerged a picture of army life that belies the common conception that the regular soldiers of the British Army constituted a helpless, tortured mass whose sole purpose was to die, at the behest of their incompetent officers, in a wantonly sacrificial mode of war.[29] Increasingly, it has been shown that officers, far from being exclusively the gilded and over-privileged sons of a corrupt aristocracy, were often recruited from very diverse social backgrounds and frequently endured many of the hardships normally associated with private soldiers. As Alan Guy's *Oeconomy and Discipline: Officership and Administration in the British Army* would highlight, for officers of more humble means—of which there were many in the army, particularly during wartime—a commissioned rank brought significant financial burdens that were magnified by the army's arcane fiscal system. These placed considerable economic strains on men whose pay often did not meet the sometimes extravagant expectations of those honored with the king's commission.[30] Suffering for want of a sufficient salary was thus felt by many soldiers throughout the spectrum of the army's ranks. Developing this study of the diverse origins of officers' backgrounds further, Linda Colley's *Britons: Forging the Nation, 1707–1837* revealed how significant numbers of the army's officers (and, indeed, recruits) actually came from what she describes as the "Celtic fringes" of the British Isles. As that historian demonstrated, the service offered one of precious few avenues of advancement for Scots and Irishmen inhabiting the geographical (and economic) edges of Great Britain in the eighteenth century. The by-product of this "Celtic enlistment" was, somewhat ironically perhaps, the strengthening of the "British" identity.[31]

The fact that the army was actually often far from what could (at least contemporarily) be considered excessive in its application of martial law is indicative of its approach to crime, punishment and the real rights that soldiers did possess. This, in many ways, also reflected its civilian counterparts in courts the length and breadth of the country. Through reference to the works of British legal historians such as Douglas Hay and E. P. Thompson and by extending this knowledge into analyses of military law, new military historians such as Stephen Brumwell have now been able to argue that the criminal justice system of both army and society was actually something of a legal pantomime that subtly protected the existing social order. It was based *not only* on the precepts of justice and (or through) terror—factors most commonly associated with civilian and military law at this time—but also on the careful application of *mercy*.[32]

It is modern British military historiography therefore, that further helps dismiss the idea that Braddock's defeat (and the overall failure of the 1755 campaign) represents the core and inevitable failure of British military tradition when it was applied to American martial, cultural and environmental parameters in 1755; dispelling longstanding and ill-contrived myths and stereotypes in the process. The army was undoubtedly an enormously complex institution which, nonetheless, was a very professional fighting force—even if it was noticeably small on its peacetime footing. As shall be shown later in this work, it also had significant experience of fighting irregular wars in Scotland and Ireland and had in these conflicts evinced an ability—sometimes albeit belatedly—to overcome the numerous and difficult conditions it faced.[33] That is not to say that the British Army did not have its flaws and weaknesses, several of which were indeed exposed in the planning and application phases of the Braddock Plan. These, however, are often exaggerated well beyond their real significance.

The principle concern of this book is, of course, with Edward Braddock's defeat, and this will occupy a significant section of the body of this work. Although a subject that already has a very extensive historiography—as diverse in opinions as to the cause of Braddock's eventual defeat as they are numerous in number—the catastrophe at the Monongahela provides the key real evidence that supports the overall premise of this monograph.[34] Indeed, when one examines the difficulties Braddock endured in acquiring funds, supplies, recruits for his regular regiments, native allies and even honest brokering between himself and his colonial allies, it becomes apparent that his setback really was representative of core failings not only within the colonies and their *bodies politic*, but also within the wider construct of the British Atlantic World. It must be stressed that these included divergences in approaches to warfare that become so counterproductive to the British response to the engagement of July 9, 1755.

Perhaps ironically, several noted historians, in response to the idea that Braddock was defeated because of his failure to adapt to American conditions and tactical customs, have suggested that the Anglo-American army was routed because their general did not adhere sufficiently to *European* martial traditions on the day of engagement. Few scholars, however, actually see in the defeat, or at least fully appreciate, the sometimes very negative impact that Braddock's colonial units—and the American civilians his army encountered on the march—had on the outcome of the Battle of the Monongahela.[35] Indeed, though Braddock's Virginian and Maryland forces are so often lauded for their behavior (in contrast to the "dastardly recoats" of the British Army), it is clear that Americans, both civilian and military, undermined the British effort on the logistical, diplomatic, political *and* martial levels. The first three elements have been sketched out earlier in this work, but often a forgotten component of the failed campaign is the truism that American soldiers (and civilians) sapped British morale on the long march to the Ohio Valley by feeding the Braddock's soldiers gruesome tales of Indian barbarity and their almost mythical prowess in backcountry warfare—an example of blue on blue "PSYWAR," to delve into modern military lexicon. On July 9, the irregular instincts of the Americans who served in Braddock's ranks also added to the consternation and panic that eventually swept through the British column when they met (in combat) a largely Native American French army. By reverting to an irregular mode of warfare, particularly at a time when many of Braddock's officers would have been attempting to re-establish *conventional* order upon their beleaguered men, the general's colonial contingent in reality undermined British martial cohesion.

An examination of the historiography of Braddock's defeat must surely highlight two further important titles which detail the campaign either in isolation or as part of a wider survey of the "nadir" years of 1754–1758. These are David L. Preston's, *Braddock's Defeat* and George Yagi Jr.'s Ph.D. thesis *Britain's Military Failure*.[36] Preston's work, which rightly challenges the assumption that the Fort Duquesne campaign was Braddock's to lose, does so by placing particular emphasis on the importance of Daniel de Beujeu's Canadien officers (most of them battle-hardened veterans) and their Indian allies. His assertion that the British were outthought by their adversaries on the day holds significant weight, but it is also the case that Braddock's (and his army's) response to the engagement was significantly hindered by the aforementioned clash of military cultures that occurred *within his own ranks*—something to be examined later in this work. Yagi's thesis has numerous merits too, and his belief that failings in British ministerial and colonial policy (as imposed by the Newcastle Ministry) was responsible for military setbacks during the 1754–1758 campaigns again possesses considerable merit. However, it is the assertion of this work that rather than being something that can be laid at the feet of an individual, an army, or even a body politic, British failure during the campaign of 1755 was symptomatic of far wider failings and weaknesses within the British Atlantic World of the eighteenth century. These included, as previously cited, the virtual absence of metropolitan fiscal and coercive authority in the colonies; the significant power that assemblies wielded in colonial political life; the foreign policy and financial concerns and priorities of the British ministry; legacy factors such as "wise and salutary neglect" (and its consequences) which made the prosecution of a distinctly centralized war effort in a climate of "diffused sovereignty" so difficult; martial divergences between Old and New World (including between allies); failed colonial Indian diplomacy and private vested interests that would, in combination, stymie not only Edward Braddock's campaign in the Ohio, but also the missions of William Johnson and Shirley in New York.

Notes

1. Francis Parkman, *Montcalm and Wolfe: The French and Indian War* (Boston, MA: Da Capo Press, 1995), xxxiii. Parkman's style of history has received some rather harsh scrutiny in more recent years; notably from Francis Jennings, who has been, perhaps, his most ardent critic.
2. This is particularly true of Britain's national conscience.
3. One prominent eighteenth-century French foreign minister would comment that "The King believes that it is possessions in America that will in the future form the balance of power in Europe..." Quoted in James A. Henretta, *"Salutary neglect:" Colonial Administration under the Duke of Newcastle* (Princeton, NJ: Princeton University Press, 1972), 323.
4. This argument was expressed by Francis Parkman and the renowned George Bancroft. See Francis Parkman, *Montcalm and Wolfe* and George Bancroft, *History of the United States of America, from the Discovery of the American Continent*, Vol. IV (10 vols. Boston: Little, Brown and Company, 1942).
5. Benjamin Franklin in *The Pennsylvania Gazette*, May 9, 1754.
6. Franklin's famous "Join, or Die" political cartoon was a further attempt by the wily Pennsylvanian statesman (a great believer in the persuasive power of political cartoons) to enjoin eight of the colonies to form a union in the face of the threat the French seemingly posed to the British provinces. Benjamin Franklin, "Join, or Die," *Pennsylvania Gazette* (Philadelphia, PA), May 9, 1754.
7. Francis Jennings, *The Ambiguous Iroquois Empire: The Covenant Chain Confederation of Indian Tribes with English Colonies from its beginnings to*

the Lancaster Treaty of 1744 (New York: W.W. Norton,1984), 11. Jennings, quite correctly, pioneered the now widespread consensus that the Iroquois were certainly not the homogenous Indian Empire they were depicted as being by contemporary commentators: "the Romans of the Western World" according to De Witt Clinton.

8. This had indeed been apparent for some time and was especially true of the Mohawk–New York relationship. See Fred Anderson, *The Crucible of War: The Seven Years War and the fate of Empire in British North America, 1754–1766* (New York: Alfred A. Knopf, 2000), 24. In addition to Jennings's previously cited *Ambiguous Empire*, there are a number of notable studies of the so-called Iroquois Empire during this time-frame. To be particularly recommended is Daniel K. Richter, and James H. Merrell (eds.) *Beyond the Covenant Chain: The Iroquois and their Neighbors in Indian North America, 1600–1800* (Syracuse, NY: Syracuse University Press, 1987).

9. For the ill-feeling that developed between the two men see "Colonel Washington to Governor Dinwiddie, 10th June 1754" in Robert Alonzo Brock (ed.), *The Official Records of Robert Dinwiddie: Lieutenant-Governor of the Colony of Virginia, 1751–1758*, Volume III (Richmond, VA, 1883), 197–200.

10. See, as an example, Lyman Copeland Draper, Ted Franklin Beleu (ed.), *The Life of Daniel Boone* (Mechanicsburg, PA: Stackpole Books, 1998).

11. Guy Fregault, Margaret M Cameron (trans.) *Canada: The War of Conquest* (Toronto: Oxford University Press, 1969); Douglas Edward Leach, *Arms for Empire: A Military History of the British Colonies in North America, 1607–1763* (University Park: Penn State University Press, 1973) and J. H. Parry, *Trade and Dominion: The European Overseas Empires in the Eighteenth Century* (New York: Praeger, 1971).

12. This idea is broadly discussed in Ian K. Steele *Guerrillas and Grenadiers: The Struggle for Canada, 1689–1760* (Toronto, 1974) and Stanley Pargellis, "Braddock's Defeat," *The American Historical Review*, Vol. 41, No. 2 (Jan., 1936), 253–269.

13. The full list of draftee regiments is quite baffling, belying the caliber of the units Braddock was expected to command. They included the 20th, 11th, 10th, 28th and 26th Regiments of Foot. See Thomas E. Crocker, *Braddock's March: How the Man Sent to Seize a Continent Changed American History* (Yardley, PA: Westholme Publishing, LLC, 2011), 52.

14. Dallas Irvine, "The First British Regulars in North America," *Military Affairs*, Vol. 9 (Winter, 1945) 337–354 and Ian McCulloch. "The Development of British Light Infantry in North America during the Seven Years War," *Canadian Military History*, Volume 7, (1998), 44–45.

15. See "Extract of a private letter from Boston, in New England, dated August 18," *The Public Advertiser*, 3 October 1755, in Darnell N. Davis,

"British Newspaper accounts of Braddock's Defeat," *The Pennsylvania Magazine of History and Biography*, Vol. 23, No. 3, (1899), 319–320.
16. Leach, *Arms for Empire*, 79.
17. Lawrence Henry Gipson, *The British Empire before the American Revolution*, VI, *Years of Defeat, 1754–1757*, 71.
18. Braddock would later lament, in a conversation with George Washington that it, "would be endless to particularize the number of instances of the want of public and private faith, and the most absolute disregard of all truth which I have met with." See Lee McCardell, *Ill-Starred General: Braddock of the Coldstream Guards* (Pittsburgh, PA: University of Pittsburgh Press, 1958), 212.
19. See James Henretta, *Salutary Neglect: Colonial administration under the Duke of Newcastle* (Princeton, NJ: Princeton University Press, 1972); Jack P. Greene, *The Quest for Power: The Lower Houses of Assembly in the Southern Royal Colonies, 1689–1776* (Chapel Hill: University of North Carolina Press, 1963); and Jack P. Greene, *Negotiated Authorities: Essays in Colonial Political and Constitutional History* (Charlottesville: University of Virginia Press, 1994).
20. This was a theme also explored in Stanley Pargellis's *Lord Loudon in America* (New Haven, CT: Yale University Press, 1968), which also linked back to the Braddock campaign as part of its analysis. William Johnson's and William Shirley's parallel campaigns in New York also failed largely because of disputes and problems linked to these issues.
21. The Duke of Newcastle who, when Secretary of State for the Southern Department (1724–1746), kept a firm grip on the dispensation of patronage, also took away from governors the ability to create their own power bases. Many of the men who had been appointed to "patent offices" actually worked with local assemblies, further weakening executive authority. See Steven Sarson, *British America 1500–1800: Creating Colonies, Imagining an Empire* (London: Hodder Arnold, 2005), 203.
22. Fred Anderson, *The Crucible of War: The Seven Years War and the fate of Empire in British North America, 1754–1766* (New York: Alfred A. Knopf, 2000) and John Phillip Reid, *The Constitutional History of the American Revolution*, 4 Vols. (Madison: University of Wisconsin Press, 1986–1993).
23. Arguably, this divergence of imperial vision first emerged from the embers of the War of the Austrian Succession as Britain began to adopt a more authoritarian approach towards its empire. See Stephen Conway, *War, State and Society in Mid-eighteenth century Britain and Ireland* (Oxford: Oxford University Press, 2006), 230.
24. Eric Hinderaker, *Elusive Empires: Constructing Colonialism in the Ohio Valley, 1673–1800* (New York: Cambridge University Press, 1997), xi.

25. See, for example, Francis Jennings, *Empire of Fortune: Crowns, Colonies and Tribes in the Seven Years War in America* (New York: W.W. Norton, 1988) 208–10, 422.
26. Michael Roberts, "The Military Revolution 1560–1660" in Clifford J. Rogers (ed.) *The Military Revolution Debate: Readings on the Transformation of Early Modern Europe* (Boulder, CO: Westview Press, 1995), 13–36 and John Shy, *Toward Lexington: the Role of the British Army in the American Revolution* (Princeton, NJ: Princeton University Press, 1965).
27. Sir John Fortesque *A History of the British Army* 2nd edition (19 vols. New York: AMS Press, 1976).
28. John Brewer, *Sinews of Power: War, Money, and the British State, 1688–1783* (New York: Alfred A. Knopf, 1988).
29. Old habits were slow to evolve, however. Though Sylvia Frey in her work *The British Soldier in America: A Social History of Military Life in the Revolutionary Era* (Austin: University of Texas Press, 1981), took a bottom-up approach to officer–men relations, she overemphasized the helplessness of the enlisted man's plight. Thus her book bears greater resemblance to many negative stereotypes of the British Army depicted in numerous earlier general histories of the period.
30. Alan Guy, *Oeconomy and Discipline: Officership and Administration in the British Army 1714–1763* (Manchester: Manchester University Press, 1985).
31. Linda Colley, *Britons: Forging the Nation, 1707–1837* (New Haven, CT: Yale University Press, 1992).
32. See Douglas Hay, "Property, Authority and the Criminal Law," in Douglas Hay, Peter Linebaugh, John G. Rule, E.P. Thomson & Cal Winslow, *Albion's Fatal Tree: Crime and Society in Eighteenth-century England* (New York: Random House, 1975), 17–63; E.P. Thompson, *Whigs and Hunters: The Origin of the Black Act* (New York: Pantheon, 1975) and Stephen Brumwell, *Redcoat: The British Soldier and War in the Americas, 1755–1763* (Cambridge: Cambridge University Press, 2002).
33. See John Grenier's analysis of the British campaign in the Scottish Highlands. John Grenier, *The First Way of War: American War Making of the Frontier* (Cambridge: Cambridge University Press, 2005), 107–111.
34. David L. Preston's *Braddock's Defeat: The Battle of the Monongahela and the Road to Revolution* (New York: Oxford University Press, 2015) and Crocker, *Braddock's March*. For other detailed works on Braddock's campaign see, Lee McCardell, *Ill-starred General: Braddock of the Coldstream Guards* (University of Pittsburgh, 1958), Paul E. Kopperman, *Braddock at the Monongahela* (Pittsburgh, PA: University of Pittsburgh Press, 1992) and Crocker, *Braddock's March*.

35. See Peter Russell, "Redcoats in the Wilderness: British Officers and Irregular Warfare in Europe and America, 1740–1760," *The William and Mary Quarterly*, 3rd Ser., Vol. 35 No. 4 (October, 1978), 629–652 and Pargellis, "Braddock's Defeat," 253–269.
36. David L. Preston, *Braddock's Defeat: The Battle of the Monongahela and the Road to Revolution* (New York: Oxford University Press, 2015) and George Yagi, A Study of Britain's Military Failure During the Initial Stages of the Seven Years' War in North America, 1754–1758 (Ph.D. thesis: Exeter University, 2007).

CHAPTER 2

The Causes of the French and Indian War and the Origins of the "Braddock Plan": Rival Colonies and Their Claims to the Disputed Ohio

The principal catalyst for the French and Indian War that befell North America in 1754 was the issue of sovereignty over the Ohio Valley. As both European powers inexorably pushed their traditional colonial boundaries into hitherto "unsettled" lands, the geographic confines of the continent ensured that, eventually, the French and British Empires would meet in the interior of the continent. The strategic and economic value of the Ohio Valley was certainly not lost on contemporary commentators. As English botanist John Mitchell would outline in his reflective work of 1757, *The Contest in America between Britain and France,*

> Nature itself has conspired to render the river Ohio hereabouts a place of consequence of all the people in North America that are within reach of it, far and nigh... To these ponds and other salt springs hereabouts, great flocks and herds of deer and wild oxen constantly resort... This draws numbers of huntsmen here to pursue their game, the chief employment of these parts. The traders again follow the huntsmen for their skins and furs. These are the chief causes of war...[1]

In truth, even this particularly astute analysis does not fully do justice to the profound importance of the Ohio country to Britain's burgeoning American empire. In essence, the disputed lands of the Ohio provided the only possible means of access to the interior of the continent and were therefore pivotal to the empire's future prosperity. This was because the

Appalachian Mountains, a natural wall or barrier that physically locked British America to the east coast of North America, made internal navigation and settlement acutely problematic. By the 1750s colonial statesmen, merchants, landed gentlemen (particularly those of Virginia and Pennsylvania) and the British government itself (though initially hostile to the idea of an expensive, sprawling, territorial empire), understood that the fertile expanses of the Ohio had to become indisputably British if their American colonies were to avoid being hemmed in along the eastern seaboard of North America—and choked into submission by the French and their native allies. For Virginia and Pennsylvania in particular, two rival colonies with strong public and private vested interests in the region (through land claims), the avoidance of economic stagnation and the potential social upheaval this would entail depended upon acquiring new territories that would meet the demands of their agrarian economies and growing populations. Virginia, a colony that depended upon the labor-and-land intensive tobacco plant for its economic prosperity, perhaps had the most to lose from ceding control of the Ohio to the French or, indeed, to Pennsylvania (and other neighboring colonies). This contested region provided a new and unique opportunity for ambitious speculators, planters and merchants looking to profit from the lucrative and virtually uninhabited lands that sat on the colony's western frontier.[2]

Virginia's (and by extension Britain's) claim to the disputed lands of the Ohio Valley could be traced to the First and Third Charters of the Virginia Company. In 1609 and later 1612, these decreed that all lands constituting the colony of Virginia would be inalienably the territory of England. Any future territories discovered (stretching from Cape Comfort [Virginia] to the furthermost western sea of the North American continent) would also form an undisputable element of England's new-found realm.[3] For much of the seventeenth and eighteenth centuries however, Virginia and its fellow English, later British, colonies were simply numerically unable to exploit their claims to the American interior. Consequently, colonial officials, like their French counterparts, understood that what was required to maintain their sovereignty over bordering regions was a form of indirect control that would keep these areas nominally British until such time as the land could be populated by new waves of colonists.

In contrast to Virginia, which was established for its potential mercantile benefits, Pennsylvania had originally been founded (though not exclusively, it must be added) by the pacifist Quakers, a group who initially sought freedom from religious persecution in the Old World. The colony quickly proved to be a successful venture and by the 1750s its prosperous economy was based largely on domestic agriculture and an embryonic industrial base concerned with the manufacture of textiles, among other things.[4] From their first manifestation in America, Pennsylvania and its governing class, dominated by the proprietary Penn family, did not participate in the land grabs that were associated with other British colonies like Virginia, and therefore enjoyed a more peaceful coexistence with local native tribes. Nonetheless, as time progressed and the attractions of the Quaker colony became widespread knowledge in Europe, the province saw a large influx of peoples who did not necessarily share the Quakers' tolerant and pacifist religious theology. Accordingly, by the 1720s, Pennsylvania had required further lands and resources to accommodate these new, hopeful and ambitious colonists. Just as Virginia would quickly realize, access to such territories depended upon establishing a presence in the Ohio region, and Pennsylvania, with numerous internal demands for more land to accommodate its new immigrants, in addition to a burgeoning class of merchants who saw the region as an opportunity to exploit the lucrative Anglo-Indian fur trade that existed there (not forgetting those who foresaw immense land-speculation possibilities), was determined to press its claim to the Ohio territories. This would naturally bring it into dispute with its neighbors, which included Virginia, Maryland and New York.[5]

Of course, the Virginia–Pennsylvania rivalry was one of many such transcolonial jealousies that were synonymous with the distinct British provinces that had been established along the east coast of North America by the time of the outbreak of the French and Indian War. Rather than being a homogenous entity, British North America was epitomized by these quasi-autonomous states, each possessing its own unique social structure, geopolitical priorities, and economic ambitions. Travelling through British North America in the eighteenth century, English clergyman Andrew Burnaby would exemplify the antipathy that stemmed from this distinctively separate segment of the British Empire when he commented in his work, *Travels Through the Middle Settlements in North America*, that "Nothing can exceed the jealousy and emulation which they [the colonies] possess in regard to each other."[6] Appreciating the depth of such "jealousies," he predicted that "Were they left to themselves, there would soon be a civil war from one end of the continent to the other." History would show the accuracy of this succinct vision, even if it was a little premature; civil war would not erupt in America until 1861.

In truth, the widespread divisions that existed within British America were hardly tempered by the *laissez faire* attitude (at least prior to 1748) the British government had adopted towards the administration of its American possessions. By 1751, nine of Britain's North American colonies were royal colonies. Maryland and Pennsylvania were proprietary colonies of the Calverts and Penns respectively, while Rhode Island and Connecticut had their original charters that allowed their legislatures to appoint governors. Yet, even within the royal colonies, the reality was that power, over many decades, had been devolved into the hands of lower assemblies; with the ability of governors to exercise their prerogative influence likewise truncated. With the exception of the Navigation Acts and other mercantile dictates, in addition to policies related to imperial defense, the colonies had thus been left to run their own affairs through their local legislatures, with minimum interference from the metropolitan government.

This dilution of central authority was further compounded by the general ineffectiveness of the governors charged with representing British interests in America. Many, indeed, chose to administer their duties in absentia; ignoring the 3000-mile gap between England and its colonies and the impossibility of implementing centrally derived dictates over such a long distance. When combined, these factors had breathed an air of autonomy and independence into local colonial assemblies. Certainly, when Chief Justice Peter Oliver of Massachusetts later observed (just prior to the outbreak of the American Revolution) that, "When Jove is distant, lightening is not to be feared," he exposed the obvious physical and practical constraints nature had historically placed upon British influence over its American Empire.[7] Combined with the loose reins the mother country itself had steered its American possessions with prior to 1755, in addition to the notable lack of coordination between the differing bodies that exercised various forms of authority within the empire, executive power was thus essentially hamstrung, forcing those governors who chose to remain in America to form local alliances.[8] This, concurrently, led to what Jack P. Greene has called the "domestication" of governors, in turn epitomizing the "latent dysfunction" that lay at the heart of the empire.[9]

What had emerged in British America, therefore, was a distinctly tiered form of governance, where there existed checks and balances to ensure a degree of representation for most classes of people. At the head of a typical royal colony was the governor, appointed by the crown for a varied period and who was charged (along with his council) with appropriations and expenditures within his province. His said council acted as advisors (effectively a cabinet) and in Massachusetts for example, constituted the upper house of the legislature and frequently formed the highest court of the colony (it should be noted that in Massachusetts, the lower house of the assembly actually appointed the governor's council). Beneath these councils were the assemblies, or lower houses. They represented the *people* and were elected by them according to the colonies' varying definitions of franchise. By the eighteenth century the lower houses of assembly had invariably acquired chief legislative power, but acts they passed, at least *theoretically*, could be vetoed by governors or set aside by the crown. Crucially, however, these third tiers of the colonial bodies politic had also wrested from their governors the crucial right to raise taxation and manage locally raised revenue, giving them enormous leverage in the colonial intergovernmental balance of power. This was very different to the supposed theory of imperial administration, whereby the duty of colonial assemblies was to pass acts and vote funds which the executive would then put into operation and distribute. The reality was that assemblies, by controlling the power of the purse, deprived governors of their autonomy. Indeed, George Clinton of New York was hardly exaggerating when, in 1752, he reflected that the only way for he and his colleagues to prosper (or be rewarded) was to "neglect their duty" for, by "their performance of it, they would only suffer." As another observer noted, every governor had two masters: one who commissioned him (the crown) and the other who paid him (his assembly).[10] This distinctively American arrangement, and the effect it had on supplying, funding and recruiting for military operations, would not be lost on British commanders (such as Edward Braddock) who, when they arrived in America, expected local executives to wield their authority in a way that facilitated martial expediency as opposed to legislative and constitutional tradition. As John Campbell, Fourth Earl of Loudon, and commander-in-chief in North America between 1756 and 1758, would lament, when faced by American political tradition and its effects on his own attempts to direct the war effort on that continent, "Governors here are Cyphers; their Predecessors sold the whole of the Kings Prerogative, to get their Sallaries; and till you find a fund, independent of the Province, to Pay the Governors, and new model the Government, you can do nothing with the Provinces..."[11]

For men like the above-mentioned George Clinton, who lacked the network of patronage that would have enabled them to manipulate local government, the expectations and demands of a London ministry which was, by the outbreak of the French and Indian War, scrambling to reassert control over its fractious colonists in the face of a new French threat, were impossible to enforce.[12] London could demand that its governors appropriate sums of money for colonial defense, for example, but with little real authority in the face of an intransigent assembly, such demands would prove impossible, unless they could convince members that it was in their best interests, and those of their voting constituents, to act.[13] As many have acknowledged (including the revered Benjamin Franklin, it will be remembered), this pluralism, despite its representative merits, did not always suit the expediencies of war. In turn, the constitutional, legal and taxation-related disquiet omnipresent within colonial bodies politic had a demonstrable effect in the drive to defend British interests in the Ohio and other contested regions. Indeed, metropolitan officers such as Edward Braddock, sent to command the Anglo-American war effort in North America (and possessing, superficially at least, vice-regal powers), would become enmeshed in these deep-rooted particularist disputes, as well as the vexations associated with coordinating the war efforts of so many distinct, separate and virtually autonomous colonies.[14] A purely martial analysis, based on the narrow prism of a battlefield defeat (or a military campaign), would ignore the depth of the task that Braddock faced in prosecuting a distinctly centralized war-effort in the midst of *de facto* politically independent provinces. It was a mission that also had to be completed, crucially, in a very short time-frame—magnifying the difficulties the ill-fated general would face.

Despite its reluctance to directly intervene in the administration of its American colonies, by 1750 the British government, too, appreciated the strategic value of the remote Ohio Valley to the nation's security and imperial ambitions. More interested in keeping France out of the Ohio than it was in the internal struggles of its fractious colonists, the British government had begun to fear that French hegemony in America would lead to the tipping of the all-important balance of power in Europe, which the ministry, epitomized by the Duke of Newcastle in particular, had historically spent so much time, treasure and blood to preserve.[15]

The realization of growing French ambitions in North America also, therefore, resulted in a shift in policy towards the colonies and their defense. Before the mid-eighteenth century, many British politicians, increasingly representative of the powerful merchant classes beginning to dominate politics of the period, had been opposed to expansive territorial empires and large standing armies with all the constitutional and economic difficulties they brought. The goal of empire was to trade and turn a profit as quickly as possible. As such, the conquest of vast swathes of supposedly uninhabited territories was hardly desirable for politicians and their vote-wielding constituents, who knew that bureaucrats and soldiers required copious outlays of hard-earned money. Nevertheless, it was also widely accepted that if France gained the upper hand over Britain's economically vital North American interests, by seizing what were potentially some of the most lucrative and asset-rich territories in the New World, then a large standing army and an even larger navy would have to be raised to counter the threat posed by eventual French primacy in America *and* Europe, where she was already the acknowledged foremost power and threat to Great Britain.[16]

This global geopolitical consideration ran parallel to a second, and more far-reaching, prospect of territorial confinement in America leading (eventually) to fraternally induced economic upheaval on the home front. Essentially, French control of the west would hem in the British colonists on the North American eastern seaboard, over time causing rapid population growth in a restricted area. This would drive down wages in the colonies, enabling American manufacturers to compete with their British counterparts. Industrialists in Britain would have to cut overheads or reduce wages to meet this trans-imperial economic challenge and, consequently, the specter of internal social disturbances would become a very real possibility.[17]

It is clear, therefore, why the fate of the American colonies, manifested in the question of sovereignty over the Ohio Valley, was one that simply could not be ignored by the British government, let alone by the colonies themselves, who had longstanding vested interests in the region. However, the politically fractured nature of the British provinces undermined any concerted effort to press their claims to this lucrative territory. Yet, what cannot be overlooked when examining the underlying causes of the French and Indian War is the fact that the Ohio was also considered the sovereign territory of Britain's great imperial rival, France. Indeed, this region was considered equally pivotal to France's American ambitions and, as such, the latter were just as determined to defend their perceived sovereign rights there.

New France and Its Claim to the Ohio Valley

Like its British rivals to the south, Canada (or New France), was settled in the early seventeenth century and by 1750 had grown into a colony of around 55,000 inhabitants.[18] Canadian society and its overarching political construct were very different from those found in the English (later British) colonies. As has been seen, within the English colonies there had evolved over time a distinctly devolved order of governance that brought a range of benefits and frustrations to both the colonists and their metropolitan government. By contrast, in Canada, religion and government closely resembled that of "Old France," which was an absolute, autocratic Catholic monarchy at this time. As Francis Parkman once proclaimed, New France was a true "wilderness autocracy" and, despite that scholar's sometimes evident flaws of historical analysis, it is difficult to argue with his assessment.[19] Indeed, the power structure of Canada in reality consisted of three major figureheads; the governor-general, *intendant* and bishop, who between them controlled the military, diplomatic, economic and spiritual affairs of the colony. Despite the possibility of governor–*intendant* conflict and the great (and in this case realized) danger of debilitating corruption manifesting through the unaccountable nature of this model of government, the unified and somewhat absolute command structure New France's government provided gave that colony distinct advantages in terms of directing native diplomacy and conducting a concerted war effort.[20] Benjamin Franklin's observation that early French successes in the contest for the American interior owed much to them being "under one Direction, with one Council and one Purse" exemplified the benefits such a narrow chain of command provided.[21]

Strategically, New France enjoyed a very strong, centralized position, as it was established along the major waterways of North Eastern North America: the St. Lawrence River and, by the outbreak of the French and Indian War, the Lake Champlain waterway. At the tip of the St. Lawrence was Quebec, administrative capital of the colony and the largest settlement in France's North American empire. Montreal was the second city of the colony and was a settlement of particular diplomatic and economic significance. It was perfectly sited on the continent's main fur trading routes and was a useful means of tempting native traders away from English posts and settlements along frontier New York and New England. It was also the colony's *entrepot*, supplying the *Pays d'en Haut* and other frontier communities with the goods and provisions they needed for trade and native diplomacy.

The *Pays d'en Haut*, which today broadly constitutes the Great Lakes region, though nominally a possession of the French Crown, was very sparsely populated, with settlements being limited to small forts and trading posts. Such examples included Forts Niagara, Detroit, Michilimackinac and Saulte Ste. Marie. In times of peace, these were lightly manned by the

Troupes de la Marine and were mainly concerned with appropriating, or cementing, New France's vital alliances with the continent's indigenous peoples; relationships that also allowed the French to retain their control of this vast region.[22]

The influence the French had, through the Jesuit Order, over the spiritual and thus political machinations of the tribes who lived among and alongside New France is worthy of note.[23] The importance of the interconnectivity of this tradition was acknowledged, and encouraged, by the very highest authorities within the Canadian government. As Philippe de Rigaud de Vaudreuil, governor-general of New France in the early eighteenth-century, would express,

> Of all the means that can be used to keep the Indians on our side, there is none more effective than giving them missionaries, because these missionaries by teaching them the principles of religion hold them by the influence they acquire over their minds and render them more peaceful…[24]

It would be quite wrong to conclude, however, that the establishment of missionaries and trading posts indefinitely won over the tribes concerned to the French cause. In reality, native groups quite rightly saw themselves as independently functioning entities, considering their role as that of *allies* of France who, nonetheless, reserved the right to switch allegiances if the benefits of an English alliance exceeded those on offer from the French.[25] By the mid-eighteenth century, many tribes in the northeast found themselves in a battle for their very existence as the pressures of a great European-style conflict were imposed onto the continental interior. Independence and the ability to forge their own policies and alliances was, for such groups, a matter of pure survival under such trying circumstances.

In addition to its St. Lawrence and *Pays d'en Haut* settlements, Canada enjoyed control of one other significant territory in North Eastern North America (or at least a portion of it). This was Acadia, Nova Scotia to the British, and here was to be found France's most expensive and elaborate North American fortress—the vaunted "Dunkirk of North America," otherwise known as Louisbourg. Despite a general belief in its invincibility, this celebrated fortress had been captured by a combined Anglo-New England force in 1745, but was returned to France via the treaty of Aix-la-Chapelle in 1748, causing a great degree of Anglo-American antipathy in the process. Since that time, copious sums of money had been spent reinforcing it, and by the outbreak of the French and Indian War,

Louisbourg once again fulfilled its role as guardian of the entrance to the St. Lawrence; protecting Canada from a sudden British naval descent on the colony.[26] Acadia itself was a flashpoint that would contribute to the outbreak of the French and Indian War and the conflict there was of the most brutal, irregular kind. The eventual expulsion of the French-Acadian population in 1755, for example, is one of the more contentious episodes in Britain's imperial history: many French Acadians were forcibly relocated to mainland Canada or Louisiana, where their situation became nothing short of deplorable.

To the south of Canada lay France's second important North American colony, Louisiana. This had been established at the mouth of the great Mississippi River; its two most important settlements were St. Louis and New Orleans. Although sparsely populated, by the mid-eighteenth century its strategic value was nonetheless indisputable. The Illinois country was becoming an important source of iron products, furs and food (the land here was conducive to farming), while the colony's significantly creolized manpower provided very useful partisan leaders who were well-versed in frontier warfare.[27]

As a tributary of the Mississippi, the Ohio River and its adjoining lands were a territory that the French considered their own. When the famous explorer Sieur de la Salle travelled down the Mississippi River in the 1680s, claiming the delta for the French crown, France believed that it had a legitimate and unassailable claim to all such domains. Strategically, it is quite striking why control of the Ohio was of paramount importance to the French. Quite literally, it linked New France and Louisiana, meaning that the two territories could trade with and reinforce one another via the interior of the continent. It was also felt that control of the Ohio would prevent the demographically superior British from "flooding" into the interior of North America, thus cutting France's possessions there asunder and overwhelming them by sheer weight of numbers.[28] Like the British though, the French would initially attempt to rule the territory indirectly, by exploiting local native alliances which, despite New France's inherent political and economic weaknesses, they were better able to maintain. For a nation that, strategically speaking, held a colony that would be described by historian Stanley Pargellis as one "large fortress," the vast numeric imbalance that existed with British America had to be offset by tactical acumen in frontier warfare, and for many years the French had been successful in that task.[29]

Indeed, the fact that a significant proportion of the male *habitants* of New France lived and hunted among Canada's indigenous peoples meant that New France possessed a pool of partisan leaders and militiamen perfectly suited to the hit-and-run spoiling raids that devastated the frontier regions of British North America.[30] This historically had served to offset the numerical imbalance between the antagonists by tying down larger English forces at frontier forts. When allied to Canada's traditional American-Indian allies, New France was thus able to call upon a lethal collection of highly skilled frontier warriors who were more than a match for any unit the British could deploy at any stage during the French and Indian War. Certainly, French successes in the "asymmetric" battles and raids of 1755–1757 (including Braddock's defeat at the Battle of the Monongahela) were often attributable to the presence and prowess of Indian warriors and Canadien militia (as well as *Troupes de la Marine* officers).

The Iroquois and the Ohio Valley: The Pre-French and Indian War Failure of Anglo-American Native American Diplomacy

By far the most demographically significant of the region's native peoples during the early colonial period was the renowned Iroquois Confederacy (sited, broadly speaking, in modern-day New York state). The Iroquois inhabited a pivotal region that lay between the competing European empires and traditionally had possessed sufficient warrior power to turn any conflict in favor of either antagonist. As such, they were coveted by both the British and French, who desperately sought to engage them in their quest for territorial gain. Hence, in exchange for recognition of their regional supremacy, in addition to copious quantities of trade goods and presents, the Iroquois were willing to exert their diplomatic and sometimes military influence as they interceded between Europeans and other native groups.[31] It would be quite wrong, however, to see this admittedly powerful group as a homogenous, omnipotent forest empire, for that would be to misrepresent the structure of this confederacy of tribes and, of course, to underestimate the complexities of Indian diplomacy in the eighteenth century. To quote Daniel Richter and James Merrell, rather than being an empire of brute force or territorial subjugation, Six Nations' pre-eminence traditionally stemmed

...less from "martial ardor" or a "thirst for glory" than from an extraordinary ability to adapt familiar customs and institutions in response to novel challenges, to convert weaknesses into strengths, and to forge alliances among themselves and with others that helped preserve native political and cultural autonomy.[32]

As Richter and Merrell alluded, an important point to consider when reflecting upon Six Nations' diplomacy and their subsequent actions is to appreciate that the Iroquois Confederacy was just that—a coalition of later six different tribes who, though bound by history and a sacred treaty, were separate entities that often had their own ambitions and strategic requirements, not too dissimilar to Britain's American colonies. For Ian K. Steele, this meant that "the confederacy's elaborate rituals promoted a broad cultural unity, but came to represent *fairly* unified diplomatic and military power."[33] Thus, when Britain, France (and, in the seventeenth century, the Dutch) appointed commissioners and diplomats to engage the Iroquois, there was no guarantee that every branch of that tribe would automatically ally itself to their cause. Ultimately, Indian diplomacy was a constantly flowing phenomenon that relied on face-to-face meetings to renew existing agreements, and this feature was particularly true of Iroquoian-speaking groups. Invariably, without the consistent renewal of alliances in these face-to-face encounters, tribal elders could not know the intentions of their brethren, and thus it would have been impossible for them to keep track of who had agreed to what arrangements. The paradox between the formal traditions of English legalisms and American-Indian verbal agreements was always striking and misunderstandings became inevitable when these two ancient traditions were thrust together as the former bartered for lands in the American interior.[34]

Generally, it was the French who traditionally enjoyed greater success when forming and successfully harnessing the advantages of alliances with bordering native tribes. There were three major reasons for this, which, ironically, grew out of New France's strategic and economic weaknesses. Most obviously, Canada had a far lighter population footprint than British America (55,000 *habitants* compared to around 1,042,000 British colonists in 1750), and was therefore considered less of a threat to native groups than its British rivals.[35] Furthermore, the traditional paucity of women within the colony of New France, particularly during the province's formative years, had resulted in many French-Canadian men marrying into native tribes. [36] Marriages with strategically valued American-Indian communities created blood links between Frenchman and Native American, strengthening the influence Canada enjoyed over local, indigenous populations. Many young Canadian men also elected to live among Indian groups, learning their customs and developing a unique appreciation of the region's topography and the skills necessary to survive in America's primeval hinterland. These men, the *Courer de Bois* of Canadian folklore, also provided significant military and diplomatic services to the colony during times of war.

The colony's economic woes also enabled it, ironically, to forge stronger alliances with Native American tribes. Because the British could sell greater quantities of cheaper and better-quality trade goods than the French, New France had to find alternative links to trade as the foundation of their Indian alliances. Such opportunities were found in service and war, with the French adopting the role of generous "fathers" as opposed to authoritarian European patriarchs. They also played numerous Native American functions, adapting to local protocols in order to assimilate into tribal traditions. Although far from perfect, and not without periods of mutual indifference, the French possessed great authority, but the Indians retained considerable voice and power.[37] It was a coexistence that brought very real economic, political and military benefits, the latter being reflected in the devastation wrought by the Franco-Indian raiding parties that plagued the British frontier prior to, and during, the French and Indian War.

Fortunately for the English (and earlier the Dutch who had first settled New Netherland), the French had not always enjoyed the same success in their attempts to enjoin the allegiance of the Iroquois. In the early seventeenth century, the then governor of New France, Samuel de Champlain, had supported the Huron against the Iroquois (the former were staunch enemies of the latter), and this had soured the relationship between the two sides for more than a century. Nevertheless, by the 1750s, years of warfare (often on behalf of the British) and a frustrating indifference of that nation's colonies towards the plight of its native allies led the Six Nations (from 1701) to position themselves as a neutral power between the French and British; using their somewhat fearsome reputation to play off the interests of the two competing European empires.[38] However, the commensurate privations associated with near-continuous war—notably a significant reduction in manpower—had taken their toll on the Confederacy, which was still eager to retain its traditional influence in the northeast; even in the face of the evolving diplomatic and political environment in the increasingly contested Ohio Valley.

Certainly, in terms of frontier security and territorial expansionism, the Iroquois had always been the most important native ally of Britain's middle and North Eastern colonies. When the latter tried to assert claims in the Ohio, the Six Nations were their only possible means of communicating with less powerful tribes in that region; a diplomatic avenue that was, by the mid-eighteenth century, increasingly archaic. Although these "other" groups (such as the Delaware, Miami, Mingo and Shawnee), had been, until the mid-1750s, *de facto* vassals of "Greater Iroquoia," they were becoming increasingly emboldened by the waning influence of the Six Nations and were eager to repatriate diplomatic powers that would enable them to independently meet the territorial pressures of growing European expansion into their tribal homelands.[39] Perhaps understandably, in view of the erstwhile conventions of native diplomacy, the British colonists and their various Indian agents allowed themselves to be convinced of Iroquois regional supremacy on the basis of their former dominance of northeastern Indian affairs (in addition to the obvious practicalities of negotiating with one confederacy as opposed to a significant array of smaller tribes). This belief in the all-encompassing power of the Six Nations would be illustrated by Thomas Hutchinson's proclamation to the "Great and General Court of the Assembly of Massachusetts" that the Iroquois had assured him that "They are a numerous people, a terrible body of men, and able to burn *all* the Indians in Canada."[40] Hutchinson and his assembly genuinely believed this bravado which truly betrayed British ignorance of shifting diplomatic patterns among native nations.[41]

As Daniel Richter and James Merrell noted in the introduction to their celebrated work, *Beyond the Covenant Chain*, there was, in fact, "no forest empire ruled by Iroquois Caesars," and the Confederacy's so-called imperial pretensions were "a fiction jointly promulgated by Anglo-American and Native American politicians."[42] Applied to British Indian diplomacy in the 1700s, this meant that, at a time when the British should have been diversifying their approach to native alliances, the metropolitan government and its colonies instead opted to entrust their fortunes to the tried-and-tested Iroquois pact. This misjudgment not only of the evolving geopolitical situation in the Ohio, but also of the flowing nature of Iroquois and Indian diplomacy (which was less rigidly structured than its European counterpart), naturally served to alienate smaller regional groups who were concurrently seeking to assert their own rights as sovereign entities.[43]

For the smaller tribes of the Ohio who had long suffered from core failings of Anglo-American diplomacy, and who, prior to 1754 had vacillated between the European antagonists, British failings (including, it seemed, indifference), brazenly illustrated by the destruction of Pickawillany in 1752, left them little choice other than to make overtures towards the French—or at least remain neutral in the forthcoming conflict—if they were to preserve their homelands and way of life. The inability, principally of the various governmental bodies of the colonies, to cement alliances with Ohio tribes who were, potentially, more disposed towards the British cause, was one of the major reasons why the Anglo-American advances into the Ohio were confounded in 1754 and 1755.

Edward Braddock, the ministry's appointed *de facto* viceroy for North America in 1755, would enjoy no greater success in this field than had his colonial and metropolitan predecessors. Though Braddock undoubtedly appreciated the need for irregular allies in the alien American interior, and he did attempt to enlist Native Americans into his force sent to capture Fort Duquesne in 1755, his European martial instincts and outlook made him a clumsy operator within this very delicate diplomatic and cultural sphere.[44] Nevertheless, Braddock, through his Eurocentric attitudes, merely intensified what was a longstanding regional native resentment towards the British and their colonies. Over many years, this antipathy had been exacerbated by a disjointed Indian policy within the provinces and London's belief, based on the advice of its governors and officials, that the Covenant Chain (or Chains) established with the Iroquois provided a legal right to—and guaranteed ownership of—all contentious lands sited on their colonies' frontiers.

In reality, as Iroquois power waned in the face of European wars and inter-tribal tensions, their diplomacy became splintered. Rather than speaking with one voice, their leaders were increasingly unable to control their own diplomatic future as they slowly surrendered control of their borderlands to the British through contentious and divisive treaties such as that forged at Lancaster in 1744.[45] Subsequent European settlement in these areas merely highlighted how far the Confederacy's power had declined and how tenuous their grip over such territories had always been—encouraging marginal tribes to forge their own paths as they fought a desperate struggle for survival. Failure to adapt to this growing reality highlighted how diplomatic weaknesses evident across the British Atlantic undermined Indian diplomacy at a time of profound geopolitical evolution within the northeast's tribal groups. This was something that would have a demonstrable impact upon Edward Braddock's campaign of 1755 and, indeed, those of William Johnson and William Shirley in New York; where factionalism again undermined native diplomacy, costing each of the prongs of the Braddock Plan substantive Native American support.

1749–1754: The Failure of Britain's Colonies to Press Their Advantages in the American Interior

The 1748 Treaty of Aix-la-Chapelle that closed the inconclusive, but bloody, King George's War had done little to ease the colonial rivalry between France and Britain, particularly in North America's contested regions.[46] This agreement, so contentious to many Britons at the time, was little more than a temporary fix to the deep-rooted enmity that existed between the two nations in the New World and, indeed, the Old.[47] Consequently, in the years leading to the outbreak of open hostilities in 1755, the colonists of both kingdoms slowly crept into the Ohio territories, testing and probing for weaknesses in their adversary's resolve, seeking any advantage that could be gained in the quest for imperial pre-eminence.

It was the British colonies who initially pressed their numerical and economic advantages in this disputed region. Following the treaty of 1748, a string of colonial traders and land speculators had flowed into the Ohio Valley, providing the natives with the European goods they craved at very competitive prices, while at the same time attempting to draw the latter away from rival French agents. The loss of influence among the indigenous peoples sited along its isolated frontiers was unacceptable to the French, who relied upon native warriors to secure their North American ambitions.

Their response, Celeron de Bienville's epic 1749 Ohio expedition, was only a temporary fix to the longstanding problem of British encroachment, and the years that followed his somewhat futile demonstration of force would see traders and speculators from Virginia and Pennsylvania course into the Ohio Valley in ever-greater numbers. These included the agents of the powerful Ohio Company (founded in 1747), which sought to divide and sell vast tracts of land in the disputed territory that, in turn, would earn enormous profits for the 20 rich tobacco planters who initially financed the enterprise.[48]

Indeed, after receiving, in 1749, approval from the Board of Trade (and then the king) for a grant of 200,000 (rising to 300,000) acres of land in the Ohio, the company began to press its goals in earnest. At the 1752 Logstown convention, the Ohio Company, represented by Christopher Gist, with George Croghan and two other officials (representing the colony of Virginia; Croghan, a Pennsylvanian trader, claimed to represent that colony) sought to wrest from the natives the right to establish a strong trading post (a fort to all intents and purposes) at the junction of the Allegheny and Monongahela Rivers; the Forks of the Ohio. This was to be linked to other company-posts, such as Wills Creek, by a road that was to be constructed through the Alleghenies. The positions, essentially, would provide Virginia with a secure and fortified base from which it could colonize the Ohio.[49]

Logstown also gave the Iroquois, and their half king Tanacharison, an opportunity to reassert Six Nations' interests in a region where their influence had clearly been eroding. Certainly, a British post at the Forks of the Ohio seemed particularly desirable providing, as it would, the supplies needed to preempt any future French pretensions to the land; while at the same time keeping increasingly resurgent Delaware, Shawnee and Miami tribes in check. And yet, in order to attain the acquiescence the tribes that inhabited the Ohio, the "Half King" had to make significant concessions that in previous generations would have been unthinkable. One such compromise was to acknowledge the Delaware's right to elect their own "king" who would henceforth speak for the tribe on matters of diplomacy. This meant that although the Iroquois had represented *all* of the tribes at the Logstown convention, eventually agreeing to the Virginian request for permission to establish a post at the Forks of the Ohio, any future negotiations between the British and the area's smaller tribes would be conducted on very different terms than had hitherto existed—if they were to have any meaning. Native diplomacy was changing, but the British and Iroquois were slow to grasp the new political realities that would soon dominate the frontiers of European America.[50]

While Virginia and its Ohio Company bartered for rights to lands in the Ohio, the French had hardly remained inactive. As the British trickled into the region in small parties, the French knew that they had to act decisively if they were to prevent the tidal wave of British settlers that would inevitably follow the initial traders and speculators into the lands of the *Belle Riviere*. In 1752, and with the aggressive Marquis Duquesne now at their head, the French resolved to send a clear warning to their wavering

Indian allies and the British traders sent to tempt them away from their traditional "Onontio." They did this by striking at one of the major symbols of Britain's emerging diplomatic and economic supremacy in the Ohio region, the Miami village and fortified British trading post of Pickawillany.[51] Rather tellingly, while the expedition's commander, Charles Langlade, descended upon the Miami with his imposing force, that tribe pleaded with Pennsylvania and Virginia for arms and aid; to no avail. Pennsylvania was overwhelmingly pacifist and militarily reticent on this account, while Virginia's elite simply did not see the need to become embroiled in what they now conveniently viewed as a "private war." Unsurprisingly, the disaffected Miami once again became a French "satellite tribe."[52]

For Governor-General Duquesne, the elimination of Pickawillany was just one facet of a broader strategy to drive the British from the Ohio. Following Langlade's success, he ordered the large-scale mobilization of Canada's militia and dispatched parties of French soldiers to begin the construction of new forts in the Ohio country. These posts (Presque Isle, Riviere aux Boeufs and Fort Machault) took advantage of New France's topographical control of the waterways that led into the interior of the continent and hence made supply and reinforcement somewhat easier than it was for the British, who were hemmed in by the Alleghenies and had few access points to the American interior.[53] A final fort was also planned for the Forks of the Ohio (construction to begin in 1754) and this would serve to "join the chain," securing the interior of the continent for France and, with native help, keeping the British out of the west in perpetuity.

In view of Duquesne's bold actions, Virginia's governor, Robert Dinwiddie, in his correspondences with Britain's Board of Trade, continually bemoaned the increasing violence British traders were being subjected to in the Ohio, expressing his deep concern that the French "... would encourage the Indians to murder our traders in cold blood" and had already, on numerous instances, "met our traders in the woods and robbed them of all their skins and goods."[54]

As Dinwiddie was very well aware, there still existed a peace treaty between England and France and a *coup de grace* simply could not be administered without the express permission of a British Government that was in no haste to engage in a new war with France. Yet, with the specter of encirclement threatening its invaluable North American possessions, the ministry, led by Thomas Pelham Holles, Duke of Newcastle, did acknowledge that some counter-response to France's intrusions was required. Typically of a Newcastle administration, however, the initial British reaction was somewhat conservative and represented a wider desire on the part of the cautious First Minister to avoid escalation of the conflict. Therefore, hoping to find an American solution to the unfolding crisis, Dinwiddie was given the authority and armaments required to establish a fort at the Forks of the Ohio (exactly where Duquesne planned to build a French post) and was provided with instructions to drive the French from "the *undoubted limits* of His Majesty's dominions." His fellow colonial governors were also instructed to provide him with appropriate assistance.[55]

In colonial America the prosecution of metropolitan dictates was never as simple as a signed proclamation or order and, to undertake Newcastle's instructions, Virginia's beleaguered governor needed to obtain the assent of the Virginian House of Burgesses to raise the funds needed to implement London's orders. Dinwiddie, however, because of the infamous Pistole Fee dispute that raged between himself and the Burgesses, was hardly on amicable terms with his lower house, with many in that legislative body expressing reservations that his planned descent upon the Ohio was simply a means of aggrandizing the wealth of the Ohio Company's influential financiers (himself included), rather than protecting the sovereign rights of the colony or, indeed, Britain.[56] As a result of this impasse, his options were limited. Hence, in the absence of the raw force required to push the French from the Ohio, Dinwiddie took the more passive choice of dispatching a diplomatic enterprise that was to formally request the French to vacate the disputed territories.

This ill-fated expedition, led by 21 year old George Washington, ultimately demonstrated the weakness of Britain's position in the Ohio.[57] After enduring all of the dangers and difficulties commensurate with a foray into the North American interior, Washington, with limited practical means to prosecute the orders contained in his instructions, received a hardly surprising dismissal from the steely veteran *Troupes de la Marine* commanding officer of Fort Le Boeuf, Captain Jacques Legardeur de Saint-Pierre. Accordingly, the young Virginian, presenting Dinwiddie's demands to the resolute Saint-Pierre, was peremptorily sent back to Virginia with the unequivocal warning that,

> ...whatever may be your instructions, I am here by virtue of the orders of my General; and I entreat you, Sir, not to doubt for one moment, but that I am determined to conform myself to them with all the exactness and resolution which can be expected from the best officer...[58]

Dinwiddie promptly dispatched Saint Pierre's riposte to the appropriate London authorities, who, seeing the gravity of the unfolding situation, gave their governor permission to raise sufficient troops to construct and defend a fort at the Forks of the Ohio. He also dispatched Washington's account (and the French retort) to his fellow colonial governors, who responded with the typical parsimony that had become a trademark of the British colonies in North America. Several doubted his claim that the contentious French forts had actually been built on British territory, while even within his own colony, Dinwiddie faced an initial political impasse.[59] After some wrangling and because their governor, following receipt of London's permission, had already begun preparations for a second mission to the Ohio, the Burgesses finally agreed to raise £10,000 to pay for a second, more potent expedition of 200 soldiers to physically wrest control of the Ohio from the French.[60]

This crucial mission was to be led by a middle-aged former mathematics tutor, Colonel Joshua Fry. The rising George Washington was to command the Virginian militia and was to act as Fry's second in command, receiving the rank of lieutenant colonel to complement his position. Concurrently, Captain William Trent, a Pennsylvania-born fur trader, was to raise 100 men, march to the Forks of the Ohio and fortify that strategic linchpin. By April 1754, he had indeed built the newly christened Fort Prince George at the forks.[61]

This was to be the extent of Virginia's success. On April 22, Washington's army received the shocking news that a large French force of over 1000 men with 18 pieces of artillery had captured Prince George.[62] Yet Washington, encouraged by news that Colonel Fry was soon to provide him with much-needed reinforcements, pressed on to the Great Meadows. Unfortunately, Fry would die after falling from his horse, leaving the inexperienced Virginian in command of this most crucial of missions. It was a happenstance that would have major repercussions for the remainder of the campaign; the first of which was the infamous skirmish at "Jumonville's Glen" that led to the death of the commander of a small French scouting party, Joseph Coulon, Sieur de Jumonville, along with ten of his countrymen.[63]

The French reaction to Washington's ill-advised assault on Jumonville's party (an action Dinwiddie had expressly asked his subordinate to avoid) was swift and ruthlessly efficient. With the young Virginian and his small army entrenched at the Great Meadows, a sizable force of French and Indians surrounded their beleaguered adversaries, who were holed up inside, and in waterlogged trenches around, the woefully inadequate but aptly named Fort Necessity. Though reinforced by 100 regular soldiers of the South Carolina Independent regiment, commanded by Captain James Mackay, the situation of the British was desperate. The abrasive relationship that developed between the party's two leading officers (Mackay, holding a regular commission, felt he was the senior officer and confronted Washington on this) worsened matters, as did the refusal of the regulars to dig trenches around the fort; at least, without receiving extra pay. It portended martial divergences that would become ever more problematic as greater numbers of British regiments were deployed to North America.[64]

Unsurprisingly then, the conclusion of this rather sorry affair was a humiliating defeat. After a bloody engagement fought under torrential rain, Washington, having lost 31 of his men killed and 70 wounded to French and Indian marksmen, was forced to surrender.[65] Following the translation (or mistranslation) of the French-written surrender document by Jacob van Braam (who only spoke French *fairly* well) Washington, in addition to finding himself forced into a capitulation, also inadvertently admitted responsibility for the "murder"—or "assassination"—of Jumonville.[66] It was a purely accidental oversight on the part of America's future first president but one which, nevertheless, had serious—and somewhat embarrassing—ramifications for the British government. More immediately, and just as critically, the French were left in undisputed control of the coveted Ohio region and now had the opportunity to consolidate their position. The stage had been set not only for the Braddock Plan of 1755 (and Braddock's defeat of July 9), but also the French and Indian, and the later global Seven Years, War.

Notes

1. John Mitchell, *The Contest in America Between Britain and France* (London, 1757), 182–183, 188.
2. I say "virtually uninhabited" from the perspective of European colonists at this time. In reality, the Ohio was home to many Native American groups.
3. Third Charter of the Virginia Company, 1612 in Louis B. Wright and Elaine W. Fowler, *English Colonization of North America: Documents of Modern History* (London: Edward Arnold, 1968), 35.
4. Fred Anderson, *The War that made America: A Short History of the French and Indian War* (London: Penguin Books, 2005), 11–16.
5. Matthew Ward, *Breaking the Backcountry: The Seven Years War in Virginia and Pennsylvania, 1754–1765* (Pittsburgh, PA: University of Pittsburgh Press, 2003), 22–24.
6. Rev. Andrew Burnaby, *Travels through the Middle Settlements in North America in the Years 1759 and 1760 with Observations on the State of the Colonies* (Dublin, 1775), 202–203.

7. Claude H. Van Tyne, *The Founding of the American Republic: The Causes of the War of Independence* (Florida: Simon Publications, 1922), 10.
8. Within the colonies there were the aforementioned governors, councils and assemblies, while Britain itself hosted the Admiralty, which dealt with enforcement of the Navigation Acts; the Secretary of State for the Southern department, who had political oversight over the colonies; the Privy Council, whose role sometimes merged with the aforementioned Cabinet office and the Board of Trade (and various other committees) that reported to and recommended actions to the Privy Council. Parliament regulated colonial trade but did not really take an active role in colonial development—at least prior to the 1760s.
9. See Jack P. Greene, *Negotiated Authorities: Essays in Colonial Political and Constitutional History* (Charlottesville: University of Virginia Press, 1994). There was a belief among many contemporary writers that the foundations of the British Empire were built on the principles of consensus and accommodation. The absence of metropolitan coercive force in the colonies during their first century and a half of existence reinforced a sense that informal cultural and economic ties (in addition to shared traditions) were sufficient to hold the empire together. See Christine Daniels and Michael V. Kennedy, *Negotiated Empires: Centres and Peripheries in the Americas, 1500–1820* (London: Routledge, 2002), 277. These theories of the "consensual empire" are further expanded upon in Paul Lankford (ed.), *The Writings and Speeches of Edmund Burke*, Volume II: *Party, Parliament and the American Crisis, 1766–1774* (Oxford: Clarendon Press, 1981). For the paradoxical opinion, see Thomas Pownall, *The Administration of the Colonies*, 4th Edition (London: J. Walker, 1768).
10. Eric Robson, *The American Revolution in its Political and Military Aspects: 1763–1783* (New York: W.W. Norton, 1966), 11.
11. Daniel J. Boorstin, *The Colonial Experience* (New York: Random House, 2000), 360.
12. When serving as Secretary of State for the Southern Department (1724–1746) the Duke of Newcastle, by retaining a considerable right to dispense "patent offices," had stripped even greater authority from the governors supposed to represent metropolitan interests in the colonies. Lieutenant Governor William Gooch of Virginia would write how this made governors "despicable" and of "little service to the crown" as it removed their ability to reward "merit" and create "Influence." See Jack P. Greene, *Peripheries and Center: Constitutional Development in the Extended Polities of the British Empire and the United States, 1607–1788* (Athens: University of Georgia Press, 1986), 46–47.
13. Herein lies a core constitutional divergence that made the American post-1688 Glorious Revolution (or, more accurately, series of revolutions)

settlement different to that experienced by Britain. Essentially, governors could not co-ordinate with provincial legislatures in the way the crown could and did with Parliament in London—for this would have put them at odds with their metropolitan masters. Even when they acquiesced with local legislative demands, as indeed many had little choice but do, governors could not institutionalize the executive–legislative coordination that had emerged in Britain. For two excellent assessments of the form of governance that emerged in British America see Jack P. Greene, *The Quest for Power: The Lower Houses of Assembly in the Southern Royal Colonies, 1689–1776* (Chapel Hill: University of North Carolina Press, 1963) and Leonard Woods Labaree, *Royal Government in America: A Study of the British Colonial System before 1783*, 2nd Edition (New York: F. Ungar, 1964).

14. Neither was the necessity of "negotiation with local assemblies" specified in Braddock's orders.
15. Jeremy Black, *Debating Foreign Policy in Eighteenth-Century Britain* (Aldershot: Ashgate, 2011), 150–153.
16. Contemporary John Mitchell, who had extensively travelled through the American colonies, summarized this widespread belief when he proclaimed, "…if we give up any part of our plantations, or suffer them to fall into the hands of the French, their trade and commerce, shipping and seamen must prosper and encrease [sic], as much as ours would decline and decrease…" See Mitchell, *The Conquest in America between Great Britain and France*, viii. John Huske, a prominent American merchant and later member of parliament warned that Britain's "Landholders, Manufacturers, Artificers, Merchants" should reflect that if the colonies were lost, "they will lose one Third of their Property and Business in general." [John Huske], *The Present State of North America* (Boston, 1755), 56–57.
17. Fred Anderson, *The Crucible of War: The Seven Years War and the Fate of Empire in British North America, 1754–1766* (New York: Alfred A. Knopf, 2000), 17. As the colonies were supposed to provide a captive market for British manufactures, it is understandable why this would have been considered such a threat to British economic prosperity.
18. Guy Fregault, Margaret M Cameron, (trans.) *Canada: The War of Conquest* (Toronto: Oxford University Press, 1969), 35.
19. Francis Parkman, *Montcalm and Wolfe* (Boston: Little Brown, 1884), 12–13. For a critique of the failings of Parkman's methodology and his evident weaknesses as a historical scholar see, Francis Jennings, "Francis Parkman: A Brahmin among Untouchables," *The William and Mary Quarterly*, 42, no.3 (1985), 306–328.
20. Nevertheless, this method of government also allowed for great abuses of power, and French metropolitan officers frequently wrote of the "evils" that ensued from wanton corruption. See Pierre Pouchot, Michael Cardy

(trans.), Brian Leigh Dunningan (ed.), *Memoirs on the Late War in North America between France and England* (New York: Old Fort Niagara Association, 1994), 94–95; Louis Antoine de Bougainville (*Tantum potuit suadere malorum auri* "So much does the hunger for gold make one the slave of evil") in Louis Antoine de Bougainville, Edward P. Hamilton, (ed., trans.), *Adventure in the Wilderness: The American Journals of Louis Antoine de Bougainville, 1756–1760* (Norman: Oklahoma University Press, 1990), 255. Also, "Louis-Joseph de Montcalm to the Marshal de Belle Isle, Montreal, April 29, 1759," in Thomas Thorner and Thor Frohn-Nielsen (eds.), *A Few Acres of Snow: Documents in Pre-Confederation Canadian History* (Toronto: Toronto Press Incorporated, 2009), 56–58.

21. Benjamin Franklin in *The Pennsylvania Gazette*, May 9, 1754.
22. The *Troupes de la Marine*, not to be confused with the marines who served on French naval vessels and in sea ports, were colonial independent companies usually raised in France but officered by Canadians. The former were administered by the French Ministry of the Marine. See Rene Chartrand, Eugene Leliepvre, *Louis XV's Army (5): Colonial and Naval Troops* (London: Osprey Publishing, 1998) and Stuart Sutherland, "Troupes de la Marine," in *The Canadian Encyclopaedia*, Volume IV (Edmonton: Hurtig Publishers, 1988), 2196. The *Troupes de Terre* were the French regular regiments deployed from France to the New World from 1755 onwards.
23. As Allan Greer suggested, unlike the English colonies based to the south, what the French wanted was not swathes of Native American land, which they could not occupy due to their small population anyway, but furs and, after the 1680s, American-Indian service in war. The Jesuits played a very significant role in drawing native groups, particularly refugee tribes like the Huron (who, through conflict with the Iroquois had been forced to settle in Canadian Indian reserves), to the French cause. See Allan Greer, *The People of New France* (Toronto: University of Toronto Press, 1997), 77.
24. "Minutes of the Council of Marine, Paris, 5 January 1718" reprinted in Charles de Raymond, Joseph L. Peyser (ed.), *On the Eve of Conquest: The Chevalier de Raymond's Critique of New France in 1754* (East Lancing: State University of Michigan Press, 1997), 14.
25. As Armstrong Starkey argued, the "Christianization" of even Canada's most stalwart native allies was not always as comprehensive as many historians once believed. In Starkey's own words, "...many Indians may have accepted Christianity as an accommodation with a superior power while retaining the fundamental beliefs of their native culture which shaped their conduct in war." Likewise, Europeans "adopted the Indian way of war without conceding their European identity..." See Armstrong Starkey, *European and Native American Warfare, 1675–1815* (London: University College London, 1998), 13. For Allan Greer, Canada possessed two kinds

of native allies: the refugee tribes who had settled in the vicinity of Canada's St. Lawrence settlements in the sixteenth-century and the aforementioned tribes of the *Pays d'en Haut*. The latter were more numerous and less closely tied to French interests than the former, who were spiritually and physically dependent on New France for their survival. See Greer, *The People of New France*, 77–78.
26. Though whether it was worth the expenditure to maintain this isolated post was an issue of contention. Writing after the siege of 1758, Bougainville would argue that, "I think if Isle Royale is returned to France, there is no need of a fortress, but only a simple post with a commander and one hundred men for the police of the fisheries." Bougainville, Hamilton (ed.), *Adventure in the Wilderness*, 273–274.
27. Anderson, *Crucible of War*, 17.
28. For the Marquis de la Galissoniere, "The Utility of Canada is not confined to the preservation of the French colonies, and to rendering the English apprehensive of theirs; that colony is not less essential for the conservation of the Spanish possessions in America, especially Mexico." See Marquis de la Galissoniere, "Memoir on the French Colonies in North America, 1750," *American History from Revolution to Reconstruction and Beyond*, http://www.let.rug.nl/usa/documents/1701-1750/marquis-de-la-galissoniere-memoir-on-the-french-colonies-in-north-america-december-1750.php accessed March 13, 2016.
29. Stanley Pargellis (ed.), *Military affairs in North America, 1748–1765: Selected Documents from the Cumberland Papers in Windsor Castle* (London: D. Appleton-Century Company, 1936), xiv–xv. Even the acerbic James Wolfe, commander of the successful 1759 venture that captured Quebec, would write admiringly that, "every man in Canada is a soldier." Quoted in Bernard Horn (ed.), *The Canadian Way of War: Serving the National Interest* (Toronto: Dundurn Press, 2006), 32.
30. For a further analysis of the experiences of French colonists among the Native Americans see Michael Cardy, "A French Officer among the Iroquois in the Early 18th Century," reprinted from: *North Dakota Quarterly*, 55 (Summer 1987).
31. "Trade goods" consisted of items of value to native tribes: clothing, alcohol, guns, gunpowder and personal ornaments. See Fintan O'Toole, *White Savage: William Johnson and the Invention of America* (London: Faber and Faber, 2005), 57.
32. Richter and Merrell, *Beyond the Covenant Chain*, 8.
33. Ian K. Steele, *Warpaths: Invasions of North America* (Oxford University Press, 1994), 113.
34. British understandings of land ownership, echoing theories outlined by philosophers such as John Locke, were tied to a belief that private property

was linked inextricably to life and liberty. Because Indians, as Locke would have seen it, existed in a "State of Nature," they suffered from a "deficiency of government," exercising little dominion and thus possessing "very moderate sovereignty." This, in British eyes, gave them *imperium* over Native American lands. See John Locke, "The Second Treatise of Civil Government, 1690" in Peter Laslett (ed.) *Locke: Two Treatises of Government* (Cambridge: Cambridge University Press, 2003), 265–429.
35. For Population figures see Fregault, *Canada*, 35.
36. Gregory Evans Dowd, *War Under Heaven: Pontiac, the Indian Nations and The British Empire* (Baltimore, MD: Johns Hopkins University Press, 2002), 26–27.
37. Ibid., 26–27.
38. Anderson, *The War that Made America*, 10.
39. Many of the Delaware were refugees who had been pushed into the Ohio by the mass immigration of European colonists to the colony of Pennsylvania in the early part of the eighteenth-century.
40. "Governor Thomas Hutchinson's speech to the Great and General Court or Assembly of the province of Massachusetts Bay, April 2, 1754," in Armand Francis Lucier, *French and Indian War Notices Abstracted from Colonial Newspapers: 1754–1755* (Bowie, MD: Heritage Books, 2007), 40.
41. The Iroquois could indeed be high-handed with their so-called vassals. Following Delaware outrage over the infamous "Walking Purchase" (1737), which was ratified by the Six Nations in 1742, Iroquois headmen are reputed to have responded to Delaware protestations as follows:

> Cousins, Let this Belt of Wampum serve to Chastise You; You ought to be taken by the Hair of the Head and shaked severely till you recover your Senses and become Sober; you don't know what Ground you stand on, nor what you are doing.... We conquer'd You, we made Women of you, you know you are Women, and can no more sell Land than Women. Nor is it fitt you should have the Power of Selling Lands since you would abuse it. This land that you Claim is gone through Your Guts. You have been furnished with Cloaths and Meat and Drink by the Goods paid you for it, and now you want it again like Children as you are.... For all these reasons we charge you to remove instantly. We don't give you the liberty to think about it. You are Women; take the Advice of a Wise Man and remove immediately... Depart the Council and consider what has been said to you.

"Iroquois-Delaware Grand Council, Philadelphia, 1742," in *Minutes of the Provincial Council of Pennsylvania*, Volume IV (16 vols. Harrisburg, PA, 1851–53), 578–580.

42. Richter and Merrell, *Beyond the Covenant Chain*, 5.
43. The British tended to see their allies as auxiliaries—both in the political and military spheres. This was deeply resented by the latter. See Richard White, *The Middle Ground: Indians, Empires, and Republics in the Great Lakes Region, 1650–1815* (Cambridge: Cambridge University Press, 1991).
44. See "George Croghan's Statement," in Winthrop Sargent (ed.), *The History of an expedition against Fort Duquesne in 1755, under Major General Edward Braddock* (Philadelphia, 1855), 407–408.
45. The infamous "Walking Purchase" of 1737 and its later ratification (1742) are two earlier examples of ill-advised Anglo-Iroquois negotiated settlements that alienated, in this case, the Delaware—demonstrating to the latter the necessity of breaking current diplomatic conventions. A map of the territories covered by the infamous "Walking Purchase" can be found in Benjamin Franklin, Carl Van Doren (Introduction), Julian P. Boyd (Historical & Biographical notes), *Indian Treaties printed by Benjamin Franklin* (Philadelphia, 1938), xxii–xxiii., v–vi. Written details are to be found on pages xxviii–xxix of this excellent resource. For the full Treaty of Lancaster see, Ibid., 53–80.
46. Part of the wider War of the Austrian Succession, King George's War had mainly been fought on the frontiers of the provinces of New York, Massachusetts Bay, New Hampshire and Nova Scotia.
47. For a useful analysis of some of the implications of the Treaty of Aix-la-Chapelle see Jack M. Sosin, "Louisburg and the Peace of Aix-la-Chapelle," *The William and Mary Quarterly*, Third Series, Vol. 14, No. 4 (October, 1957), 516–535.
48. Some of the men involved in this enterprise were very notable indeed. They included Thomas Lee, John Mercer and George Washington's brothers: Lawrence and Augustine Washington Jr. See Herbert T. Leyland, *The Ohio Company: A Colonial Corporation* (Cincinnati, 1921), 6. The Ohio Company was not the only private enterprise with speculative designs in the Ohio. The Loyal Company, which also consisted of propertied gentlemen from Virginia, had set its sights on territories that sat on the south of the Ohio River in modern-day Kentucky. They had successfully thwarted the Ohio Company's plans to exploit the west until, in 1749, the then acting governor became head of the company. On his death, and having learned a valuable lesson, stockholders in the Ohio Company quickly offered a share to the newly appointed lieutenant governor, Robert Dinwiddie. Such were the vested interests that dominated the internal politics of Britain's colonies.
49. Ibid., 14.
50. The background to the treaty of Logstown and some of its implications are given by Louis Mulkearn in "Why the Treaty of Logstown, 1752," *The*

Virginia Magazine of History and Biography Vol. 59, No. 1 (Jan. 1951), 3–20, Published by: Virginia Historical Society.

51. Pickawillany perhaps more than any other post epitomized the increasingly audacious insult that British speculators and traders represented to French sovereignty. The position, a declaration of intent with regards regional diplomacy and territorial claims, was able to supply essential trade goods at half the price French contractors could and was thus a very real threat to France's alliances with wavering native tribes in the Ohio Valley. See "Historical sketch of the post at Pickawillany" in Captain William Trent, Robert Dinwiddie, Alfred Thomas Goodman (ed.), *Journal of Captain William Trent from Logstown to Pickawillany, A.D. 1752: now published from a copy in the archives of the Western Reserve Historical Society, Cleveland, Ohio, together with letters of Governor Robert Dinwiddie; an historical notice of the Miami Confederacy of Indians; a sketch of the English post at Pickawillany, with a short biography of Captain Trent and other papers never before printed* (Pittsburgh, 1871), 39.
52. Francis Jennings, *Empire of Fortune: Crowns, Colonies and Tribes in the Seven Years War in America* (New York: W.W. Norton, 1988), 49.
53. The challenges the French had in moving men and materiel into the Ohio should not, however, be understated.
54. "Governor Dinwiddie to the Board of Trade, December 10, 1752" in Captain William Trent, Robert Dinwiddie, Alfred Thomas Goodman (ed.), *Journal of Captain William Trent from Logstown to Pickawillany*, Cincinnati: William Dodge, 73–81.
55. As such, Robert D'Arcy, Earl of Holderness and Secretary of State had dispatched a circular letter to the governors of North America in which he urged *them* to resist any French encroachments upon Britain's dominions. It was an instruction, of course, that placed great responsibility upon the governors themselves; evidently in the hope that there would be an *American* solution to the impending colonial crisis. See Stanley Pargellis, *Lord Loudon in North America*, Hamden, CT: Archon Books, 1968, 20–22.
56. For more on this controversy see, Jack P. Greene, "The Case of the Pistole Fee: The Report of a Hearing on the Pistole Fee Dispute before the Privy Council, June 18, 1754," *The Virginia Magazine of History and Biography*, 66, No. 4 (October, 1958), 399–422.
57. Like many of the old Virginian landowning aristocracy, the youthful Washington felt that his future fortunes were inextricably linked to the territories that sat to the west of "old" Virginia. Indeed, his brother Lawrence had been a stake-holder in the Ohio Company (as was George Washington himself). See, Robert M. McClung, *Young George Washington and the French and Indian War, 1753–1758* (North Haven, CT: Linnet Books, 2002), 3–7.

58. George Washington, Fred Anderson (ed.), *George Washington Remembers: Reflections on the French and Indian War* (Lanham, MD: Rowman and Littlefield, 2004), 27–28. For Washington's journal see, George Washington, *The Journal of Major George Washington, sent by the Hon. Robert Dinwiddie, Esq; His Majesty's Lieutenant Governor, and Commander in Chief of Virginia, to the Commandant of the French forces on Ohio, To which are added the Governor's letter and a translation of the French Officer's answer* (Colonial Williamsburg, 1959).
59. Governor Glenn of South Carolina was one such contemporary who would question whether the Ohio was really part of England's domain. Dinwiddie naturally resented this assertion which also intimated that he was acting in his own interest as opposed to the "wider good." See Patrice Louis-Rene Higonnet, "The Origins of the Seven Years War," *The Journal of Modern History*, Vol. 40, No. 1 (Mar., 1968), 57–90.
60. "Governor Dinwiddie to Governor Horatio Sharpe of Maryland, February 23rd, 1754" in Robert Alonzo Brock (ed.), *The official records of Robert Dinwiddie: Lieutenant-Governor of the Colony of Virginia, 1751–1758, Volume III* (Richmond, VA, 1883), 101–104.
61. "Governor Dinwiddie to Governor Sharpe, March 1st 1754," Ibid., 85–86.
62. For Washington's full initial account of the skirmish see "Colonel Washington to Governor Dinwiddie: From our camp at the Great Meadows, 29th of May, 1754" in Robert Alonzo.Brock (ed.) *Official records of Robert Dinwiddie*, Volume III, 179–182.
63. The French, hoping to diplomatically exploit the affair, would later claim this action to be an assassination, or murder. "Colonel Washington to Governor Dinwiddie, 10th June 1754," *Official Records of Dinwiddie*, III, 197–200.
64. Ibid., 197–200.
65. For a French account see, "Jolicoeur" Charles Bonin, Andrew Garrup (ed.) *Memoir of a French and Indian War Soldier* (Bowie, MD: Heritage Books, 1993), 100–102.
66. Washington's own version of the battle of Fort Necessity is also given (albeit more briefly than in his correspondence with Dinwiddie) in George Washington, Fred Anderson (ed.), *George Washington Remembers*, 16–18.

CHAPTER 3

Metropolitan Intervention: Britain's Strategy for a New Colonial War

The third chapter of this work is devoted to an examination of Britain's strategy for the campaign of 1755. To begin this assessment, it is appropriate that the great historical figures who would formulate Britain's response to unfolding events on the North American continent are studied; providing a clearer contextualization of the "Braddock Plan's" political origins. Undoubtedly, the most significant of these characters were the Duke of Newcastle and the Duke of Cumberland, deeply polarizing figures both in their own time and posterity, who, with their respective cabals, jostled for power and influence in the formulation of an American strategy for 1755. This was, essentially, a divide that in today's geopolitical lexicon would be considered a contest between "dove" and "hawk." The Newcastle faction, determined to avoid a wider war with France, would play the role of the former. Cumberland, a very capable but profoundly uncompromising soldier-statesman, would epitomize the latter analogy. Ultimately, it was the belligerent Cumberland who would win this ideological clash of constitutional titans, and General Edward Braddock, a very conventional officer, distinctly of the Cumberland fold, would be given command of Britain's quest for American pre-eminence. Soldiers from the regular establishment would also be deployed to the New World, making the British strategy for 1755 one of direct interventionism.[1]

By extension of the studies outlined above, an analysis of the strategy adopted by the ministry—including its strengths and shortcomings—will also prove essential, as will a reflection (in the guise of a mini-biography)

© The Editor(s) (if applicable) and The Author(s) 2016
R. Hall, *Atlantic Politics, Military Strategy and the French and Indian War*, War, Culture and Society, 1750-1850,
DOI 10.1007/978-3-319-30665-0_3

of the man assigned to lead Britain's war effort in North America, the aforementioned Edward Braddock. Like Newcastle and Cumberland, Braddock is a divisive figure and history, concurrently, has judged him as such. Traditionally, and most particularly in America, Braddock has been a figure of scorn whose ignorance of (and contempt for) Americans and the American way of war ultimately led to his inevitable downfall. To others, he is merely anized unfortunate general, lacking the fundamental characteristic Napoleon Bonaparte always sought in his commanders: luck. Essentially, for historians disposed towards this view, Braddock was a man of self-evident conventional abilities who was thrust into an alien environment to battle with fractious colonial governments with whom he, an archetypal European soldier, could find little common ground. His tactics and genuine abilities, if applied to a European theater of war would, in all likelihood, have delivered Fort Duquesne to the British. In America, however, where nature, politics and ill-fortune would conspire against him, Braddock, a man of little patience, unwilling to adapt to the political and strategic realities of eighteenth-century North America, was simply out of his depth.

Britain's Intercession in Colonial Affairs

George Washington's defeat at Fort Necessity was naturally greeted with consternation by Virginia's Lieutenant-Governor, Robert Dinwiddie. The setback at the Great Meadows had left France virtual master of the Ohio country and, with each passing day, Dinwiddie was only too aware that the French would spare no effort in intensifying their grip on this important territory.[2] Of further concern was the impending threat of French-Indian assaults on the exposed Virginian backcountry following this latest colonial setback. Experience had shown that the British colonies' exposed and extended frontiers were tempting targets for Franco-Indian raiding parties. The capture of the strategically vital Forks of the Ohio magnified the dangers faced by frontier Virginia and Pennsylvania.

Politically, there was little Dinwiddie could do to alleviate the situation without the consent of the Virginian House of Burgesses, who had already proven obstinate in their response to his initial request to raise and equip Washington's defeated army. Sensing that they could wrest significant advantages from the unfolding Ohio crisis, the Lower House, in exchange for a proviso-attached £20,000 grant, attempted to exact painful political concessions from their governor in the Pistole Fee dispute that had raged within the colony from 1752.[3] For Dinwiddie, matters may have been alleviated somewhat had assistance from Virginia's fellow colonies been forthcoming. This, unfortunately, was not the case and the beleaguered lieutenant-governor was left frustrated by the reality that, of all his fellow provinces, only North Carolina voted to appropriate significant funds for colonial defense; with the rather telling stipulation that the monies they raised could only be disbursed within the boundaries of that province.[4]

In London, however, the deteriorating situation in America was hardly passing unnoticed. Britain's First Minister at this time was the politically savvy Thomas Pelham-Holles, Duke of Newcastle, a figurehead who can be fairly described as one of history's more colorful and controversial characters. A staunch Whig, Newcastle was something of a career politician, serving the first three Hanoverian Georges in an expansive career that saw him appointed to an array of governmental positions. Initially, he had learnt the art of politics under the guidance of one of eighteenth-century Britain's most successful politicians, Robert Walpole. It was from this Goliath of British constitutional history (in addition to his other mentor and ally, Charles Townsend) that Newcastle would learn the art of political manipulation he would utilize so successfully throughout his career. Indeed, it was Walpole who first appointed him to a cabinet post, giving him the title of Secretary of State for the Southern Department (a position that included responsibility for the American colonies) in 1724.

The alliance with Walpole lasted for 20 years but would not survive the strains that flowed from the "War of Jenkins's Ear," which began in 1739. As part of its colonial strategy for 1742, the British had launched a disastrous attack against the Spanish settlement of Cartagena in South America, with the aim of capturing that distant outpost of Spain's extensive but vulnerable American empire. Unfortunately, the expedition would fail amidst a severe outbreak of disease and would descend into a particularly notorious, and shameful, fiasco.[5] Although Newcastle had formulated and ordered the ill-fated attack, it was Robert Walpole, figurehead of British politics for the better part of 21 years and a target for rising, hawkish "Patriot Whig" stars like William Pitt, who was forced to withdraw from office. The resignation of Walpole would leave Newcastle and his half-brother, then First Minister Henry Pelham, virtual political masters of Britain until the latter died in 1754, upon which Holles, who first had to dispatch the threat posed by his longstanding rival Henry Fox, attained his now-deceased brother's position.[6]

To many contemporaries and indeed subsequent historians, Newcastle has been viewed as representative of the worst excesses of political patronage and self-aggrandizing empire building that often passed for politics in the eighteenth century. Nowhere is this more apparent than in the writings of Horace Walpole, a renowned man of letters and one of that era's best-known political commentators.[7] However, although there is some legitimacy in the assertion that Newcastle was political avarice's greatest champion (he did have a propensity for staffing the bureaucracy with government supporters and using secret service funds as a source of bribery), it would be a rather unjust and naive over-simplification of longstanding eighteenth-century political traditions to denounce him as any worse than any other politician of significant influence who enjoyed the degree of patronage he held at this particular time in history. Certainly, Newcastle would manipulate the system to serve his own and the Whig political interest very well, but he also acted in a way he felt best served the nation *and* the crown. These political inclinations manifested themselves in his overriding view that public opinion should be tranquilized rather than embraced; it was a tendency that sat rather uneasily with his enemies who saw it as further evidence of his purely atavistic and authoritarian designs.[8] Of further concern for his rivals was Newcastle's staunch support of the Royal prerogative. Throughout his period in office, he actively opposed any extension in the legislative power of the House of Commons, which, in the eyes of his adversaries, made him the potential puppet of a would-be autocrat; and thus a dangerous man once ascended to a high station.[9]

Nevertheless, akin to many of his era, Newcastle's real underlying beliefs dictated that civil order upheld by strong central authority was the best method of ensuring individual freedom for ordinary Britons.[10] His main fear had always been that if authority were weakened, the nation would be at the mercy of the "mob" and would require a substantial military force to maintain peace and order. When it is remembered that large standing armies were anathema to most Englishmen, they being traditionally associated with the truly autocratic monarchies of Catholic Europe, Newcastle's concerns in this regard were hardly baseless. Fundamentally, they reflected a worry (and quandary) that existed deep within the national psyche at this time.

And yet, like many astute men who have held the levers of power, Newcastle knew only too well that political mastery was a temporary trapping. Consequently, throughout his career he was able to demonstrate a willingness to accommodate his political adversaries where timing and circumstances required such a course of action. In his determination to undermine his long-time rival, the then Secretary of State for the Southern

Department, the Duke of Bedford, Newcastle, in the late 1740s, sought an alliance of convenience with the President of the Board of Trade, the Earl of Halifax. By pandering to Halifax, no great friend it must be added, Newcastle was able to undermine Bedford and, in 1751, finally forced him from office.[11] More evidence of this adaptability emerges from his conduct during the Seven Years War. From 1757 to 1761, having earlier been forced from office by the disasters that befell British efforts in that conflict, he would re-enter government with arch-rival William Pitt, forging a pact that oversaw Britain's eventual triumph in the "Great War for Empire" (as Pitt would later call it). In hindsight, therefore, perhaps the much-maligned Newcastle should be viewed as a flawed man who was nonetheless the skilful tactical manipulator of a profoundly imperfect political system; as opposed to the wholly corrupt, buffoonish and somewhat dangerous wheeler dealer portrayed by Horace Walpole (and indeed historians such as Archer Butler Herbert, who described the duke as "as perfect an ass that ever held high office").[12]

In the realm of foreign policy, like his former patron Robert Walpole, Newcastle was something of a dove, though not as averse to conflict as his old patron had been. As such, he generally opposed Britain's direct embroilment in Europe's seemingly perpetual wars that offered little national advantage but came at an exorbitant cost. This cost could indeed include one's political career—as he himself had witnessed first-hand, with the fall of his old mentor. Nonetheless, when warfare did erupt, Newcastle, a "traditional Whig" who extolled the merits of the old system of foreign policy (or the "Newcastle System" as it had become popularly called by the mid-eighteenth century), felt that Britain's interests were best served by maintaining a balance of power on the European continent; thus it was towards that theater that he expended most of his efforts. As a loyal servant of his Hanoverian masters, he also allowed his strategic judgment to be clouded by the need to protect the king's beloved Hanover.[13] This, and the pro-Austrian policy it bred (Hapsburg Austria being France's traditional rival at this time), had led him to commit substantial numbers of British troops to the continent during the War of the Austrian Succession; a policy that brought him into conflict with a new breed of emerging Whig strategists (epitomized by William Pitt), who felt that Britain's best hope of undermining Bourbon power was to assault France's vulnerable colonial outposts in North America.[14]

Consequently, when the previously cited peace of Aix-la-Chapelle was signed in 1748, it did little to assuage the concerns of Newcastle's detractors. Britain's position on the continent had weakened as the War of the Austrian Succession progressed and when the articles of the treaty were finally signed, she was forced to return to France the important post of Louisbourg (Nova Scotia), which had been captured by an Anglo-American force in 1745. Although France ceded Madras and withdrew from the Low Countries in return for this concession, many felt Louisbourg a prize that, from a solely British perspective, far outweighed the compromises to which the French had acquiesced. Naturally, therefore, the terms of the Treaty of Aix-la-Chapelle were greeted with incredulity by the duke's political adversaries, and indeed by many in the powerful merchant classes who felt that colonial wars were better for business.[15]

After so many years in politics, by the outbreak of hostilities in America in 1754, Newcastle was certainly no novice when it came to the chessboard of international diplomacy. One of the more spurious charges levelled against him with regards to the American aspect of this perilous art was his ignorance of the importance of that expanding continent. Quite often denounced as a man of "abysmally limited capacities," his often-cited contemptuous response to the idea that Annapolis (Nova Scotia) be defended—"Annapolis, Annapolis! Oh, yes, Annapolis must be defended; to be sure, Annapolis should be defended ... where is Annapolis?"—is frequently seen as indicative of a wanton indifference to Britain's colonies.[16] And yet, by the 1750s the duke *was* acutely aware of America's significance to Britain's geopolitical standing and had been so for many years. Certainly, even before word reached him of Washington's defeat, Newcastle had made it very clear that he would not forebear abandoning the Americans to their fate and was determined to prevent France from gaining pre-eminence on the North American continent.[17] In a discussion with Lord Chancellor Hardwicke in August of 1749, he would express a mounting fear of growing French pretensions in Europe and America. Commenting on the controversial peace treaty of 1748, Newcastle candidly divulged his concern that Britain's ancient enemy had only come to an agreement in order to strengthen her navy, buy allies in Europe through subsidies, restore her trade and extend her territorial limits in America. Britain, weakened by such manoeuvres, would find no redress because France could rely "upon Her great superiority." As such, they were, depressingly from a British perspective, "the absolute Masters of Europe."[18] Again, in the following year, and despite his peaceful predilections, he would warn his brother, First Minister Henry Pelham, of the risks of ceding ground to the French in America—in this instance, in Nova Scotia, if we lose our American possessions; or the influence or Weight of Them in Time of Peace; France will, with great Ease, make War with us, whenever they please hereafter: And as long as we stick to our treaties; the French may talk Big; And, at a Distance, their Officers act hostilely, or at least, impertinently; But they will not enter into a Serious War. I should be as sorry to see That as You can be.[19]

Outlining a resolution adopted by the Cabinet Council in a letter to Horatio Walpole on June 29, 1754—one evidently expressing a resolve to respond to French encroachments in the Ohio—he would, on the eve of conflict, again clearly convey his (and the government's) belief that Britain should endeavor to protect its American colonies and interests,

The first point we have laid down is, that the colonies must not be abandoned, that our rights and possessions in North America must be maintained and the French obliged to desist from their hostile attempts to dispossess us.[20]

Negligence of the colonies from a global-strategic standpoint was not therefore something that the duke could be charged with.[21] Yet there were other pressing realities that he felt would directly affect Britain's ability to engage the French in another conflagration. One consideration was that such a war could prove financially ruinous, particularly after the War of the Austrian Succession, and Newcastle, stung by earlier claims made by his rivals that he was unfit to direct the Treasury (he being First Lord of the Treasury), was determined to prove his fiscal frugality. Naturally, therefore, he had little desire to embroil Britain in a fully-fledged and expensive colonial war that posed a real risk of spreading to Europe.

Neither did the broader diplomatic situation seem promising, as the treaty of Aix-la-Chapelle had left Austria, Britain's traditional ally, deeply disgruntled and in no hurry to engage in a new conflict on London's behalf. The Dutch Republic, another longstanding friend of Great Britain, was also reluctant to confront the French.[22] That nation, precariously close to monolithic France, would, if war erupted, likely face a potentially devastating French onslaught into its vulnerable homeland—as had happened during the previous conflict when Bergen op Zoom and Maastricht fell to French forces. Clearly, another conflict would not be attractive to the already hard-pressed Dutch. To assuage Austria, a simultaneous alliance was being proposed with Russia, and this could have proven very useful in Europe. However, the benefits of such a coalition would principally be felt on the continent, and not America, where the current crisis was really unfolding. Meanwhile, the possibility of a Bourbon pact (between

France and Spain) became more acute when, in April 1754, the Marquis of Ensenada authorized attacks on British loggers in Honduras. Such a coalition would truly present a perilous threat to Britain's colonial interests.[23]

These were some of the dilemmas that Newcastle and his ministry faced. Though there were financial resources available to him to prosecute operations in America, he needed to formulate a method of deterring the French from further American expansionism without antagonizing an already delicate European diplomatic situation. For Newcastle, direct conflict should be avoided, but, paradoxically, Britain must show enough resolve to persuade the French that a colonial war would inflict greater damage on their interests. Slowly, therefore, the idea of using limited numbers of soldiers from the British establishment to tip the balance of power in America began to gather momentum, as it seemed to provide the swiftest, least risky (and yet most decisive) solution to the emerging colonial crisis.

Deploying British regulars to America had in fact always been a possibility but, among other things, was considered an extremely expensive option. There were also practical concerns that "regular battalions were not likely to be of much value in the forest warfare then being waged on the American frontier."[24] This sentiment was echoed by Sir John Ligonier, Lieutenant-General of the Ordinance, who argued that any American engagements should be fought by colonial militias who were familiar with the local terrain; Britain's military input should be to provide arms and regular officers who could offer advice to irregular colonial forces.

Ironically, the main obstacle to such a strategy came from within the colonies themselves. To prosecute a colonial-led offensive against the French in Canada, there would have to be a greater measure of uniformity within British America than had hitherto been apparent, and this was hardly forthcoming.[25] Colonies such as Maryland and New Jersey, for example, were unwilling to share the burden of the costs of war, often citing the fact that the French did not pose a significant threat to their territories. Meanwhile, Pennsylvania and Virginia were embroiled in a heated dispute over land rights in the Ohio country, something that was further compounded by the suggestion of several other governors that certain parts of the Ohio might not be British after all.

Despite calls for greater colonial unity, there was also a paradoxical danger to the drive for centralization that Newcastle and others in government feared stoking; and it was one the French themselves would allude to on the formal conclusion of the French and Indian War in 1763. If the

British were to encourage political integration within their colonies, then it was considered highly probable that such a union would lead to a growing spirit of colonial nationalism that in turn could develop into a very real internal threat to British control over its American empire. Indeed, a continent of over one and a half million people, possessing its own military force and the means of funding it would hardly require British assistance of any kind if it were to establish these two prerequisites of sovereign nations.[26] It is somewhat ironic, then, that this perceived threat to the British Empire would indeed become a reality in the 1760s, with a growing resistance to imperial authority that would culminate in the American War of Independence from 1775.

Facing such difficulties, it would have been easy for Newcastle to vacillate at this point, but the stakes in America were just too high. Time and again, the colonists had shown that they were unable to defend their frontiers even with the assistance of British subsidies; the recent Washington debacle had simply reinforced this impression. Consequently, Holles, hoping to establish British supremacy in the Ohio before opening any negotiations with France, came to the realization that the deployment of limited numbers of regulars to America was one of the few viable options that could reverse the tactical position on that continent.

This too was fraught with challenges, not the least of which was the considerable obstacle posed by none other than George II himself, who was unsettled by the prospect of sending his few professional battalions to fight a war 3000 miles from his kingdom. To acquire the king's assent, therefore, Newcastle had to turn, albeit reluctantly, to a man who was, ironically, one of his most ardent of rivals, the equally polarizing Duke of Cumberland, Captain-General of the British Army and favorite son of George II.

Cumberland is another of those great figureheads of eighteenth-century British politics who would divide opinion both among his peers and subsequent commentators. To many of his parliamentary contemporaries, such as Pitt, Hardwicke and indeed the Duke of Newcastle, Cumberland's post as Captain-General of the army, the fact that he was the favorite son of the king (possessing great influence with George II) and his undoubtedly impressive political abilities made him a dangerous opponent who posed unique constitutional challenges.[27] By the 1750s, his royal rank (and its corresponding influence) had enabled him to accumulate the nucleus of a political faction that, after 1751, would challenge the "Old Guard" of British politics. It would grow in significance to include men such as the Earl of Sandwich

(First Lord of the Admiralty until 1751), the Duke of Bedford (one time Secretary of State for the Southern Department), Lord Halifax (President of the Board of Trade) and Henry Fox (Secretary of War). In time, this rising faction would look to expand its political power not only by engaging the aid of its traditional adherents but also by persuading army officers who held seats in Parliament that their careers (and personal interests) would be best served by towing the Cumberland-cabal line.

From this perspective it is evident why this soldier-statesman, a man of royal lineage and political ambition, would be considered such a threat by the traditional Whigs within Britain's establishment. After all, military rule had been a disaster in England during the 1650s, while no Briton sought a form of governance akin to the militarized Catholic autocracies of mainland Europe. Despite the fears of some very notable contemporaries, Cumberland was hardly an aspiring Nero (or even a Louis XIV). For instance, though he would use his influence in Parliament to make himself Regent, in general his decisions were formulated in view of his absolute loyalty to the throne and a thoroughly professional mindset when it came to the execution of his duties as captain-general of the army.[28] In this latter role, he made numerous reforms to the service, which improved the professionalism of officers and the discipline of the soldiers who formed the rank and file.[29]

It was, however, as an administrative general that Cumberland served best, for Cumberland the field commander was something of a mixed success. In 1746, at the Battle of Culloden, he had successfully overseen the crushing of the Bonnie Prince Charlie-inspired Jacobite rebellion, finally ending Stuart pretensions to the throne of Great Britain. His tactics, including a unique bayonet drill specifically aimed at counteracting the Highlander's ferocious broadsword and targe assaults, undoubtedly played a role in ending that rebellion. Yet this victory had also been severely tarred by the brutality with which he had suppressed the rebellious Highlanders who formed the backbone of the Stuart cause; his exactions in the Highlands would rightfully earn him his infamous, and some may suggest telling, "Butcher" nickname.

In Europe, when faced by the more disciplined and professional soldiers of the French army, Cumberland's tactical proficiency would prove suspect and his defeat at the Battle of Fontenoy during the War of the Austrian Succession was the first real indication of his limitations as a general in the field. Fears over his suitability for field command would indeed be confirmed in 1757 when, following another defeat at the Battle of Hastenbeck, he would be forced to sign the Convention of Klosterseven, whereby he disbanded his army, virtually ceded control of Hanover to France and left Britain's then ally (Prussia) exposed to French attacks from the west. After this debacle, he was forced to resign from his post as captain-general of the British Army.[30]

When compared to the Duke of Newcastle, Cumberland, with a long history of military service and the mindset of an uncompromising soldier, was an undisputed "hawk" in the field of international politics. His lack of diplomatic tact was something that greatly concerned the former, whose plan for evicting the French from the Ohio was based less on out-and-out war and more on a British show of force. Nonetheless, Newcastle had to gain Cumberland's support if he were to persuade the king to deploy British soldiers to far-flung America—where there would be little chance of a quick recall if the French threatened to invade the British Isles.

Personal differences, and indifferences, had to be set aside when Robert Dinwiddie's correspondence outlining Washington's humiliating defeat finally reached London, making some kind of solution to unfolding events in America essential. On receipt of Dinwiddie's depressing news, and its corresponding pleas for aid (including a request for substantial numbers of British regulars), Newcastle and Cumberland acted without delay, and within a week had convinced the king that Britain's rights in America could only be maintained by the deployment of regular soldiers to that far-flung continent.[31] Nonetheless, agreeing upon an American strategy that would put these soldiers to the most effective use would prove more problematic, as the dovish preferences of the Newcastle faction became superseded by the more aggressive predispositions of the Cumberland cabal. The plan of operations that emerged from this conflict of ideas would have profound consequences for the pivotal campaign of 1755.

The "Hawks" Take Control: The Cumberland-Fox Drive for American Pre-eminence

The news of George Washington's defeat at Fort Necessity was followed by three weeks of frantic discussion as to what Britain's response should be. This debate was to be dominated by three major points of profound relevance: the possibility of creating a union of the colonies; whether American troops should be deployed to meet the emergency but be taken into British pay; or whether regular British regiments should be sent to North America to retrieve the deteriorating situation. On the first account, deliberations raged around an earlier suggestion made by the Board of Trade concerning the feasibility of a colonial union. This had been submitted as a formal plan on August 9 1754, and in part argued for the creation of a permanent fund of provincial money for the building and maintaining of a line of forts and for treating with Indians; hence securing the colonies' frontiers. Measures were also to be taken for the raising and paying of troops to meet any invasion.

To command this series of fortifications, a Commander-in-Chief was to be appointed in England and would have recourse to the American "central fund" to facilitate his duties. The plan, seeking to offset the inevitable concerns of colonial assemblies troubled by a potential loss of self-governing rights, also took great pains to make the union one imposed by the colonies themselves.[32] Hence, what it really consisted of was a series of *suggestions* which provincial commissioners might use as the basis of their own general convention. The legality of the plan they framed would derive from the acts of the various assemblies to which it would be submitted before any royal approval. The powers of the Commander-in-Chief were likewise limited as he could normally draw upon any colonial treasury only for funds assigned by commissioners as the quota of that colony. Likewise, before he could employ an increase in forces or funds to meet an invasion, the Commander-in-Chief would have to consult with the various commissioners to apportion the expense an invaded colony claimed was needed to defend its sovereignty.

The Board of Trade was fully aware that the alternative to such a consensual scheme would inevitably involve the intervention of an Act of Parliament, either to levy a tax upon the colonies or to reduce the four remaining chartered colonies to royal status; thus creating a standard pattern. This would have raised enormous opposition on two fronts; from among the colonies who would have seen their freedoms truncated, and from the House of Commons, which, for political reasons, the ministry often withheld information from with regards American matters.

The plan, despite some of its evident wisdoms, was rejected by the ministry who ultimately doubted its workability. The Earl of Hardwicke, for instance, thought that any agreement reached by the commissioners should be approved by the ministry before it was submitted to colonial assemblies. Furthermore, he felt that the governor, council and assembly of any invaded colony ought to be able to decide upon the amount of aid their neighbors should give in the face of an invasion. Charles Townsend, who enjoyed considerable experience in colonial matters, argued that the colonists would never agree upon reciprocal expense and that colonial assemblies, even if a plan were agreed by commissioners, would refuse to pass acts of supply or, alternatively, would attempt to encroach upon the prerogative in exchange for their consent in passing acts permitting a Commander-in-Chief to draw on their treasuries.[33] Townsend also felt that an effective plan of union should *compel* the colonists to provide permanent revenue—something the Board of Trade's plan had fervently argued against. For the Duke of Newcastle, the plan, ironically, threatened to create too close a unity among the colonies. Such a union, he argued, would lead to a corresponding call for independence among the newly united provinces. Meanwhile, the Duke of Cumberland, favoring a strong-armed approach, advocated sending a man of exceptional qualities to oversee the unification of the colonists; a *generalissimo* "after the manner of the Spaniards" as he referred to it. Under this political master would then serve a separate commander-in-chief of military forces. Ultimately, Cumberland's proposal was rejected by the king who knew that though the Earl of Halifax fitted this description, his conditions for such a service would be impossible to bear.[34] Thus the plan was discarded and the idea of a colonial union was postponed until after the French threat to Britain's sovereign rights in North America had been dealt with by force of arms.

Necessarily, the most serious problem now concerned what a military force for the defense of Britain's territorial rights on that remote continent should, in fact, consist of. Whether American forces (in British pay), or British troops from the regular establishment in Ireland be deployed to America therefore became the issue at the core of strategic planning. William Murray, the attorney general, proposed raising 20,000 men in the colonies under British half-pay officers, all to be commanded by a British general. Lord President Granville emphatically agreed with this assessment and the two likeminded allies concurrently convinced the Duke of Newcastle and the Earl of Hardwicke of the wisdom of this measure. Their formal resolution correspondingly declared that:

> ...In the present Situation of Affairs in North America, It seems advisable to send a Commanding Officer of Rank, with a number of Half-Pay, or other Officers, with Money, Arms, and Ammunition; and Directions to concert with the proper Persons at Virginia, etc., upon the measures to be taken, for the defence of His Majesty's Colonies, and dispossessing the French, from the Settlements made, or Possessions taken, on any Parts of His Majesty's dominions there.[35]

Dinwiddie's earlier pleas for help had, however, specifically requested British troops and there was, at least initially, talk of sending the 42nd Highland regiment to America and of raising additional independent Highland companies for service on that continent—with William Pitt leading the calls for such a move.[36] The king, however, refused to part with a British regiment for a service that offered little chance of a swift recall if matters turned for the worse in Europe. The Earl of Hardwicke and the Duke of Cumberland also opposed the move, remembering only too vividly how recently the Highlanders had raised their Claymores for the Stuart cause.[37] Consequently, it was agreed that a British general should be posted to America along with British officers. Troops would be raised in America and the Treasury would meet the expense.

One important point did still remain unresolved and, to all intents and purposes, it was *the* pivotal question: namely, whether British half-pay officers would aid the Americans in drilling troops, or whether they would be regimented with them to the complete or partial exclusion of American officers. This was an issue that threatened to create enormous difficulties for any commander appointed to lead the campaign, as it would inevitably prick colonial sensitivities. Indeed, George Washington's fractious relationship with Captain James McKay of the Independent South Carolina Regiment had recently provided a very real indication of the trouble this would cause between Anglo-American units in the field. There was of course the option of raising distinctly American regiments from within the colonies, paid for by the crown and officered by the colonists themselves. The precedent for this had been set by Governor William Gooch's albeit unsuccessful expedition of 1740 against Spanish possessions in the Caribbean and Central America, which utilized a distinctly American Regiment. Although militarily a failure, it nonetheless demonstrated the possibilities of any future Anglo-American partnership. By using provincial officers, the expedition pre-empted the aversion to enlistment that many American soldiers felt towards service under non-American commanders.[38] Playing to colonial ideals of "Britishness"—self-governing communities led by local elites serving a common sovereign—the expedition fundamentally demonstrated the "signs of a greater integration of the British Atlantic World, or even a further unifying of the extended British nation."[39]

Somewhat unfortunately, Britain was concurrently moving away from its hitherto light-touch approach towards its colonies as it sought to centralize authority in its North American empire. This was epitomized by the Earl of Halifax's appointment as President of the Board of Trade and a subsequent re-evaluation of colonial policy that sought to curb what he regarded as the American tendency to "imbibe Notions of Indepen[den]cy of their Mother Kingdom."[40] The placing of a bounty on indigo production (ostensibly to boost the British textile industry), the Iron Bar Act of 1750 and the Currency Act of 1751 were all clearly indicative of this desire to rebalance political power within the empire.[41] The preliminary stages of what would become the French and Indian War also provided Halifax with an opportunity to implement several important colonial reforms he had previously outlined in 1752. Significantly, these had called for the creation of a colonial governor-general, which, in turn, was a step towards the earl's longstanding goal of creating a continental military union. This, he believed, would "help the colonies to put forth a concerted effort in the event of a war with Canada."[42] When such personal resolutions were applied to the planning phase of what would become the Braddock Plan of 1755, the promising by-products of the albeit unsuccessful Gooch expedition were thus overlooked; his mission was viewed as yet another disastrous Anglo-American failure that exemplified the need for direct British interventionism in provincial affairs.

Considering this rather complex and deep-rooted military and political backdrop, it required the iron will of the Duke of Cumberland to settle the controversial question of force structure, and his proposals soon acquired the king's approval.[43] His solution was one loosely reminiscent of that adopted in 1711 by Robert Harley's administration, which deployed 5300 regulars, carried by 31 transport ships and defended by 14 ships of the line, in an ill-fated assault on Quebec.[44] Consequently, Edward Braddock, a politically reliable figure, was named as the general officer to command in America and, instead of half-pay officers, two regiments from the Irish establishment, the 44th and 48th Regiments of Foot, were to be sent to the colonies. These regiments, over-officered but under-manned on their peacetime establishment (300 men apiece), were to be brought to full strength in America. Considering the traditional paucity of recruits in the colonies, this idea was soon modified so that part of the increase would be made good by 200 draftees from other regular regiments who were swiftly dispatched to Cork. The remaining men needed to fill the 44th and 48th were to be raised in America.[45] In addition to these units, and again on the urging of Robert Dinwiddie, five military engineers under the command of Chief Engineer James Montresor were also deployed to the colonies, to oversee the constructions of roads, the maintenance of fortifications and the "conduct of sieges."[46]

Cumberland's ever-growing influence would morph the initial objectives first advocated by Newcastle, Hardwicke and indeed, the duke himself. This preliminary military strategy, a collaborative effort between Newcastle and Cumberland, had called for the removal of French encroachments in three stages, and by military standards was a comparatively moderate one—suiting the more "dovish" inclinations of Newcastle and his likeminded Whig allies.[47] British soldiers, commanded by Edward Braddock, were to drive the French from the Ohio and then proceed northward to destroy Fort St. Frederic in upper New York. This French fort, built at the southern tip of Lake Champlain, provided a launch pad for French-Indian raiding parties who menaced that colony's frontiers and was indeed a constant threat to the frontiers of all the northern colonies of British America. The fall of Fort St. Frederic was to be followed by the final element of this conservative and fundamentally "Newcastle strategy," which was to drive the French from the forts they had constructed in Nova Scotia.[48]

To augment the regular units he would take with him to America, Braddock was given permission to raise colonial levies and his position as commander-in-chief included the proviso that he would enjoy authority over all local governors, allowing him to oversee the defense of British North America as a whole. This last facet of the plan superficially gave Braddock powers akin to those of a viceroy; meaning he could centralize colonial administration and rationalize the colonies' defense—something that many forward-thinking colonists, such as Benjamin Franklin, had been urging the colonies to do themselves.[49] To streamline the prosecution of Indian affairs, a move previously recommended by the Board of Trade, Braddock was given supervision over all Indians and thus enjoyed the power to appoint Northern and Southern superintendents of Native American affairs.

What made this plan appealing to dovish politicians such as Hardwicke and, at least initially, the hawkish Earl of Halifax (President of the Board of Trade, which supervised the administration of the colonies), was the fact that it placed the focus of operations on America itself (as opposed to Europe) and required the centralization of the colonies' political administration, something Halifax in particular had always desired. For the cautious Newcastle, the great hope was that, by proceeding in stages, Braddock's concentrated forces could eliminate the troublesome French posts singularly. After each conquest, he could press the French back to the negotiating table, where, it was hoped, they would see the hopelessness of their situation and make the strategic concessions Newcastle desired; thus avoiding a wider European conflict.

For Cumberland and his ally Henry Fox (Secretary of War and a habitual enemy of Newcastle), this tentative plan lacked the decisiveness they felt was truly required to defend Britain's interests in America and, with an ever-increasing say in geopolitical matters, they were able to squeeze the Duke of Newcastle to the periphery of strategic planning. By October 1754, they had sufficiently tinkered with the original strategy so that its evolved manifestation now suited their more belligerent inclinations.[50] What Cumberland and Fox's new plan called for was a simultaneous four-pronged assault on France's most strategic (and menacing) possessions in the disputed regions of North America. Starting with the Ohio, an Anglo-American army led by Edward Braddock would be required to capture Fort Duquesne and re-establish British sovereignty there with the building of a new British fort that would possess,

> A strong garrison of three independent companies now in *Virginia*, sustained by such a part, or the Whole of the Provincial Troops, be left defend it, & to protect the Indians in those parts, as well as British settlements lately broken up.[51]

It was here that the British regulars Braddock would take with him from Ireland were to be concentrated, as it was felt that a decisive blow struck in this theater would solve one of the major grievances of the simmering tensions between Britain and France. After the capture of Fort Duquesne, all remaining French encroachments in the region were also to be effaced.

The second prong involved breaking French power on Lake Ontario, which in theory would cut the French colonies along the Mississippi and St. Lawrence asunder. Consequently, the object of this assault was Fort Niagara, a pivotal regional *entrepot* that was the guardian of the *Pays d'en Haut* and which also served to tempt native traders away from the English at nearby Oswego. The capture of Niagara was to coincide with a thrust against Crown Point (Fort St. Frederic) at the southern tip of Lake Champlain. This latter assault had been contrived in the Northern colonies (acting under the influence of Governor William Shirley of Massachusetts) who undertook, on their own initiative, to put a wholly provincial army into the field under the command of a general of their own choosing. Since planning for this attack was already well underway before Braddock reached America, it was incorporated into the official strategy of 1755, and enjoyed the token approval of the commander-in-chief when he arrived in the colonies. Nonetheless, the decision to adopt this provincial prong of attack created huge political troubles that eventually intensified the infamous rivalry that emerged between Shirley and William Johnson. The latter would become Braddock's appointed Superintendent of Northern Indian affairs and also commanded the assault against St. Frederic (Crown Point). Shirley, of course, commanded the Niagara expedition. By default, therefore, there emerged a split command in New York and this would have dire consequences for the unity of Indian management as both commanders, vainglorious Goliaths of colonial society, quarreled violently over the control of Britain's Native American allies.

The final element of this fourfold assault concerned the disputed territory of Nova Scotia. The principal objective of the Acadian campaign was the capture of the strategically vital Fort Beausejour, which commanded the Bay of Fundy and was described by Lieutenant Colonel Charles Lawrence, commander of British forces on that peninsula, as a base from which, "they [the French] have made all their incursions upon us, and committed every kind of outrage."[52] Indeed, the presence of a large ethnic French community in this region, supplied and sheltered by a strong fortified position, made the dangers faced by the British here particularly acute. As early as August 1754, a letter from Lawrence to Halifax clearly outlined the threat posed by Beausejour and proposed the elimination of this troublesome post. That this suggestion should become an instruction integrated into Braddock's orders for the campaign of 1755 should therefore come as no surprise. Hence, in addition to his orders to "correspond constantly with Col. Lawrence who commands H:M:'s forces in that Province," Braddock was to supply the latter with reinforcements from his own units if Lawrence required supplements to his force.[53]

Such a large-scale operation called for many more soldiers than could be provided by the 44th and 48th regiments (who were to be sent from the Irish establishment and were to be financed by the Irish parliament). Thus, to meet the requirement for additional manpower, Braddock was to assume control of all British forces already on the American establishment, in addition to the regiments of Shirley and Pepperrell, which were being raised in the colonies in anticipation of the assault on Niagara. Braddock would also have at his disposal a common defense fund which would be raised by the colonies themselves and would be used to support the operations of his forces. If extra money was needed, and many suspected it would be considering the hostilities anticipated from the colonies in raising such a fund, he could draw from the paymaster-general. Colonial governors were required to provide quarters for his troops in addition to transport, supplies and a complement of 3000 men that would be drafted into the general's regiments to supplement their strength. These levies could be taken from colonial militias if volunteers were not forthcoming.

When the above revised strategy was resubmitted to Lord Halifax, he quickly discarded his erstwhile preference for Newcastle's more moderate plan and cast his lot with the Cumberland–Fox faction—despite reservations he harbored of a campaign against Fort Duquesne that involved a long march over primeval forested terrain which incorporated the daunting Laurel Mountain and the Youghiogheny River.[54] Although far more ambitious than the initial "Newcastle strategy," the plan's call for greater colonial unity plus a provincially-raised central fund were measures that Halifax had long endorsed. Fundamentally, he had always been a hardline "hawk" who possessed a deep, xenophobic hatred of the French; this modified plan pandered to his ardent belief in assertive metropolitan authority and his imperialistic desire for colonial aggression against Britain's long-term adversary.[55] Arguably, this strategy resembled the military wing of his post-1748 reforms to imperial administration.

Indeed, Halifax's desire for colonial bureaucratic centralization was spurred by his previous failures to bring the colonists to heel in his drive to unify the administration of British North America. When he looked to the colonies and their methods of governance, he did so with a contemptuous sneer, seeing avaricious, self-interested provinces, concerned only with their own aggrandizement and possessing little concern for the interests of the crown. Certainly, one of his earliest aims as President of the Board of Trade from 1748 had been to cut the power of the local assemblies, which he felt were responsible for the perpetual political deadlocks that hamstrung efforts to assert Britain's interests in America. Like Cumberland and Newcastle, he was a man of the prerogative and consequently believed that the basic institution of colonial administration should not be the local assembly but the imperial bureaucracy which was immune from the control of those they ruled.[56] This, of course, was notably different to the widespread American belief that the "Rights of Englishmen" included devolved legislative power for local assemblies; as was historically guaranteed by their colonial charters. So, for instance, while Halifax may have supported the establishment of a colonial central fund for General Edward Braddock in 1755, he was evidently indifferent to the inevitable provincial demand that this be done by mutual consent and involve a degree of accountability. Here lay one of the major flaws of the Braddock Plan, one which highlighted the failure of the British government to fully appreciate that geography and metropolitan neglect (spanning much of the seventeenth and eighteenth centuries) had resulted in a very different idea of "Britishness" emerging in the American colonies. The provinces would never simply appropriate funds and submit them unquestioningly into the hands of another body or individual; such an action ran completely contrary to their ideals of liberty and diffused sovereignty—principles the assemblies of British America had fought so long to preserve. Unsurprisingly, when Braddock arrived in America, he soon understood that his supposed provincial central fund would never materialize on anything near the scale the ministry had hoped. Until the rise of William Pitt, this clash of two distinct political cultures—Parliamentary and executive ascendency versus the colonial model of government (one limited by the customary restraints of consent and fundamental law)—would severely undermine the ability of British commanders to fully implement the strategic goals of their metropolitan government.

Ideology aside, as Newcastle had always feared, the large-scale mobilization of British soldiers and the logistical effort this entailed could only arouse the suspicions of the French—leading to an increased probability of conflict escalation. By appealing to Cumberland for assistance in convincing George II to deploy regulars to America, Newcastle had opened the door to the more hawkish elements of the ministry who had always wanted to adopt a more belligerent pose on that continent. The above-cited strategy, hammered out in Cumberland's private chambers (with the First Minister increasingly acting as an anxious onlooker), was far more aggressive than Newcastle's original diplomacy-driven and strategically tentative plan. And yet it was not quite the unrestrained free-for-all that Newcastle had feared. The ministry had, from the succession of George I in 1714, been tied to the notion that "Britain-Hanover" was, essentially, a distinct "state." Britain, as a result of this "Hanoverian focus," had historically been required to provide large commitments of ground forces and costly subsidies to foreign powers in its efforts to defend the Electorate; all of which had appeared to come at the expense of maritime and colonial expansion (and was thus furiously contested both inside and outside of parliament by Tories, urban radicals and the Whig opposition).[57] The Duke of Cumberland, favorite son of George II, was also bound by the need to placate his father and would never have jeopardized the security of his patriarch's precious Electorate by ordering a full-scale assault on France's American possessions.

Such was another major failing of the "Braddock Plan"; its tactical over-ambitiousness yet, concurrently, strategic conservatism. Certainly, the logistical obstacles faced by all of the armies engaged on the four ventures outlined in the Braddock Plan would have been challenging feats in a conventional European war—they were magnified ten-fold by the primeval topography of America. Deploying regular soldiers to fight on such terrain was in fact a well-acknowledged risk and fears over the army's readiness to fight a so-called "wilderness war" would also prove somewhat prophetic. This detachment from America's geographical realities was exemplified by Braddock's "secret instructions" which showed little appreciation of the immense challenges a campaign on the fringes of European America would entail.[58] In addition to driving the French from the Ohio (not just Fort Duquesne, it must be stressed), Braddock was required to ensure the "immediate Reduction of Niagara and Crown Point" and coordinate with Colonel Charles Lawrence in Nova Scotia who was to reduce Fort Beausejour and "master the whole province."[59] The instructions required the coordination of Anglo-American units on a geographical scale unimaginable to those who asked Braddock to perform such deeds. Neither did it show any understanding of colonial politics and the impossibility of getting provincial assemblies to coordinate their efforts by surrendering, to all intents and purposes, cornerstones of theirs—and their vote-wielding constituents—"liberties" as freeborn Englishman (including exemption from arbitrary appropriation).

Furthermore, the Braddock Plan did not make provision for any assault on the major military and economic bastions of New France; namely, the St. Lawrence settlements of Quebec and Montreal and the imposing Acadian fortress of Louisbourg. Fundamentally, the Ministry's aim was to roll back the edges of New France, not eliminate it wholesale and this was done to avoid provoking the French into commencing operations against Hanoverian interests in Europe—where Britain was particularly vulnerable. History has shown how deeply flawed this premise was, as an assault on any French territory in the New World would, irrespective of its remoteness or ambivalent sovereign status, result in reciprocal hostilities. As a strategy, it also negated several advantages the British may have enjoyed in North America. By throwing Braddock's albeit under-strength Irish regiments onto the frontiers of European America, the ministry had, at a stroke, negated the tactical advantages such soldiers may have enjoyed when conducting a conventional military campaign. Instead of allowing the redcoats the option of fighting conventional sieges and pitched battles, Braddock's army was to hack its way through unfamiliar terrain to fight an enemy (a largely Native American foe as it transpired on July 9, 1755) perfectly suited to the forests of America.[60]

As the Earl of Halifax seems to have concluded, if a backcountry campaign had to be fought (in order to avoid a costly wider war), then it should have been directed against French positions in New York. To reduce Fort Niagara would have severed links between Canada and its Ohio territories, forcing the abandonment of posts such as Fort Duquesne which would have been left isolated and virtually impossible to restock with supplies and reinforcements. It was not and, as a consequence, Edward Braddock and his army were sent to fight a campaign that was fundamentally flawed.

Despite the desires of Cumberland and Newcastle, the deployment of Braddock and his regulars to America, supported by a squadron commanded by Admiral Augustus Keppel, made the descent into a wider armed conflict, at least on the North American continent, inevitable.[61] Indeed, when word reached Versailles that British plans were afoot for some kind of action in America, the French would raise a squadron of ships to transport 3000 French regulars (commanded by the experienced Saxon General Jean-Armand, Baron de Dieskau) to reinforce Canada. Notwithstanding the efforts of Vice-Admiral Edward Boscawen, the major part of this convoy successfully made fall in New France, providing a much needed reinforcement for that beleaguered colony and enabling it to make defensive and offensive preparations of its own.[62]

For the British, the challenge now was to meet the military, logistic and indeed political challenges they would face in their ambitious plan for American pre-eminence. This daunting task would principally fall upon the shoulders of Edward Braddock, a man who would enter the annals of history as either an unfortunate hero or a foolish, brutish martinet; depending on the conclusions one draws from the polarized opinions that have surrounded this British officer. Whether the prejudices formulated of Braddock are fair representations of his character and abilities is something that requires discussion.

Edward Braddock III: A Brief Biography

The choice of Edward Braddock to command such an important mission may seem, on reflection, a questionable one. History has taken a deeply polarized view of this ill-fated figure, with the more negative analyses of him generally focusing on his defeat on the banks of the Monongahela and his prickly, often hot-headed encounters with American assemblies; in addition to his general contempt (at least prior to his death) towards American soldiery and the American way of war. Perhaps unsurprisingly, therefore, many of the most derisory reflections of Braddock are to be found in American histories of the conflict where he, as Dallas Irving once observed, was equated with a quintessentially American caricature of the typical British officer of the eighteenth century; a "Colonel Blimp" who led his "stupid brutes" to disaster.[63]

As contemporary officer Charles Lee would argue, such sentiments were always excessive and did great injustice to Braddock's professionalism.[64] So strong were the former's opinions on this matter that he even hoped that, "there will come a day when justice will be done to this man's memory, who has left few behind him that are his Equals, in Courage, honesty and Zeal for the Publick, his death was a cruel stroke to us in particular, and a very unhappy stroke for the Nation in general."[65]

Lee had a very pertinent point. Braddock was certainly not a one-dimensional character and the over-reliance of certain historians on colonial prejudices, in addition to the application of the de-contextualized barbs of Horace Walpole are, quite often, the source of many unflattering stereotypes of Braddock as a man and general. Ever-ready to find a scapegoat for a catastrophe and, in truth, hamstrung by incomplete (or patchy) evidence concerning Braddock's pre-Monongahela career and life, historians have had little to analyse of the general except these small gobbets of information; explaining why their commentaries of this unfortunate commander have so often been defined by harsh judgments that frequently bordered on vitriol.

Early Career

In actuality, Edward Braddock was a profoundly conventional eighteenth-century British officer, one who was professional to the core and dedicated to army and crown. He certainly was not the hapless brute so often been portrayed in so many popular histories of the French and Indian War. These latter, as mentioned, provide overly-simplified stereotypes of Braddock that owe as much to American impressions of British imperialism during and after the Seven Years War (especially the Revolutionary era) as they do on a careful analysis of Braddock the man and commander; or indeed, the institution in which he held his commission.

That said, Braddock's lack of experience in terms of senior command is perhaps one of the more substantial charges raised regarding why he should have been precluded from command of the American expedition of 1755. Indeed, although he had served in the Coldstream Guards (Britain's most senior and thus prestigious regiment) for 45 years, his career had not actually incorporated what could be defined as "strategic command." During the War of the Austrian Succession, he had been deployed to the Low Countries and was present at the Siege of Bergen op Zoom (1747), where he served as a Lieutenant-Colonel under the command of the Prince of Orange; Braddock, however, had not seen any combat during this deployment.

This somewhat superficial insinuation ignores, however, the fact that Braddock's career, at least until 1755 had, despite a lack of combat opportunities, been a rather honorable one. The sheer longevity of his service and his performance as governor of Gibraltar (1753–54) for instance, highlight a number of characteristics that would make his appointment, on reflection, somewhat less perplexing. Neither should his previous omission from command be seen as an indictment of his abilities. Braddock, irrespective of the opinions one forms of him following his defeat at the Monongahela in 1755 was, and always had been, a very brave and diligent officer; one imagines that nobody felt more disappointed by his legitimate lack of opportunities to lead a sizable force into battle more fervently than he himself.

Edward Braddock III, the quintessential "career soldier," entered the army at the tender age of 16, beginning his vocation, like many young officers, as an Ensign. Despite his youth, the young Edward Braddock would have been fully aware of the type of lifestyle he was committing to, for his father, General Edward Braddock II, had also served as a British officer. The senior Braddock was a highly respected figure whose service more than warranted his appointment to such an elevated post. His father's influence therefore had a profound impact on the younger Braddock, who evidently had always sought to follow in his footsteps. Having grown up in a military household and having been well versed in martial tradition, the younger Braddock was, to all intents and purposes, a "son of the army."[66]

The service Braddock Junior was entering at such a delicate age was hardly the revered institution it is today. Although officers enjoyed far more respect than enlisted men, who were treated rather contemptuously for much of the eighteenth century, the army as a whole was viewed with a deep mistrust by many of its countrymen. Professional soldiers were feared as the potential "shock troops" of a would-be tyrant and with the specter of Oliver Cromwell and James II still looming large in the national psyche, the presence of a large standing army was something that ran contrary to the ideals of "English liberty."[67]

One of the notable features of the officer corps was its general reflection of the socially stratified nature of society-at-large in the eighteenth century. This meant that to acquire the very highest ranks in the British Army, one often had to be a landed gentleman and a man of fiscal means, and a degree of patronage from an appropriate quarter was also advantageous. Lower down the officer corps, however, the army was more meritocratic than many give it credit for. By the middle of the century, most regimental commissions were held by men drawn from the middle classes, while there were also a sprinkling of Huguenots, Irishmen and Scots in the service whose numbers (in the case of the latter) would become somewhat substantial by the conclusion of the Seven Years War.[68] Furthermore, many Non-Commissioned Officers—who possessed the necessary experience, education, desire and capital—could and were awarded the king's commission, particularly during periods of exigency; and consequently built stable careers based on their own competencies and professional endeavors.

However, it would still be quite wrong to state that the service was a fully-fledged meritocratic institution. It was not, and money, even further down the pecking order, was a crucial factor in so many aspects of an officer's life. The reason why financial prosperity was frequently a prerequisite of advancement was simply because commissions (or indeed promotions) were often purchased after the demise, retirement or withdrawal of a previous incumbent; generally, therefore, officers required merit *and* hard cash to advance. As the cost of a commission also depended on the seniority of the rank desired, it was not unknown for proficient officers to be passed over for promotion if they failed to acquire the necessary financial means to purchase a more senior rank.

Again, there were paradoxes in this rather obscure system. Indeed, the purchase of commissions was hardly a "free market enterprise." There were measures that controlled who could purchase what rank and no officer could buy a commission more than one rank above his own. Sellers were expected to offer their commission to the next officer in seniority (in their own regiments) while each rank carried a clear tariff.[69] Those on the career ladder were also expected to have completed a minimum period of service before they could progress to the next rank; one could not become a captain without having served 10 years as a subaltern, for instance. Ultimately, however, it was the crown that reserved the right to block any purchase which did not meet its approval. It was a role that George I, George II and the Duke of Cumberland—who had taken great pains to improve the caliber of the officer corps—took very seriously. All three made regular inspections of the army and knew the names and capabilities of most of the 2000 officers serving in 1755. Politicians who dared interfere in this vast system of patronage were likely to receive a swift riposte from the reigning sovereign who jealously guarded their role as "supreme commander" of the British Army.

For a nation still haunted by the aforementioned specter of Oliver Cromwell and Stuart absolutism, the patronage system also went some way to allay the fears of the political classes. Essentially, it ensured that men who progressed through purchase (at least to the army's very highest ranks) were likely to be men of land, property and influence, with a stake in the country and thus more inclined to uphold the status quo; their interests were those of the state and the social class that dominated politics. Furthermore, such men were unlikely to seek to overthrow a system upon which they depended for their prosperity as they stood to lose considerably from any subversion of Church, State or King.[70] Purchase and patronage also encouraged officers to act professionally as, in the event of their being "cashiered" (thrown out of the army), they would be prevented from selling their rank and would thus forsake a considerable sum of money.

For prospective officers of more moderate fiscal means, there were other financial challenges which extended beyond the significant initial outlay of purchasing a commission. British officers, far from being overpaid, landed gentleman of extensive privilege were, overwhelmingly, professional "middling" individuals tasked with the unenviable requirement of balancing the demands of the service with their social obligations as "gentlemen." Such requirements were particularly stressful in view of the inadequate pay officers received; something which was compounded by the exorbitant expenses associated with holding a commissioned rank.[71]

From this perspective, Edward Braddock III was very fortunate. His father was a general in the army and this ensured that he had the means to pay for his commission and the patronage to support his transition into the officer corps. As such, he also avoided the alternative routes of acquiring a "gentleman's position" which would have proven far more arduous and indeed perilous than the path to commissioned status he took. The first possibility (briefly discussed above), working through the ranks, would have required considerable skill, luck, patience, extraordinary commitment and exceptional conduct. Persons on this route would also have to continually prove that they were worthy of becoming a "gentleman." Traditionally seen as a birth-rite, the "gentleman's club" was notoriously difficult (and expensive) to break into—though not as foreboding as it inevitably was for men of "lower" social status in other European armies.[72]

Braddock also avoided the second option faced by other young British officers hoping to acquire a commission—volunteering. Volunteers were often junior members of the gentry who served as cadets in the hope they could distinguish themselves in battle and progress that way. Though they could thus earn their commissions without having to pay a penny, they would necessarily have to take huge risks (well beyond the norm) in the drive for recognition; and such opportunities usually only arose in periods of war. Consequently, becoming a volunteer could prove to be something of a forlorn hope for many an ambitious young squire. Edward Braddock III, who avoided these more arduous routes into the officer corps, could, therefore, consider himself rather fortunate.

Nevertheless, even for men of a martial legacy and upbringing, there existed professional (and social) barriers that defined how far a career could progress, particularly within the army's most prestigious regiments. This was reflected by the fact that, although aristocrats occupied only a quarter of junior posts within the army, they nonetheless filled over half of the senior commissioned ranks.[73] Despite his good fortune in having enjoyed an influential degree of patronage from his esteemed father, the fact remained that Edward Braddock III was still technically a "commoner" and not a member of the aristocracy. By 1753, he had, as a result of his obvious merit, progressed to the rank of Lieutenant-Colonel in the Coldstream Guards—a highly desirable position in itself. However, his lower status precluded him from command of that most senior of army regiments, for only a man of noble blood could hope to hold such a prestigious post. Therefore, frustrated in his ambitions to achieve a rank he evidently felt he had earned through service, he resolved to leave his beloved old unit.

Braddock would not have to wait too long to acquire his sought-after colonelcy. The Royal Horse Guards had been for some time without a colonel (the previous incumbent, Charles Lennox, having died in 1750) and this provided an opportunity for the ambitious Lieutenant-Colonel. As often occurred in such circumstances, there followed a period of reshuffling as the king sought to fill the vacancy for this esteemed regiment with an appropriate person of noble standing. Consequently, command of The Blues was given to Sir John Ligonier, meaning the Honourable William Herbert succeeded him as colonel of the Second Dragoon Guards. Concurrently, this created a vacancy in the 14th Foot; the opportunity Braddock had been waiting for had finally arrived. For someone of lesser means, purchasing a colonelcy would have provided enormous financial difficulties, but Braddock had the good fortune of holding a lieutenant-colonelcy in the Coldstream; the sale of this commission had a fixed value of £5000, enabling him to easily afford a position he had coveted for some time.[74]

In the year or so that separated his promotion to colonel and his deployment to America, Braddock was posted to the important strategic post of Gibraltar, where he commanded the considerable garrison there in the governor's absence. This no doubt honed his understanding of the administrative and technical facets associated with senior command and siege warfare. Nonetheless, Gibraltar was never going to replicate the rigors of a campaign in North America where he would face unique difficulties few British officers had encountered before. Indeed, strategically, the Cumberland-inspired plan Braddock was to implement would have challenged even the finest of tacticians—one of which he was not. Perhaps more fairly, he had not *yet* been tested for these tactical qualities. The European frontiers of America consisted of virtually unchartered terrain that covered many hundreds of miles and crossed a mountain range (the Appalachians) that was bisected at best by narrow Indian trails. Even the most basic supply requirements would prove debilitating over such distances, a factor that would be exacerbated by the colonies' reluctance (and inability) to provide wagons and necessaries for his small army.

Braddock's superiors would have had some familiarity with these disconcerting problems. The Board of Trade had been made aware over many years (by the continual complaints of governors) that it was impossible to force anything on the colonists without their express consent. Consequently, the capture of the Forks of the Ohio and establishing a base there could and should have been deemed a sufficient success for someone of Braddock's abilities and temperament.[75] Unfortunately, Fort Duquesne was simply not enough for the ambitious Cumberland. Braddock's instructions required him to coordinate this difficult expedition with three other virtually simultaneous assaults across a continent that physically dwarfed Britain and Ireland. Rather ambitiously, his mandate also assumed that the colonial assemblies would fall in line and prostrate their legislative rights before the orders of their new de facto Viceroy. In reality, however, Braddock's position would require a great deal of patience, tact and an ability to negotiate for authority, characteristics he simply did not possess. That experienced men like the Earl of Halifax could not, or would not, foresee the political and indeed martial tensions Braddock's appointment would create is also testimony to the over-ambitiousness of the latter's instructions and the determination of the resolute earl to implement the new colonial policy that he had been devising since 1748.

So why in fact was Edward Braddock chosen for command of the critical American expedition of 1755? Ultimately, when all factors are considered, what made him the ideal choice for the American expedition was the fact that he was very much a Cumberland protégé. His previous conduct as an officer—rigorous adherence to discipline and administration (in addition to his political reliability and single-mindedness)—appealed most to the equally uncompromising duke, who no doubt felt that Braddock could lick the apparently fractious and recalcitrant colonists into shape. Furthermore, when one considers the logistical trials the British Army would face on the North American continent, an administrative general (someone who did things by the book) would seem a perfectly logical choice for a posting that posed unparalleled hazards and difficulties; ones unimaginable to many of Braddock's contemporary Britons.

Beyond the Army

Understanding Braddock the "private man" proves to be an elusive task for analysts of this period. There are a number of contemporary commentators who give insights into his character, but biographies are rather sparse indeed. Instead, Braddock's character is often examined in the context of wider narrative histories concerned principally with recounting the events of his march to Fort Duquesne. What primary evidence does exist concerning his persona mainly takes the form of contemporary anecdotes, gossip and various documents produced during and after the campaign in the Ohio. The latter, however, must always be examined with a great deal of scrutiny. They were often written by officers who had a great deal to lose after the Monongahela debacle, and thus were concerned with deflecting potential censure away from the conduct of their authors. When one also understands that cliques had emerged in Braddock's officer corps as the campaign gathered momentum, this level of inspection becomes ever more pertinent.

As figures rose and fell on the international stage, so they would likewise fall under the acerbic penmanship of Horace Walpole. It is from this meticulous (if bitingly cynical) commentator that we learn of several rather interesting anecdotes that help develop a fuller picture of Edward Braddock. One such tale concerns one of the latter's two sisters, Frances (or Fanny) Braddock. The unfortunate Fanny was something of a *cause célèbre* in her time, being renowned in Bath as a devotee of gaming. Initially, she had been a woman of some means, having been left half of her father's estate, a total of around £3000, following his eventual demise.[76] Unfortunately, being rather flighty and overly trusting in nature, she had fallen in with a renowned gambler and debtor who would draw on the naïve Fanny when imprisoned for his debts; only to elope and leave her confounded. Eventually, her despondency spiraled and she took to playing cards to fill the void in her life. Inevitably, her debts span out of control and her mental health likewise suffered. Tragically, her ill-judgment, exacerbated by her deteriorating fortunes, became too much to bear and she was finally driven to the point where she ended her own life; doing so with what Walpole described as a "truly English deliberation ... Leaving only a note upon the table with those lines 'To die is landing on some silent shore, etc.'".[77]

Braddock's reputed response, "Poor Fanny! I always thought she would play till she would be forced to tuck herself up," at first reflection seems heartless if not cruel. Fanny, after all, was his sibling and there is no evidence to suggest he had ever renounced her for her choice of suitor; or indeed for the addiction she had to Bath's notorious gaming tables. Nonetheless, in view of the social conventions of his day, Braddock's reaction can be understood, if not justified. When one considers that a scandal such as this could draw him (a young, ambitious Lieutenant in the Coldstream Guards at this time), into an orbit of gossip, inspection, notoriety and unwanted fame—and when one reflects on the impact such unwanted renown would have had on his all-important reputation—it is perhaps understandable why he would have been eager to quickly shrug off (or curtail) any scandal associated with his now legendary sister.[78] Failure to distance himself from Fanny's legacy risked far more than the condemnation of his reputation and to be mocked by fellow officers or gentlemen could bring additional perils of its own. As shall be seen, Braddock was indeed willing to risk all for his honor.

His reaction to his poor sister's tragic demise, therefore, can certainly be understood. Less excusable, however, and also cited in the letter quoted above, was Braddock's treatment of a Mrs. W. H. Upton, who had been keeping him. It can be assumed that the two enjoyed some level of intimacy and it would seem that financially speaking, Mrs. Upton was the healthier partner. Braddock had, to quote Walpole, been "going to great lengths with her pin money" and always sought more until,

> One day that he was very pressing, she pulled out her purse and showed him that she had but twelve or fourteen shillings left; he twitched it from her, "Let me see that!" Tied up at the other end he found five guineas; he took them, tossed the empty purse in her face, saying, "Damn you for a bitch, did you mean to cheat me?" and never went near her more...[79]

What we see here is Braddock as something of an opportunist, latching on to a wealthier partner only to abandon her when she showed the prudence that would surely prove necessary if she were to avoid financial ruin at the hands of her partner's largesse. We also see his often-cited intransigence and brutality, and also a belief that, whatever the circumstances, he was right and that to contest him was inexcusable. Furthermore, he clearly demanded obedience without question and his discarding of the poor Mrs. Upton in spite of her previous generosity towards him supports this view. In Braddock's mind, her ostracism was undoubtedly justified. Despite the fact that there do not appear to have existed any pre-marital covertures between them, she had "cheated" *him* out of *her* money, showing insubordination and disrespect which concurrently disqualified her as desirable company. Unsurprisingly, after his defeat at the Monongahela, these uncompromising characteristics would be documented by a number of his subordinate officers (and several provincial attachés) who served under his command. It would seem that Braddock never had any disguise about his person, both in his private and professional lives.

Walpole's final anecdote, again highlighting Braddock's obstinacy and even recklessness, places him in a duel with a Colonel Samuel Gumley, an officer in the Royal Dragoons. Apparently, the two had previously been good friends, but for some obscure reason had reached the stage where honor needed to be settled in the time-tested gentlemanly way of the eighteenth century—a duel. Accordingly,

> Gumley, who had good humour and wit, (Braddock the latter) said, "Braddock you are a poor dog! Here take my purse; if you kill me you will be forced to run away, and then you will not have a shilling to support you." Braddock refused the purse, insisted on the duel, was disarmed, and would not even ask his life.[80]

Without question, none of these anecdotes portray Braddock in a particularly favorable light. He appears haughty, arrogant, treacherous, stubborn and, generally, a bit fatuous. And yet as Walpole alludes in the next sentence of the above letter, Braddock was good at his job—he was a more than competent soldier. Indeed, as the often scathing Walpole acknowledged "...However, with all this brutality, he has lately been governor of Gibraltar, where he made himself adored, and where scarce any governor was endured before."[81]

As Walpole suggested, Gibraltar was no easy posting and was generally unpopular with officers and soldiers alike. The "Rock," a hot and barren strategic outcrop in the Mediterranean, was notorious for its poor living quarters, rampant disease and terrible food. Garrison returns for the years 1740–1748 show that the regiments posted there were losing 17 percent of their men to sickness. As such, it was also a hotbed of desertion with the soldiers assigned to garrisoning the isthmus viewing their service as little more than a punishment.[82] So to have kept a general good order in this often-fatal posting and to have been "adored where scarce any governor was endured before," belies Braddock's undoubted merits as a British officer. It truly was quite an achievement.[83]

Likewise, although Braddock's mission to the Monongahela would fail disastrously, it would be quite wrong to assume that he would be vilified by all of the colonists with whom he would serve on this ill-fated expedition. Of the said colonial contemporaries who met and dealt with Braddock, two names stand out both for their subsequent fame and, more importantly, the proximity they had to the general. Both would acknowledge his flaws as a man and officer, but would paradoxically reinforce the view that Braddock was not the cruel, clownish martinet portrayed in so many other contemporary (and subsequent) accounts of him.

The first of these considerable figures, George Washington, had joined Braddock's expedition as an aide de camp and, despite a severe bout of dysentery, served most of the campaign at the general's side; he was with Braddock when the commander-in-chief was shot from his horse and mortally wounded at the Battle of the Monongahela. Writing many years later in his *Reflections on the French and Indian War*, Washington would say of his commander that he was a man,

> ...whose good and bad qualities were intimately blended. He was brave even to a fault and in regular service would have done honor to his profession— His attachments were warm—his enmities strong—and having no disguise

about him, both appeared in full force. He was generous and disinterested—
but plain and blunt in his manner even to rudeness...[84]

For Washington, Braddock was clearly an officer to be respected, but his contempt for the American way of war was, in the former's eyes, responsible for his failure in 1755. Here again are to be seen the positive and negative traits outlined by our civilian anecdotes. Braddock was brave and diligent but haughty and intransigent when faced by contrasting opinions—characteristics that quite possibly cost him his life.

The second significant colonial analysis regarding Braddock (and his conduct during the fateful campaign of 1755) is provided by that astute Pennsylvanian statesman, Benjamin Franklin. Franklin would find himself as something of a go-between during the Duquesne expedition, attempting to reconcile the impatient orders of a disciplinarian British field officer to the consensual political machinery of his colonial assembly. Perhaps reflecting the prejudices that existed between Pennsylvania's legislature and the London-appointed commander-in-chief, Franklin commented that,

> Our Assembly apprehending, from some information, that he (Braddock) had conceived violent prejudices against them, as averse to the service, wish'd me to wait upon him, not as from them, but as postmaster-general, under the guise of proposing to settle with him the mode of conducting with most celerity and certainty the dispatches between him and the governors of the several provinces...[85]

Nevertheless, on the whole Franklin's assessment of Braddock the man and commander were very fair—particularly when compared to many of his countrymen. Certainly, Franklin never exhibited any notably virulent animosity towards the general, acknowledging that he was a good officer caught up, tactically, in the wrong campaign. Similar to Washington, if criticisms were to be made, they would concern Braddock's total reliance on and preference for the British way of doing things. This included his belief that colonial assemblies should be made wholly subservient to the requirements of the commander-in-chief, and his staunch adherence to the tactics of the "Old World" *Frederician* military school employed by his soldiers. Like Washington, Franklin would note that Braddock's greatest failing was his intransigence in the face of contrary evidence and advice.[86]

If such a thing as a summary of a character can to be made, one could legitimately argue that Braddock was a good conventional officer who was certainly respected by many of his fellow soldiers as a fair and diligent commander. He undoubtedly placed great emphasis on discipline and was a stickler for careful administration. That he managed to marry the said predisposition for fairness with his authoritarian traits was no easy task. Like his conscientiousness, Braddock's personal courage could never be questioned, even though his bravery was sometimes reckless. This is evident in the Gumley incident and, later, the events leading to his death on the banks of the Monongahela. Unrestrained courage was, therefore, another of his positive *and* negative traits.

For all the accusations of his detachment from the realities of American campaigning that followed the Monongahela defeat, Braddock was well aware of the mortal dangers he would face on the North American continent before he was actually deployed there. Indeed, he evidently realized that the mission he was to command in America was, quite possibly, beyond his very conventional capabilities. This conclusion is based on a conversation he had with his friend George Anne Bellamy, a famous young actress with whom Braddock also enjoyed something of a paternal relationship. Braddock had first met Bellamy when she was a very young child and the two had grown notably close as the years passed (there had even been scurrilous rumors circulated that he had begun an affair with the young actress when she was 14 years old). So familiar did they become that the normally haughty Braddock would often refer to her as "Pop"; thus it can be assumed that he felt confident enough to speak freely in her company. Tellingly, before leaving for America on his fateful expedition, Braddock would express, in a rare moment of personal candidness, what may have been his true feelings about his perilous mission. According to Bellamy,

> The General told me he should never see me more; for he was going with a handful of men to conquer whole nations; and to do this they must cut their way through unknown woods. He produced the map of the country, saying at the same time, "Dear Pop, we are sent like sacrifices to the altar."[87]

To counter the popular perception of Braddock as a somewhat "brutish man" she also recounted, in the third volume of her autobiography, how the general possessed a strain of empathy; supporting accounts of his good conduct in Gibraltar. As the two were walking through a park one day, Bellamy recalled how,

> ...we heard a poor fellow was to be chastised; when I requested the General to beg off the offender. Upon his application to the general officer, whose

name was Dury, he asked Braddock, How long since he had divested himself of brutality and insolence in his manners? To which the other replied, "You never knew me insolent to my inferiors. It is only to such rude men as yourself that I behave with the spirit which I think they deserve."[88]

Evidently, Braddock was not quite the callous brute of popular imagination. Interestingly, Bellamy's first anecdote also suggests that he was hardly blind to the unique challenges of a military campaign in North America. His self-inspection shows that he was more than aware of the tactical flaws inherent in the hugely ambitious and speculative "Braddock Plan." Without question, Edward Braddock was a very good regimental-level officer and he may have made a fine general in a more traditional, set-piece European theatre of war. Indeed, the first of Bellamy's recollections, as mentioned, unveiled his awareness of the logistical challenges he would face on the frontiers of European America. Contrast this with the Duke of Cumberland's sweeping designs which bore little understanding of the environmental perils of an American campaign, then Braddock's strategic and tactical capabilities are, to a certain extent, vindicated.

Nonetheless, there were several fatal flaws in Braddock's martial and personal qualities and, as shall be shown later in this work, when faced by the unfamiliar terrain of a new continent; the hostility and intransigence of colonial assemblies; and the absolute necessity of personal adaptability in the face of his allies *and* an enemy who simply did not recognize the traditional formalities of European warfare, he was simply out of his depth. In the absence of adaptability, Braddock had to rely on the traits that had hitherto served him so well in his career—an inherent sense of duty, personal courage and strict disciplinarian inclinations—if he were to stand any chance of prosecuting the Braddock Plan he was to command. The latter attribute was one the Duke of Cumberland, in discussions with Braddock prior to his dispatch to North America, stressed was perhaps the most important of all given the nature of the service on that continent. As the steely Duke pressed upon his subordinate, "the Strictest & most exact Discipline" was "always necessary, but can never be more so than on your present Service." This was essential to "prevent any Pannick in the Troops from Indians, to whom the Soldiery not yet being accustomed, the French will not fail to make attempts towards it."[89] It was advice that Braddock would follow into his makeshift grave.

In consideration of the above-cited anecdotes, one cannot help but be drawn to the conclusion that Braddock was a very well-schooled European officer—certainly at the regimental level. To be a good officer, a man needed courage, gentlemanly virtues (in other words, social status and standing), an ability to set a fine example for the soldiers under their command and a good private and professional reputation. In an eighteenth-century context, it is evident that he ticked virtually all of the right boxes, the largest of which, arguably, was the excellent reputation he had cultivated for himself as commanding officer of the Gibraltar garrison. With advantageous political connections to the Duke of Cumberland, a man who took great pride in the reformations he had made to the army as an institution, Braddock, the quintessential "Cumberland soldier," was a perfectly logical choice for the American expedition. His abilities as an organizer (or administrator) also hinted that he would be the best choice for a profoundly "logistical" military campaign in Britain's politically fractured and topographically daunting American empire.

Before concluding this brief biographical sketch of General Edward Braddock it is apt to pose one further significant question; and one which should be asked of all Braddock's detractors. That is whether there existed another British general who at this time (1755) could have met the unique challenges posed by American warfare. Many of the celebrated officers who would enjoy successes in Braddock's wake were in fact fortunate in that they were able to draw on the reams of tactical commentary compiled after the Monongahela defeat. Were Wolfe, Forbes, Amherst and Howe (for instance) placed in Braddock's shoes, one should wonder whether they would have enjoyed a more successful outcome than their unfortunate predecessor did. American warfare was, essentially, an alien concept to the British Army in 1755 and few contemporaries in either Great Britain or its army would have thought, prior to July 9, that a largely Native American force (dismissed as unruly "savages" by complacent observers—including Braddock) would rout such a considerable force of professional British soldiers. Indeed, the doctrines (and application) of *petite guerre* that had been encountered and embraced in wars in Ireland and Scotland in the seventeenth and eighteenth centuries had been dismissed by most within the army's officer corps, who refused to grasp the merits of what they considered a "barbarous" method of fighting. This meant that the British army in North America, whoever commanded it, would rely on European tactics to overwhelm the French and their Indian allies in the American backcountry. Considering these factors, it may very well have been that at the time of his appointment, Edward Braddock III was the best candidate for a very difficult job. It was a charge that also, it will be remembered, exposed the commander-in-chief to the very British–Atlantic political divergences that had frustrated experienced metropolitan politicians, such as the Earl of Halifax, who from 1748 had sought to establish a hugely ambitious "new colonial policy."[90] As I have previously argued, that men so experienced in colonial affairs (as Halifax undoubtedly was) could not reshape British America to accept and fit this new imperial vision in reality—and from the perspective of this book—also exemplifies the enormity of the leadership challenges Edward Braddock faced as he sought to execute what can be essentially described as the military wing of Halifax's colonial reforms.

Notes

1. Jeremy Black, *America or Europe? British Foreign Policy, 1739–63* (London: UCL Press, 1998), 81–104.
2. "Dinwiddie to the Earl of Halifax, August 15th, 1754" in Robert Alonzo Brock (ed.), *The Official Records of Robert Dinwiddie: Lieutenant-Governor of the Colony of Virginia, 1751–1758*, Volume III (Richmond, Virginia, 1883), 281.
3. More specifically, the Pistole Fee (equivalent of a Spanish coin worth approximately $4.00) was demanded by Dinwiddie in return for attaching the "official seal" to patents for land. He had only obtained the acquiescence of the "Council" when passing this fee and this brought him into conflict with the colony's lower house. The Burgesses saw the fee as a form of taxation that had been passed without their consent; which was a breach of the principle of freedom from arbitrary taxation. See Jack P. Greene, "Landon Carter and the Pistole Fee dispute" in *The William and Mary Quarterly, Third Series, Vol. 14, No 1* (Jan, 1957), 66–69 and "The Case of the Pistole Fee: The Report of a Hearing on the Pistole Fee Dispute before the Privy Council, June 18, 1754," *The Virginia Magazine of History and Biography*, 66, No. 4 (October, 1958), 399–422.
4. Dinwiddie would express his disappointment with the responses of Virginia's fellow colonies in a letter to the Board of Trade. Pleading for assistance, he suggested that, "The other colonies (saving North Carolina) have not given any Assistance, and I fear do not intend to do anything, unless oblig'd by an Act of Parliament for a general Poll Tax of half a Crown..." See "Governor Dinwiddie to the Lords of Trade, July 24th, 1754," in Brock (ed.) *The Official Records of Robert Dinwiddie*, III, 239–243. It would seem that Dinwiddie was drawing the same conclusions as the Earl of Halifax as he reflected upon the indifference of the British colonies to their collective defense.
5. A good review of the environmental challenges posed by a tropical war is provided by J. R. McNeill, "The Ecological Basis of Warfare in the Caribbean," in Maartin Ultee, *Adapting to Conditions: War and Society in the Eighteenth-century* (Alabama: University of Alabama Press, 1986), 26–32.

6. Thad W. Riker, "The Politics behind Braddock's Expedition," *The American Historical Review*, Vol. 13, No. 4 (Jul., 1908), 742–752.
7. It would be fair to say that Walpole despised Newcastle. For instance, in his memoirs for 1755 he compares Newcastle to the Duke of Buckingham (1592–1628), even referring to him (Newcastle) as a "*Stellionatus*" (a lizard with star-like spots—tricky/cunning/deceitful). See Horace Walpole, John Brooke (ed.), *Memoirs of King George II, March 1754–1757* (New Haven, CT: Yale University Press, 1985), 99. Historian George L. Liam estimates that Walpole referred to Newcastle on at least 250 occasions in his fêted letters. See George L. Liam, "Walpole and the Duke of Newcastle," in Warren Hunting Smith (ed.), *Horace Walpole: Writer, Politician and Connoisseur: Essays on the 250th Anniversary of Walpole's Birth* (New Haven, CT: Yale University Press, 1967), 59. A more balanced review of Newcastle's relationship with his one-time mentor Robert Walpole is provided by Clyve Jones, "The Duke of Newcastle's Letters on the Fall of Walpole in 1742," *The Electronic British Library Journal* (2013), art. 1, 1–9, http://www.bl.uk/eblj/2013articles/article1.html, accessed 15/04/2013.
8. Reed Browning, *The Duke of Newcastle* (London, 1975), 187–188. Also, see Francis Jennings's brief assessment of Newcastle's political machinery in Francis Jennings, *The Ambiguous Iroquois Empire: The Covenant Chain Confederation of Indian Tribes with English Colonies from its beginnings to the Lancaster Treaty of 1744* (New York: W.W. Norton, 1984), 112–116.
9. Newcastle's own words express his contempt for demagoguery, "I shall not … think the demands of the people a rule of conduct, nor shall I ever fear to incur their resentment in the prosecution of their interest. I shall never flatter their passions to obtain their favour, or gratify their revenge for fear of their contempt." See Samuel Johnson, *The Works of Samuel Johnson, LL.D.*, Volume XIII (13 vols. London: John Stockdale, 1777), 166.
10. The Duke's core ideological beliefs were hardly unique and echoed somewhat the earlier political ideas expressed by seventeenth-century philosopher Thomas Hobbes, who had also argued for strong, central, governmental authority.
11. Thad W. Ricker, "The Politics behind Braddock's Expedition," *The American Historical Review*, Vol. 13, No. 4 (Jul., 1908), 743.
12. Archer Butler Herbert, *Braddock's Road and three relevant papers, Historic Highways of America*, Volume 4 (Cleveland, OH: Arthur H Clark Company, 1903), 34–35.
13. After the War of the Austrian Succession, Newcastle became even more entrenched with regards this "system." See T. R. Clayton, "The Duke of Newcastle, the Earl of Halifax, and the American Origins of the Seven Years War," *The Historical Journal*, Vol. 24, No. 3 (Sep., 1981), 571–603.

14. See Reed Browning, "The Duke of Newcastle and the Imperial Election Plan, 1749–1754," *The Journal of British Studies*, Vol. 7, No. 1 (Nov., 1967), 22–47.
15. Summarising the popular view perhaps, one commentator would exclaim "Is this Treaty Honourable? With reluctance I speak out the shame of my country, it is far from Honourable ... When I dipped into it I really took it to be a *French* Edict ..." Such was the widespread incredulity with this treaty. See "*A Letter from a gentleman in London to his friend in the country: concerning the treaty at Aix-la-Chapelle, concluded on the 8th of October, 1748*" (London, 1748). Considering the weak position Britain found itself in by 1748, at least on the European continent, Newcastle's concessions were actually quite brilliant and did much to save face in the halls of Europe's great courts.
16. Thomas E. Crocker, *Braddock's March: How the Man Sent to Seize a Continent Changed American History* (Yardley, PA: Westholme Publishing, LLC, 2011), 47 and Archer Butler Herbert, *Braddock's Road and Three Relevant Papers*, 34–35.
17. Browning, *The Duke of Newcastle*, 207. Newcastle's strategic awareness of the importance of the colonies was also stressed by T. R. Clayton. Clayton highlighted the fact that Newcastle, even after being succeeded by the Duke of Bedford in the Southern Department, was kept abreast of colonial developments by intelligence documents he frequently received concerning French encroachments in the New World. See T.R. Clayton, "The Duke of Newcastle, the Earl of Halifax, and the American Origins of the Seven Years War," *The Historical Journal* Vol. 24, No. 3 (Sept., 1981), 471–603.
18. Quoted in Ibid., 575.
19. Ibid., 576.
20. Quoted in Lawrence Henry Gipson, *The British Empire before the American Revolution*, Vol. VI, *The Great War for the Empire: The Years of Defeat, 1754–1757* (New York: Alfred A. Knopf, 1968), 55.
21. Newcastle can, however, be censured for allowing colonial policy to be determined by private interests and systematically neglecting the administration of the colonies' political machinations. Neither did he specifically oversee the implementation of the mercantilist principles of the Acts of Trade and Navigation Acts. This *laissez faire* attitude naturally helped widen the aforementioned chasm between the British and colonial Americans as the latter became rather used to being loosely governed; and would consequently resist Britain's attempts to centralize their administration. See James A. Henretta, "*Salutary Neglect:*" *Colonial Administration under the Duke of Newcastle* (Princeton, NJ: Princeton University Press, 1972).

22. See "The Anglo-Dutch Relationship, 1750-1850," in Bob Moore & Henk van Nierop (eds.), *Colonial Empires Compared: Britain and the Netherlands, 1750-1850* (Aldershot: Ashgate Publishing, 2003), 11-33.
23. The geopolitical situation that existed at this time was masterfully summarized by Julian S. Corbett in his renowned work, *England in the Seven Years War*. Fundamentally, in the event of a breach with France, it was essential for Britain to avoid being seen as the aggressor. See Julian S. Corbett, *England in the Seven Years War: A Study in Combined Strategy*, Volume I (London: Longman's Green and Co: 1907), 22-23.
24. Colonel H. C. B. Rogers, *The British Army of the Eighteenth-Century* (London: George Allen and Unwin, 1977), 23.
25. In August 1753, Robert D'Arcy, Lord Holderness and Secretary of State for the Southern Department, had advised William Shirley, Governor of Massachusetts, that it was the King's wish "that all his provinces in America should be aiding and assisting each other, in case of any invasion." It must be added that this proclamation reflected a desire to avoid costly British overseas commitments and not a yearning for a homogenous British North America. See "Holderness to Shirley, 23 August 1753," in Charles Henry Lincoln (ed.) *Correspondence of William Shirley, Governor of Massachusetts and Military Commander in America, 1731-1760*, 2 Vols (New York: Macmillan, 1912), Vol. II, 13.
26. See Henretta, *Salutary Neglect*, 339.
27. Indeed, Cumberland was a very able man. That the often-scathing Horace Walpole would rank him with Pitt, Granville, Mansfield and his father Sir Robert Walpole as one of the five great men he had known is testimony to his evident abilities. His command of a large army in Europe during the 1750s did cause great unease for many Britons who evidently saw his advocacy of military "continentalism"—defending British liberties in Germany through confronting absolutist France there—as a surreptitious guise to mask his *real* intention of truncating English liberties. Hence Lord Chesterfield's expressed fear that, should George II die while his son was on campaign in Germany, the latter could return "attended by an Army of nine thousand men ... Richard the Third had but seven thousand upon a like occasion." See Philip Dormer Stanhope, Lord Chesterfield to Newcastle, 4 August 1757 in Romney Sedgwick (ed.), *Letters from George III to Lord Bute: 1756-1766* (London. Macmillan, 1939), xlix.
28. See Evan Charteris, *William Augustus Duke of Cumberland: His early life and times (1721-1748)* (London, 1913), vii-ix.
29. The officer class and their performance "pre-Cumberland," was something of a deep concern; warfare, it would seem, was regarded as a gentlemanly pastime and as such, officers were rather sloppy in their appearance and discipline. Cumberland, therefore, had to go back to basics in his reforms, administering everything from the way in which junior officers

addressed their superiors to the "baggage" they could take with them into the field. See Sir John Fortesque, *A History of the British Army: Volume II, First Part—to the close of the Seven Years War* (London, 1899), 566–567.
30. Matthew Ward, *Breaking the Backcountry: The Seven Years War in Virginia and Pennsylvania, 1754–1765* (Pittsburgh, PA: University of Pittsburgh Press, 2003), 159.
31. Clayton, "American Origins of the Seven Years War," 592.
32. This plan is briefly discussed in George Louis Beer, *British Colonial Policy, 1754–1765* (New York, 1907), 24–26 and, more recently, George Yagi, A Study of Britain's Military Failure During the Initial Stages of the Seven Years' War in North America, 1754–1758 (Ph.D. thesis, Exeter University, 2007), 19–50. The full plan can be read in E. B. O'Callaghan (ed.), *Documents Relative to the Colonial History of New York, Procured in Holland, England and France*, Volume VI (Albany, 1855), 903–906.
33. This was, after all, frequently their favorite means of extracting concessions from governors as Robert Dinwiddie had discovered first-hand when, in exchange for revenues to support his Ohio expedition of 1754, the House of Burgesses demanded he concede defeat in the infamous "Pistole Fee" dispute.
34. See Alison Gilbert Olson, "The British Government and Colonial Union, 1754," *The William and Maryland Quarterly*, Third Series, Vol. 17, No.1 (Jan, 1960), 22–34.
35. Quoted in Pargellis, *Lord Loudoun in America*, 29.
36. See "Dinwiddie to Earl Granville, July 24th, 1754," in Brock (ed.), *Official Records of Robert Dinwiddie*, III, 249–250. Dinwiddie's biographer, John Alden, has, with some justification, argued that it was Dinwiddie himself who did much to influence the evolution of the Braddock Plan. It was he who had first recommended to Henry Fox that a "generalissimo" be sent to America and Fox, a close ally of the Duke of Cumberland, duly passed on his intelligence and opinion. See John Richard Alden, *Robert Dinwiddie: Servant of the Crown* (Charlottesville: University Press of Virginia, 1973), 89.
37. William M. Torrens, *History of Cabinets: From the Union with Scotland to the Acquisition of Canada and Bengal*, Volume II (London: 1894), 192.
38. "William Shirley to the Duke of Newcastle, Dec. 14th, 1745" in Charles Henry Lincoln (ed.), *The Correspondence of William Shirley, Governor of Massachusetts and Military Commander in America, 1731–1760*, Volume I (2 volumes, New York, 1912), 295.
39. Stephen Conway, *War, State and Society in Mid-eighteenth-century Britain and Ireland* (Oxford: Oxford University Press, 2006), 230.
40. Quoted in Timothy J. Shannon, *Indians and Colonists at the Crossroads of Empire: The Albany Congress of 1754* (Ithaca, NY: Cornell University Press, 2000), 78.

41. Jack Greene, "An Uneasy Connection: An Analysis of the Preconditions of the American Revolution" in Stephen G. Grutz and James H. Hutson (eds.) *Essays on the American Revolution* (Chapel Hill: North Carolina University Press, 1973), 32–80.
42. See Jack P. Greene, "The Origins of the New Colonial Policy, 1748–1763" in Jack P. Greene, J. R. Pole (eds.), *A Companion to the American Revolution* (Oxford: Blackwell Publishing, 2000), 107–108.
43. Cumberland's role in this matter is discussed briefly in Dominic Graham's analysis of the Beausejour expedition. See Dominic Graham, "The Planning of the Beausejour Operation and the Approaches to War in 1755," *The New England Quarterly*, Vol. 41, No. 4 (Dec., 1968), 551–556.
44. I refer to the "Walker Expedition." See Ian K. Steele, *Guerrillas and Grenadiers: The Struggle for Canada, 1689–1760* (Toronto: Ryerson Press, 1974), 39–40. There was, of course, no single overall commander-in-chief of all forces in North America in this particular campaign.
45. Winthrop Sargent, *The History of an Expedition against Fort Duquesne in 1755, under Major General Edward Braddock* (Philadelphia, 1855), 134. Unfortunately, the hope of raising sufficient levies in America was to be disappointed.
46. Douglas W. Marshall, "The British Engineers in America: 1755–1783," *The Journal of the Society for Army Historical Research*, 51 (Autumn, 1973), 155.
47. Newcastle was also extremely concerned by the potential cost of any large-scale assault on French encroachments in the New World. There was a surplus of £100,000 to meet the French threat in America and Newcastle, as far as was possible, was desperate to keep expenditure within this sum in order to avoid referring matters to the House of Commons—where he lacked any reliable allies. See Pargellis, *Loudon in America*, 22.
48. Anderson, *Crucible of War*, 68.
49. Franklin's "Albany Plan of Union" advocated just that. He hoped that by creating a grand Assembly headed by a "President-General," the colonists would develop a common spirit that would help meet the French threat to the North. The Board of Trade, advocating its own Plan of Union, never sought official approval for Franklin's plan from the Crown; they instead proposed that governors, along with select members of their councils, order the raising of troops and building of forts. Funding would come from the Treasury; the money would later be repaid by a parliamentary tax levied on the colonists. Neither plan met the approval of the Ministry. See Benjamin Franklin, John Biglow (ed.), *The Autobiography of Benjamin Franklin* (Philadelphia, 1868), 294–301.
50. Cumberland did not have a position in the cabinet so Fox served as the "cabal's" representative in his stead.

51. "Sketch for the operations in North America. Nov. 16 1754" in Pargellis (ed.) *Military affairs in North America*, 45–46.
52. "Lieutenant-Colonel Charles Lawrence to Halifax, August 23rd, 1754" in Pargellis (ed.) *Military affairs in North America*, 26–30.
53. For a complete transcript of Braddock's instructions for the campaign of 1755 see the previously cited "Sketch for the operations in North America. Nov. 16 1754" in Ibid., 45–48.
54. Clayton, "American Origins of the Seven Years War," 596.
55. Halifax clearly favored a campaign in New York—which would sever French links between the Ohio and Canada and also bring greater control over the Iroquois confederacy. See Gipson, *The British Empire before the American Revolution*, VI, 60.
56. Jennings, *Empire of Fortune*, 115.
57. See Black, *America or Europe?* 81–104.
58. For Braddock's secret instructions see O'Callaghan (ed.) *Documents relative to the Colonial History of New York*, VI, 920–922.
59. Ibid., 920–922.
60. Neither did it allow for British naval advantages to be directly brought to bear (as was evidenced in the pivotal sieges of Louisbourg [1758] and Quebec [1759]).
61. For Keppel's mission objectives see, "Instruction from the Lords of the Admiralty to Admiral Keppel" in Pargellis, *Military Affairs in North America*, 48–53.
62. Unfortunately, the dispatch of British forces to America was published and announced by Henry Fox (now Secretary for War) in the *Gazette* with, as Philip Yorke stated, "as much parade as possible." See Philip C. Yorke, *The Life and Correspondence of Philip Yorke Earl of Hardwicke Lord High Chancellor of Great Britain*, Vol. II (3 vols. Chicago, University of Chicago Press: 1913), 257.
63. Dallas Irvine, "The First British Regulars in North America," *Military Affairs*, Vol. 9 (Winter, 1945) 337–354.
64. Lee, a controversial figure during the later War of Independence, will, like Edward Braddock who he so readily defended in 1755, remain one of the more polarizing figures of American history.
65. See Paul E. Kopperman, *Braddock at the Monongahela* (Pittsburgh: University of Pittsburgh Press, 1992), 94.
66. For an excellent biography of Braddock see Lee McCardell, *Ill-Starred General: Braddock of the Coldstream Guards* (Pittsburgh: University of Pittsburgh Press, 1958).
67. Alan J. Guy, *Oeconomy and Discipline: Officership and Administration in the British Army 1714–1763* (Manchester: Manchester University Press, 1985), 3–9.

68. As Linda Colley suggested, the prevalence of Scots and Irishmen within the officer corps was due, in no small measure, to the relative poverty that existed on the "Celtic fringes" of the British Isles. See Linda Colley, *Britons: Forging the Nation, 1707–1837* (London, 1992), 128–129.
69. See Anthony Bruce, *The Purchase System in the British Army, 1660–1871* (London: Royal Historical Society, 1980).
70. Henry Pelham would summarize this belief when, in 1744, he voiced his deeply ingrained beliefs on the subject to Parliament, declaring, "I have always heard it admitted that our liberties can never be in danger as long as they are entrusted to men of family and fortune ... Has it not always been with good reason urged that our liberties are in no danger from our standing army because it is commanded by men of the best families and fortunes." Quoted in Guy, *Oeconomy and Discipline*, 89.
71. See Ibid.
72. Indeed, to use the French model as an example, the 100,000 noblemen France possessed by the middle of the eighteenth century dominated the ranks of the officer corps of the French Army. Jealous of their perceived rights, they were hostile to the idea of promotion through merit and actively fought to retain their privileges. The French Revolution effaced this "tradition." See William Doyle (ed.), *Officers, Nobles and Revolutionaries: Essays on Eighteenth-Century France* (London: Hambledon Press, 1995), 63–66.
73. J. A. Houlding, *Fit for Service: The Training of the British Army, 1715–1795* (Oxford: Clarendon Press, 1981), 104.
74. For a costing of various commissioned ranks in the Coldstream see Daniel MacKinnon, *Origin and Services of the Coldstream Guards*, Volume I (London, 1833), 347.
75. Whether Fort Duquesne should have been considered the crucible of the campaign remains an issue of contention. Stanley Pargellis, for instance, concluded that Braddock's expedition should have been concentrated in New York, where a wholly provincial expedition, concocted by Governor William Shirley of Massachusetts, was already being prepared in anticipation of an assault on Crown Point. See Stanley Pargellis, *Lord Loudoun in North America* (New Haven, CT: Yale University Press, 1961), 35–42.
76. McCardell, *Ill-Starred General*, 54.
77. "Horace Walpole to Sir Horace Mann, Thursday 21 August 1755" in W. S. Lewis, Warren Hunting Smith and George Liam (eds.) *Horace Walpole's Correspondence with Sir Horace Mann, Volume IV 15th November 1748 NS 18th September 1756* (New Haven, CT: Yale University Press, 1960), 490–494.
78. According to Braddock biographer Lee McCardell, Henry Fielding's comedy, *The Covent Garden Tragedy*, has scenes loosely based on the fate

of Fanny Braddock and the notorious behavior of her brother, Edward. See McCardell, *Ill-starred General*, 63–66.
79. "Walpole to Mann, 21 August 1755" in Walpole, Lewis, Smith and Lam (eds.), *Walpole's correspondence*, Vol. IV, 492–493.
80. "Walpole to Mann, Thursday 28 August 1755," ibid., 494–496. Although a slightly comical incident, this duel—and others of its kind—were often tied, at least within military circles, to the wider issue of "honor." Honor essentially dictated an officer's relationship with his commissioned peers. As James Hendrix has suggested, in the pre-bureaucratic age, it was an officer's reputation that ultimately governed his chances for recognition and promotion (purchase and seniority notwithstanding). See James N. Hendrix, Spirit of the Corps: The British Army and the Pre-National Pan-European Military World and the origins of American Martial Culture, 1754–1783 (Ph. D. Thesis, University of Pittsburgh, 2005), 72–75.
81. Ibid., 496.
82. Houlding, *Fit for Service*, 16.
83. As David L. Preston has suggested, Braddock's service here would also have entailed frequent engagements with civilian authorities and a diverse multi-ethnic community. See David L. Preston, *Braddock's Defeat: The Battle of the Monongahela and the Road to Revolution* (New York: Oxford University Press, 2015), 51.
84. Washington, Anderson (ed.) *George Washington Remembers*, 21.
85. Benjamin Franklin, John Biglow (ed.), *Autobiography of Benjamin Franklin* (Philadelphia, 1868), 302.
86. Ibid., 249.
87. George Anne Bellamy, *An Apology for the life of George Anne Bellamy, late of Covent Garden Theatre, Volume II* (London, 1786), 204–205. Bellamy was originally born in Fingal, Ireland and was the illegitimate daughter of Lord Tyrawley. She rose to fame in 1744 following her depiction of the character "Monimia" in the play *The Orphan*. George Anne was always a feature in the "best circles" of society and made her last appearance on the stage at Drury Lane in 1785.
88. Bellamy, *An Apology for the life of George Anne Bellamy*, Volume III, 55.
89. Quoted in Houlding, *Fit for Service*, 357.
90. See Greene, "The Origins of the New Colonial Policy, 1748–1763" in Greene and Pole (eds.), *A Companion to the American Revolution*, 101–112.

CHAPTER 4

"Stupid Brutes Led by an Eighteenth-Century Colonel Blimp?" The British Army of the Eighteenth Century

As has been demonstrated in several instances within this work, the British regiments Edward Braddock led into the Virginian backwoods in 1755 have received harsh indictments in many histories of the French and Indian War, particularly those produced by American nationalist historians who have also contextualized them, and the army in general, through the prism that is the War of Independence. The latter was, of course, a struggle in which the British redcoat was the antagonist (or oppressor) in the battle for American nationhood, and is thus condemned, essentially, for being on the wrong side of history. Braddock's defeat at the Monongahela in 1755 was, therefore, in actuality one of numerous pre-Revolutionary War progenitors that helped shape the negative connotations of this historical paradigm. Indeed, Ian K. Steele's observation that "North American pride in the ways of the New World," which was based on an assumption that "in warfare, as in everything else, the men of the New World were better than the history-laden men of the Old," is noticeably evidenced by many American reflections upon the supposedly *British* defeat of July 9, 1755.[1]

Stanley Pargellis, of the vanguard of what can only be described as a revisionist school of thought regarding the Anglo-American rout at the Battle of the Monongahela, had previously applied this understanding of New World attitudes to Old World soldiery and societies when he suggested that,

© The Editor(s) (if applicable) and The Author(s) 2016
R. Hall, *Atlantic Politics, Military Strategy and the French and Indian War*, War, Culture and Society, 1750-1850,
DOI 10.1007/978-3-319-30665-0_4

Military historians hold that Braddock's defeat taught a lesson badly needed for the time: you cannot employ parade ground tactics in the bush. To almost everyone who in one connection or another remembers Braddock, this episode stands as a conflict between Old World and New World ways, with the outcome justifying the new.[2]

Dallas Irvine, a contemporary of Pargellis's, reinforced the latter's conclusions, albeit in a more vernacular tone, when he declared that the setback had been used to make the redcoats,

...appear as stupid brutes led by an eighteenth-century Colonel Blimp, while American militia simultaneously appeared as a keen yeomanry led by that paragon of all virtue and destined military hero of the fight for American liberty, George Washington.[3]

To this day, such a depiction of the British Army still has its adherents and is reflected in many of the more non-scholarly representations of the seemingly infamous redcoat that have permeated the popular culture of the twentieth and twenty-first centuries.[4]

Fortunately, these often extreme generalizations have been, and are continuing to be, eroded by modern military historiography. The result is that many of the stereotypical denunciations of the army (especially those forces deployed to North America) are shown to be grossly misguided or, at best, extreme characterizations of this institution and the men who served in it ranks. The trend emergent from "New Military" social, economic and martial studies has seen Braddock's army, and indeed the eighteenth-century British Army as a whole, receiving a more balanced evaluation. Certainly, with the study of military history no longer the sole purview of antiquarians and professional soldiers, this historiographical genre has increasingly focused upon the more academically acceptable areas of martial tradition. These, as mentioned, have included the various ways in which war shaped the process of nation-state formation, the development of the army as a social institution and the place of war and the military in society as a whole. Corresponding to such a shift in the priorities of martial studies, a change in the perception of the eighteenth-century British Army has thus been made possible.[5]

The purpose of this fourth chapter, then, is to provide an analysis of the British Army of the eighteenth century that will incorporate some of the works outlined above into its contextualization. As the regular army was expected to be the decisive factor in the prosecution of the

"Braddock Plan" of 1755, such a reflection is amply justified. In basic terms, it is hoped that a brief overview of the institution's historical origins will provide the reader unfamiliar with recent historical scholarship with a background knowledge of this fighting force. Yet this analysis will provide more than just a narrative of events; it will also elaborate upon the reasons behind what was, undoubtedly, a longstanding cultural hostility towards the British Army; one which extended to both sides of the Atlantic. Separating fact and reality from traditional prejudice and biased interpretation not only serves the purpose of providing a clearer contextualization of the contemporary hostility that existed towards the army, but also allows this frame of mind and the manner in which it has resonated in subsequent histories of the French and Indian War to be better understood.

To provide a natural flow from this analysis of the cultural origins of British (and indeed American) hostility towards professional armies, also to be examined are more specialized fields in which the British Army operated; such as its familiarity with, and implementation of, military concepts that were supposedly absent from its preparations for operations in the North American hinterland. Notably, this included an appreciation of the importance of *petite guerre* (unconventional, or guerrilla war)— a localized variety of which was to be fought in America. Indeed, for critics of Braddock's army, the unfamiliarity of the British soldier with American *petite guerre*, and the refusal of Braddock himself to adapt to it (despite colonial protestations), is a major cause of the setback he suffered on July 9, 1755. The logic follows that the British soldier, as judged by his performance on that fateful day, was fine material for the chess-piece encounters of continental Europe, but was almost pre-destined to fail in the American backcountry, where the usual conventions of regular warfare rarely applied.[6]

Such an argument, however, ignores the very real experiences the British Army had encountered in its historical campaigns in Ireland and Scotland during the seventeenth and eighteenth centuries. In both instances it had been required to adopt the tactical doctrines of *petite guerre* to meet the unique localized challenges posed by armed civilians fighting unconventional military campaigns. Unfortunately, although the army certainly was not ignorant of the theories this mode of warfare, the upper echelons of the officer corps, convinced of the supremacy of conventional war and having witnessed great British victories against the French (such as Malplaquet) and, latterly, the Jacobites at Culloden, marginalized the *real* lessons of the latest Stuart uprising. They instead continued to place great emphasis on conventional training and tactics. Some of the army's preliminary difficulties in America, therefore, lay in this attachment to convention and tradition; a factor that would be exacerbated by its latent prejudices towards Native Americans and Canadian militia, who were dismissed as "savages" by none other than Edward Braddock himself.[7] Even so, the necessity of adaptation was certainly not lost on that general who evidently placed some value on the services of native warriors in the abounding forests that spanned the borders of British America. He, however, lacked the cultural subtlety required to master the delicate balancing act that was native diplomacy, while Governors James Glenn and Robert Dinwiddie, through their intense particularism and attachment to local and personal interests, ruined any hope the general may have had of adding Iroquois and Cherokee warriors to his distinctly *Anglo-American* army. This was, ultimately, to be compounded by the fact that his colonial auxiliary units, though consisting of locally raised American soldiers, were largely untrained, raw recruits who had as much familiarity with the rigors of forest fighting as did the troops who formed the rank and file of the 44th and 48th. In short, they simply could not be relied upon to replace, or replicate, the services of indigenous warriors.[8]

The second stick used to beat the British Army of the period (often cited by neoprogressive historians such as Francis Jennings), and one which is placed within the wider context of its inherent brutality, inability to adapt and thus ineptitude for American warfare, concerns the nature of the relationship that existed between the officers and men of the rank and file. Traditionally, stereotypes of the redcoat and his plight as a serving soldier manifest themselves in lurid accounts of the wanton cruelty of the officer corps who commanded the soldiery. To say that the British regular is thus depicted as being a deeply oppressed figure that lived under a regime of ruthless pseudo-slavery—one imposed and maintained by the army's savage disciplinary code--would be no exaggeration of the attitudes that have been adopted by many historians.

Following from notable modern army scholars, such as Glenn Steppler and more recently Stephen Brumwell, it will be argued here that although the army's legal code was inhuman by *today's* standards, it was not indiscriminate and was actually based upon the English legal system that operated more widely in society-at-large.[9] By reference to notable studies of eighteenth-century English law, its implementation within wider society and, by extension, its military counterparts, "The Mutiny Act" and "The Articles of War," it will be stressed that assumptions made of the ingrained brutality of the British Army are exaggerated, and miss the very real motivating factors that also gave men the incentives to serve in what was a notably perilous occupation.

Tracing the Origins of Army Stereotyping: The Misapplication of Historical Literature

Much of the criticism levelled at the humble redcoat is derived from what may seem, at first appearance, to be rather surprising sources. Indeed, the interpretation and widespread application of rather unflattering quotes from some of the army's most well-respected (and well-known) officers has often been used to paint what has been a very negative picture of the British soldier and the institution he served. Epitomizing this trend among those who formed the officer corps of the eighteenth-century army was the celebrated James Wolfe, commander of the British expedition that finally wrested control of Quebec from the French in 1759, who seemingly possessed an almost inherent contempt for the regular soldiers he served alongside. Reflecting on the defeat of Edward Braddock in 1755, for example, Wolfe concluded that the disaster could be laid squarely upon "the cowardice and ill-behavior of the men." He further pondered: "did ever the Geneva and pox of this country operate more shamefully and violently upon the dirty inhabitants of it under the denomination of soldiers." Wolfe did not stop there. Such was his disdain for Braddock's soldiers that he even derided them as "Rascals" and "canaille."[10] Wolfe was but one of many officers who unceremoniously damned that general's enlisted men. In all likelihood he, in this instance, drew his conclusions from the literature of his fellow officers who had served on the banks of the Monongahela. Many of these, including Braddock's aide-de-camp, Robert Orme, laid much of the blame for that loss at the feet of the panic-stricken soldiery. Indeed, Braddock himself was said, in his death throes, to have condemned the performance of the British regulars and praised that of his American auxiliaries.

Wolfe's frequent exasperation with his men appeared regularly in his personal correspondence. Commenting on recruits destined to reinforce the British Army in America for the campaign of 1758, he would lament that, "The reinforcements from England and Ireland consist of about five-or-six-and-twenty hundred men, two very good battalions we have, and the rest is *la canaille* from the second battalion upon this establishment."[11] Even more harshly, at Portsmouth (in February 1758) he would bewail that,

Disorderly soldiers of different regiments are collected here; some from the ships, others from the hospital, some waiting to embark—dirty, drunken, insolent rascals, improved by the hellish nature of the place, where every kind of corruption, immorality, and looseness is carried to excess; it is a sink of the lowest and most abominable of vices.[12]

Despite this apparent vitriol, in a theme reminiscent of many officers of the period, Wolfe's chastisement of his soldiers actually derived from a very evident paternal concern for his men. Although the soldiers were denounced as "dirty, drunken and insolent rascals," what really leaps from this letter is his fatherly fear that the "infernal den" that was eighteenth-century Portsmouth was ruining his men. Like a scolding parent disparaging his children for being led astray, therefore, Wolfe's denunciations should not be taken too literally; he cared that his troops seemed to be being corrupted by their environment and wanted to put a stop to it post haste. Most British officers would have shared this sentiment.

Like James Wolfe, Bennett Cuthbertson, author of a very influential contemporary treatise on military administration, deplored what he considered the general ignorance and lack of intelligence that apparently blighted the army's rank and file. In his work, *A System for the Compleat* [sic] *Interior Management and Economy of a Battalion of Infantry*, Cuthbertson clearly expressed his exasperation with the caliber of army recruits when he wrote that "Soldiers are not to be depended on in anything, let it be ever so much so for their advantage." They also needed to be cured of the "Stubborn disposition which characterizes the peasants of most countries" and broken of their "awkward, clownish ways."[13] When it came to recruiting, he advised officers to make their own judgments about a man's age as, "the common people are in general so ignorant in this point, that it is absurd to take a peasant's word, for being only twenty-five."[14] Such, in Cuthbertson's eyes, was the general aptitude of the common soldier upon his recruitment.

Scathing as they undoubtedly were, these insults and derogatory commentaries did not represent the whole picture of soldier–officer interaction and should be placed within their contemporary context. Fundamentally, they represent the ingrained hierarchical structure of eighteenth century Britain and show only part of an officer's attitude towards the men of the rank and file. Ultimately, the British Army operated in a paternalistic way; one in which the soldiers were children and the officers father-figures. Hence, Cuthbertson, despite his disparaging remarks on the intelligence and capabilities of the soldiery, would also urge officers to act as the guardians of the men in their companies. Wolfe, so often bitingly critical, could also display great regard for his soldiers, particularly when they were afflicted by privation. As historian Stephen Brumwell related, after the siege of Louisbourg (1758), he quickly urged measures to be taken for the sustenance of 72 invalids from that siege who had been disembarked at Portsmouth without any preparations for their reception. The fabled officer was clearly genuine in his concern that "these Poor Creatures are likely to suffer every kind of distress, being put on Shoar, without Billets or Quarters."[15] This is not the response of a man who had nothing but contempt for his charges. In reality, it shows a very real paternalistic thread in Wolfe's relationship with his soldiers. Unsurprisingly, such attentive behavior earned him the gratitude and reverence of his men, and his death at the very point of victory at Quebec in 1759 was greeted by an outpouring of grief among the soldiers of his army. Care for enlistees, therefore, was reciprocated by those who constituted the rank and file.[16]

What can easily be overlooked if one focuses on the more negative comments of the army's most inspired and respected leaders is the fact that many officers, including Humphrey Bland (who wrote the most universally popular British military-manual of the eighteenth century) really believed that the British soldier was among the very best of his kind. Indeed, Bland once proudly boasted, with a dash of national stereotyping it must be said, that the troops of the British Army were less susceptible to panic than those of their continental neighbors because, "The English are naturally Active, Strong, Bold and Enterprising; always ready to go into action; but impatient when delay'd or kept back from it."[17] The Duke of Wellington, who, during the Napoleonic conflicts so famously denounced the redcoat as the "scum of the earth" (another quote frequently twisted to unfairly characterize British soldiery), would epitomize this flip-sided attitude to his enlisted men when he marveled that it was, "wonderful that we should have made them the fine fellows they are." Indeed, whether in victory *or* defeat, if the soldiers of the eighteenth-century British Army performed well, they could expect the praise of their commanding officers. After the disastrous assault on the Marquis de Montcalm's lines just outside Fort Ticonderoga in 1758, for example, General James Abercrombie, whose generalship during this battle would be severely criticized, nevertheless found time to issue general orders praising the men for their gallant behavior. It was expected that the commanding officers of the corps, who had sacrificed so much in wave after wave of futile assaults, would relay his thanks to the men—as was the widespread protocol of the period.

This is the real picture historians can draw of the humble redcoat. Certainly, though the men of the rank and file were poorly educated, and could be irresponsible, childish and were frequently drunk, in battle they were often heroic and possessed a deep and longstanding respect for officers who led them well. And yet, within society-at-large in the eighteenth century, the British Army's mere existence was often regarded with deep ambivalence, irrespective of its glories and sacrifices in the service of its king (or queen) and country.[18] Quite often, victories which were fervently celebrated by the nation at the time of their announcement, were soon forgotten as wars ended and soldiers returned to their home counties. The return of troops from overseas deployment caused a range of difficulties for towns and parishes the length and breadth of the country. In the case of those units who were kept on the establishment, communities were suddenly faced with armed soldiers who needed to be maintained within their midst. Perhaps more problematic and intimidating than this were the social and economic issues caused by those troops destined to be demobilized. The socio-economic travails caused by returning soldiers (many of whom would have been disabled by terrible war-wounds)—unemployment, poverty and, by extension, crime—contributed, quite often, to the hardening of public attitudes towards this most vulnerable caste of society. Yet there were deeper cultural traditions that underplayed public hostility towards the redcoat and these extended far beyond the social and economic concerns that followed the process of "demobbing." Within the country at large, there was an intense unease at the very notion of a standing army and this had been ingrained in the national psyche for many, many years. It is a factor that can be traced in contemporary writings and literature of various kinds; and thus echoes in the works of subsequent historians who examine the army's failures.

CULTURAL ORIGINS OF THE RESISTANCE TOWARDS A STANDING ARMY

The history of the British Army, such as it was by the mid-eighteenth-century, can be traced to the Glorious Revolution of 1688, when parliament finally acknowledged that a standing force of professional soldiers was a prerequisite of national security. Initially, this was limited to an expansion in the establishment of the existing guards and garrisons. Public opinion was deeply hostile to the notion of professional armies, and thus growth without cause was not possible. Indeed, from its very outset, this public antipathy manifested itself in an intense scrutiny of all aspects of the army's organization with, for instance, the command structure of the British Army receiving an almost zealous monitoring by an ever-suspicious parliament. Certainly, though many non-indigenous soldiers would serve in the army (both in the ranks and the officer corps), no foreigner was allowed to hold a military command. Even the vaunted English Bill of Rights, passed in 1689, provides core evidence of the paranoia that accompanied the prospect of a permanent, standing army. One of its central provisos established that, "The raising or keeping a standing army within the kingdom in time of peace, unless it be with consent of Parliament, is against law."[19]

For opponents of the fledgling army, even the stringent and constraining measures passed in the Bill of Rights were insufficient to allay long-standing fears of tyranny and the usurpation of cherished English liberty that a core force of professional full-time soldiers seemed to harbinger. Therefore, at several points during its formative years, levels of popular antipathy towards the service frequently meant that its mere existence was regularly challenged. Fundamentally, opponents were fearful of a return to the bad old days of governance by the Major-Generals of Cromwellian instigation (or, indeed, the absolutist inclinations of the restored Stuart monarchs) and dreaded the possible truncation of their rights by a potential despot who had an armed and trained force at his disposal. Consequently, although the army would survive attempts to replace it with a militia force (notably after the Peace of Ryswick [1697]), its strength and popularity fluctuated, depending on whether there existed a state of war or even an internal threat. This trend, based on a discernable link between periods of national exigency and growth in the army, was exemplified by the fact that in 1719 there were a mere 12,000 men on the establishment but, by 1720, the birth of Prince Charles Edward, and a corresponding spike in Jacobite activity, forced the government to raise this number to 18,000.[20]

Traditionally, therefore, the eighteenth-century British Army was anything but a well-respected service that the nation had taken to its heart as the protector of liberties and national sovereignty. That honor belonged to Britain's senior service, the Royal Navy, the vital importance of which few, if any, contemporary Britons would have disputed. It was, in effect, a geographical and hence strategic tradition, born from the fact that the military policy of Great Britain had always been determined by its physical location.[21] Unlike France and other major continental European powers, Britain, an island nation, did not need a large standing army to protect expansive borders or frontier fortresses. Historically, the major threat to Britain's survival had come from nations that endangered her control of her coastal approaches. This strategic reality had, and would, be exemplified at many points in the nation's history, from the threat of the Spanish Armada through to the Battle of the Atlantic of the Second World War.

Somewhat surprisingly, the emergence of an embryonic English (and later British) Empire did not lead to an exponential growth in the army. At least initially, the growth of the Empire simply further highlighted the importance of a strong, well-manned and professional navy, which would guard the trade links between mother country and its overseas possessions. Essentially, the colonies, such as they were prior to 1754, were often sited in coastal regions, meaning that a standing force of professional soldiers was hardly a prerequisite of colonial defense. Furthermore, in the case of Britain's American colonies, where there was a creeping expansion into the interior of the North American continent prior to 1754, attitudes to colonial warfare in London often mirrored the hands-off approach the British took to colonial administration as a whole. The colonies, wherever possible, were to be left to conduct their own affairs and, furthermore, would hardly have welcomed a standing force in their midst. Just like their British cousins, this was only tolerable during times of war. Even then, it was expected that soldiers, as far as was humanly possible, would be sent where they were needed and not garrisoned or billeted on the towns, ale houses and individuals of British America.[22]

For contemporary Britons, therefore, the expense of raising and maintaining a sizable force of sailors to man the Royal Navy was not an unreasonable one. Indeed, it was a necessity. Trade, and thus profit, depended on keeping Britain's sea lanes open and, for the most part, sailors (unlike soldiers) were often deployed at sea and were more likely to be out of sight and out of mind. For the eighteenth-century army however, there was little equivocation. Attitudes towards the "second service" often swung between open hostility and periodical enthusiasm (usually coinciding with periods of national emergency). When the threat of invasion subsided, the nation returned to its general ambivalence or even hostility towards professional soldiers.

The peacetime role of the army also proved a controversial one as, in the absence of a police force, soldiers were frequently called upon to maintain civil order. Unsurprisingly, this did not endear the redcoats to the public-at-large. That such a role was equally unpopular with the soldiers assigned to perform it mattered little to the general populace who were, in times of disquiet (often caused by hardship and legitimate grievance), confronted by the spectacle of armed soldiers in their midst.[23] In many parts of the country, resistance to the army's role as a policing service manifested itself in underhanded attempts to further savage the reputation of the professional soldier. Accordingly, the civilian population sometimes picked quarrels with troops in order to build upon the general unease many felt towards the army. This was not limited to social class; even officials in high local and municipal station would "in their rancor against the redcoats, stoop to lawlessness as flagrant as that of the mob."[24]

Despite the best efforts of its many detractors, the British Army would survive as an institution and, when called upon, repeatedly proved its worth to the nation's security—both at home and overseas. The War of Jenkins's Ear, which began in 1739, provided a much-needed impetus for growth, though, ironically, there were many in parliament who were clamoring for war against Spain while at the same time pressing for a reduction in the army's size. It was The War of the Austrian Succession, a conflict that called for the deployment of large numbers of redcoats to Europe, which truly necessitated a considerable expansion in the regular army.[25] Ultimately, this was a war in which external and internal threat manifested themselves at the same time, creating a unique national emergency that so nearly resulted in the restoration of the Stuart dynasty to the throne of Great Britain.

European wars were always costly affairs, a drain on public finances and the armed forces. The War of the Austrian Succession was no different in this regard and it is somewhat ironic that events that followed one of Britain's most celebrated victories ignited a chain of occurrences that nearly ended in disaster. After the famous victory at Dettingen in 1743, estimates of strength for 1744 provided for an expansion of the British Army in Flanders. Unfortunately, a short-sighted parliament failed to pass the legislation that would have allowed an increase in the army's strength, so the troops required for the ongoing continental war had to be drawn from the Home Establishment. This left Britain itself particularly vulnerable, and served as an open invitation to Prince Charles Edward Stuart, the vainglorious figurehead of the Jacobite cause, to launch a French-supported invasion. The resulting campaign, an epic march that began in Glenfinnan and ended in Derbyshire, caused near-pandemonium in London and threatened the very existence of the established Hanoverian order.[26] Although the Duke of Cumberland, reinforced by British troops redeployed from the continent, would eventually crush the pretensions of

"Bonnie Prince Charlie" at the Battle of Culloden, this final great Jacobite uprising shocked a somewhat complacent establishment into finally acknowledging the need for a permanent, and sufficiently manned, Home Country force. Thus, by the close of the War of the Austrian Succession in 1748, the army's establishment was fixed at 30,000; 20,000 men were to be based in Britain, the rest in garrisons overseas. Another 12,000 were kept on the Irish Establishment, a number which had been fixed in 1692 and remained at that level until 1769.

The Irish establishment, like its mainland counterpart, suffered from unique problems of its own; most notably in its regimental structure, which consisted of a relatively large number of under-strength regiments. Indeed, there were 37 regiments of infantry and cavalry based in Ireland which, taking into consideration that the overall size of this establishment was fixed at 12,000 men, allowed for only 300 men per regiment (on average). The reason for this was quite simple; having a large number of under-strength units in Ireland provided a nucleus of regiments upon which an expansion of the army could take place in times of war.[27] There were, however, several notable flaws in this strategy. Though the Irish establishment did provide a regimental core that could be quickly deployed to foreign and domestic emergencies, the fact remained that, the original nucleus of soldiers aside, Irish regiments would have to be quickly supplemented by new recruits—something that brought a range of potential problems.

Bringing depleted Irish regiments to full-strength could be achieved in two ways: through recruitment of raw recruits or by drafting men from other regiments. The latter option was a particularly unpopular method of recruitment and often had a negative impact on donor and recipient regiment alike. Simply put, those units donating men lost valuable manpower, while those set to receive an influx of new soldiers had the usual problems associated with assimilating large numbers of strangers. In theory at least, draftees were expected to be upstanding men, but the reality was frequently quite different. Donor regiments, quite naturally, preferred to keep their best soldiers, thus draftees often consisted of the dregs of their original regiments. At best, they could be raw recruits or misfits, at worst they were men of "bad character."[28] Officers of the period were well aware of the impact such "bad characters" had on unit morale, discipline and cohesion, and were not averse to expressing their hostility towards receiving drafted soldiers. Neither was such a fate popular with those men designated for donation. Uprooting individuals from their familiar surroundings and comrades often caused resentment among those destined for the draft. At its most serious, this could manifest itself in desertion, a problem the army's hierarchy of this period particularly feared.

The force Edward Braddock took with him to America was drawn from the Irish establishment. It experienced many of the difficulties outlined above.[29] Indeed, the regiments Braddock was to march to Fort Duquesne in 1755, the 44th and 48th, received draftees from an array of regular units and also needed to recruit, in America, 500 men apiece to bring them to a full war-strength of 1000 rank-and-file (each). This was also true of the other regiments designated to execute the grand Cumberland–Fox strategy of 1755. The American-based Shirley's and Pepperell's regiments, the 50th and 51st, were to be re-raised in America at 1000 men each; while the 40th, 45th and 47th, based in Nova Scotia, required a considerable influx of local recruits to bring them to full strength.

For the campaign of 1755, therefore, the colonies were expected to provide 4,300 men for regular service. This figure does not, of course, factor in the requirement of finding replacements for men lost through death, desertion, and discharge. Superficially, when one considers that Robert Dinwiddie, Governor of Virginia, in 1740 had estimated that the colonies could furnish 135,000 men for any war effort, this does not seem unreasonable.[30] The manner in which these men were brought into service did, however, raise considerable ire among the colonists and is one of the reasons why the British soldier has been viewed with such negative connotations on the American side of the Atlantic.

Recruiting the British Army

Hitherto, much of this chapter has been concerned with dispelling (or explaining the root cause of) many of the exaggerations and distortions that have surrounded the eighteenth-century British Army; and which have, in turn, colored numerous histories of the Braddock defeat and the wider French and Indian War. Irrespective of the often misguided hyperbole that surrounds the army of this period, what is indisputable is that, in Georgian Britain, soldiering in the ranks was considered a lower-caste occupation, with professional soldiers being considered to possess only slightly more prestige than cottagers, paupers or vagrants. There were several reasons for this. Not only was life in the army dangerous and unpopular, but soldiers were notoriously poorly paid. A Private, for instance, would earn a meager 8d a day, before stoppages, a rate that placed him among the humblest sections of society. As D. Hay and N. Rogers established in their work, *Eighteenth-Century English Society*, compared to other jobs on the bottom rung of the social scale, a soldier's lot was clearly a poor one. As of 1759, a Private could earn an annual income of £14, which contrasted unfavorably with even laborers or husbandmen, who were able to earn £16 in the same year.[31] Soldiers themselves were well aware of the paucity of this income, and the hardships it created did not pass without complaint. As one of Braddock's men would protest, the soldiers of that general's army were, "treated in a very disrespectful manner, exposed to many hardships, and by the meanness of their pay are put to the greatest inconvenience to subsist."[32]

Poor pay and conditions hardly helped the soldier's reputation, but neither did the tendency of magistrates to pardon convicted felons in exchange for a period of service in the army. Those men who had joined of their own accord—and had a real interest in the service—were thus thrust into action alongside men who quite often reverted to their former traits soon after enlistment. Rather unfairly, the appearance of such "bad characters" has been used to feed the misguided interpretation of the redcoat as, to reference once more the infamous, though often misapplied (or de-contextualized) words of the Duke of Wellington, the "scum of the Earth." Again, it must be reiterated that this is not, and never was, a true reflection of the men who compromised the majority of the rank-and-file.

Certainly, irrespective of the disdain a soldier's profession was viewed with by many contemporary Britons, the fact remained that the army at this time was still, technically, a volunteer force; though reality and necessity often bent the meaning of the term "volunteer." The infamous Press was periodically enforced in periods of wartime expediency, but many redcoats were, in essence, men who had given their consent to enlistment. In such times of emergency, the army's ranks needed to be filled quickly and the most common means of encouraging potential recruits to fill the king's regiments, Press aside, was by the use of recruiting parties.

It is quite telling that these somewhat comical units became so inspirational for playwrights and satirists (such as William Hogarth and George Farquhar), who immortalized in their cartoons and ballads the often-debauched scenes that followed such parties.[33] Usually consisting of a subaltern, a merry sergeant, a musician who drummed up a crowd and a sprinkling of veterans sporting a martial air, recruiting parties would seduce their less wily victims with promises of extravagant wealth and perpetual glory; while carefully omitting the harsh realities of meager pay, back-breaking labor, exacting discipline and the ever-present threat of death or mutilation. With abundant alcohol thrown into the mix (and frequently a few prostitutes to boot), impressionable young men were, in their stupor, easy prey for the silver-tongued officers into whose hands many a naïve youth fell. Tricks of the trade like these were in fact common knowledge throughout society-at-large and were magnificently exposed and satirized in Farquhar's celebrated play, *The Recruiting Officer*.[34]

Here, though, we must be careful not to sensationalize satire and confuse it with common practice; for the army did have, at least superficially, standards to which its prospective recruits should adhere. At least in theory, for instance, would-be soldiers had to possess minimal physical specifications to join up, though these varied according to the need for men (which was driven by wartime demands). Written orders given to officers recruiting in Pennsylvania in 1755, for example, provide an indication of some of the characteristics expected of new enlistees,

> You are to enlist no Irish, or any other country, unless you are sure they are Protestants... All your Recruits must be straight and well made, broad shouldered... you are to enlist none but shall measure 5 Feet 5 Inches without shoes, from 16 to 20, and 5 Feet 6 from 20–35.[35]

Naturally, such stringent specifications were on occasion evaded because of the desperate necessity to find men to fill the army's ranks. This was particularly true of Braddock's army which also had to find augmentations for the three Nova Scotia regiments that had to be increased to 1000 men each. Consequently, recruiting officers often turned a blind eye to deficiencies in physical standards. As the French and Indian War progressed, many in the army's hierarchy would share this ambivalence, something that was, in no small measure, a consequence of the unique environmental challenges of waging an American war. Writing to then British Commander-in-Chief John Campbell, Fourth Earl of Loudoun, John Forbes, who would in 1758 successfully lead a campaign against Fort Duquesne, wrote that, "The middle of a war is not a time to beautify Regts and if any size is taken in England that can carry a musket, there can be no reason for refusing them here, where from behind a tree a pigmy may kill a Polyphemus..."[36]

Once promised to the service, recruits were entitled to an enlistment bounty. In Britain this was "a Guinea and a Crown" while in the colonies, its provincial equivalent, "a Pistole and a Dollar," was provided. This money never really belonged to the enlistee and was siphoned off by various formalities. The crown was used to drink the king's health while the Guinea was reserved for provisioning the recruit during his march to join his new regiment. Other necessaries, such as clothing, were also detracted from this amount. With the initial agreement made, recruiting officers had four days to take their new charges before a justice of the peace for formal attestation. Enlistees could, at this point, change their minds, but had to repay their bounty plus an extra pound "smart money" for the inconvenience caused.

Recruiting in the colonies provided opportunities and difficulties that were, in certain cases, wholly different to those encountered in Britain. First, the paucity of willing recruits in America created many a headache for the army's hierarchy as it often brought them into conflict with local propertied interests. In 1755, several of Edward Braddock's regular recruiting officers both mistakenly and deliberately enlisted indentured servants as they scoured Maryland and Pennsylvania for men willing to supplement the 44th and 48th. Naturally, the indentured servants themselves leapt at the chance to break their bondage and escape their servitude. For the owners of their indentures, however, losing a servant was akin to being robbed of property (property and liberty were synonymous in the colonies at this time) and, at the behest of Governor Horatio Sharpe of Maryland, Braddock himself was forced to release four newly recruited servants enlisted by a Lieutenant Brereton at Rock Creek.[37]

Such flagrant disregard for local sensitivities, at least with regards recruiting for the regular army, were hardly isolated incidents. In Britain, recruiting parties were subject to stringent rules outlined by the Mutiny Act and any infringement of these would earn a swift chastisement. In America, recruiters utilized a whole range of manipulative tactics that their counterparts at home could only dream of. Indeed, such methods were more reminiscent of the notoriously unscrupulous German states than they were of a supposedly demilitarized Britain. The problem lay in the fact that although the Mutiny Act covered the relationship between civilians and recruiting officers it did not, at least initially, extend to the colonies. In America, the discipline of regular and provincial soldiers was encompassed by the Mutiny Act, but civilians had no definitive legal redress. As such, when recruiting parties, in their desperation to fill under strength regiments, utilized somewhat duplicitous, or at least contentious, methods of acquiring enlistees for the regulars, tensions flared and civil unrest was provoked.

Indeed, in Maryland, one contemporary story then in circulation provided a particularly telling indication of the depths to which the army could sink in its drive to find recruits and, in the case of certain recruiting officers, to line their pockets. It came to pass that an officer had allowed his sergeant to be temporarily jailed for enlisting servants; an offense of grave seriousness to the propertied classes of the colony. His temporary submission was merely a ruse, however, as the officer, "filled his [sergeant's] pocket with dollars and that night the sergeant enlisted in gaol seventy servants."[38] A wily act certainly, but one that was hardly unique. This type of behavior did, however, create huge resentment and, in several instances, led to serious riots as events often spiraled out of control. In Pennsylvania, as William Shirley would recall, a particularly serious disturbance resulted in the death of a Sergeant "in the discharge of his duty [recruiting]."[39]

Needless to say, such stories affected public opinion at the time and have echoed in the general impressions formulated of the army in subsequent history. These depictions do contain certain truths. Indeed, as recruiting soldiers were the regular troops most likely to be encountered by the average colonist, frustration directed against them and, by extension the army, was notably virulent. The fear of falling into a drunken stupor and being hauled off into the regular army was a very real one for many young colonists, and the army's often scandalous methods of enlisting provincial men into its ranks did exacerbate their suspicions.

Despite the undoubted underhandedness of British recruiting parties, the fact remains that, for much of the French and Indian War period, the service received insufficient support from colonial governors and assemblies in filling the quotas necessary to bring its regiments to full strength—another distinctly British Atlantic shortcoming. This was as much a consequence of provincial rivalries, vested interests and, less avariciously, ideals of liberty, as it was of the reluctance of individual colonists to join up. In 1754, the British government, when drawing up its great Braddock strategy for 1755, had expected that the colonies would defray the costs of recruitment (the vaunted common fund, consisting of *provincial* contributions, was to be used by the British commander for recruitment purposes) and have at readiness 3000 men for enlistment into the four regular regiments to be deployed during the campaign. It proved a naïve expectation. Virginia and Maryland would recruit 432 men for the 44th and 48th, while Connecticut and Rhode Island would raise 400 for Shirley's Regiment.[40] The rest trickled in through the efforts of recruiting parties. The common fund proved as elusive as many of those experienced in colonial affairs had anticipated; though money was raised under the pretense of being allotted to a central fund, the reality was that the colonies used it for their own purposes and very little actually reached Braddock—reflecting the strict controls provincial assemblies exerted over the appropriation and expenditure of their monies. According to Robert Orme, only £4000 in colonial currency ever passed through Braddock's hands, and this was supplied by South Carolina.[41]

The impression of British commanders like Edward Braddock that parochially inclined colonial assemblies were rather reluctant to lend their support to efforts to enlist their men into the British Army was not without foundation. Indeed, at times the excuses the assemblies gave for their reticence pushed the limits of credibility. In a 1755 *Representation to the Crown*, the Governing Council of Massachusetts rather spuriously claimed that military drafts would curtail future population growth as, "Every Man gone from the Province has really carried a family with him." Even less credibly, they argued this would hurt Britain's own economic interests as fewer colonists meant fewer consumers for British manufactures—or so the theory went. This lamentation further proclaimed that freedom-loving Americans would not make good soldiers anyway because, "our people are not calculated to be confined in Garrisons, or kept in any Particular Service" and would grow "troublesome" at their "Folly in bringing themselves into a State of Subjection" when they were previously independent and free.[42] It must be said that in the latter declaration there was an element of truth. Colonial soldiers, particularly those of New England, did possess a leveling spirit that would frequently place them at odds with the martial culture of their regular allies.

Acute economic foresight and a concern for Britain's long-term interests were, however, peripheral issues to colonial assemblies that had, for some time, been quasi-autonomous. In reality, protecting their legislative rights and other parochial ambitions was of far greater significance. Indeed, colonial legislators knew that if large numbers of able-bodied men were drafted off into regular regiments then frontier defense would suffer proportionately. Personal ambitions played a role, too, as many leading statesmen had their own designs for military glory in the field. Other, less idealistic, individuals had opportunistically foreseen the possibility of acquiring considerable wealth from lucrative wartime provincial contracts.

Also at play was the deep-rooted colonial interpretation of what "Englishness" actually meant (and the importance American colonists placed upon its provisos). Their determination to cling to this cherished ideal, even in the face of America's first large-scale Europeanized war, contributes significantly to the explanation of their reservations about allocating provincial regiments for British service.[43] Historically, colonial assemblies always sought to control, as far as was possible, the military affairs of their own provinces and had often refused to allow their soldiers to serve outside the boundaries of their own domains. It is not difficult, therefore, to imagine the discomfort that the idea of allowing their men to serve under British command in theatres of war spanning the length and breadth of European America would cause. Apart from freedom from arbitrary taxation, the notion of "liberty" or "Englishness" rested upon the ability of a representative assembly to raise, discipline and command its own forces; after all, the English Civil War had been fought partially over parliamentary command of the army. To renounce the control of their regiments to the British, who from 1754 applied their own military strictures to American troops, was to surrender one of their most idealized rights as autonomous legislative bodies—notwithstanding their own soldiers' and citizens' rights as Englishmen.

From the perspective of British military commanders, this example of the emerging divergence of British-Atlantic understandings of what "Britishness" actually meant did little to help them fill their regiments with desperately needed men. Indeed, if the army was excessive in its use of roguery to acquire American recruits, then it could be argued that the provinces too should be held accountable for their failure to set aside their localized concerns for the sake of the common good. Compromise in the face of a common danger could be considered amply justified, particularly in consideration of the fact that the colonies' own failure to protect their frontiers from French encroachments provided the woeful backdrop to the eventual decision to deploy British regular regiments to America in 1755.

Furthermore, local assemblies had hardly prohibited all recruitment into the regular army. Instead, the provinces were highly selective in the types of men they allocated to serve in British regiments; hinting at the character of many of the colonists allotted for service in the famous red coat. Indeed, the bulk of the Americans who did find their way into the British Army were anything but the frontier Spartans of local folklore; tending, instead, to be the propertyless, idle or just plain unfortunate of provincial communities.[44] Many others were the type who served for the highest bidder—though this was not always a bad thing as such individuals were less likely to be recruited into provincial ranks, and did provide a ready pool of men for British regiments. In such instances, therefore, provincial assemblies had demonstrated that their high ideals could indeed be compromised; while their notions of "Englishness" and "liberty" did not always stretch to the most disadvantaged or undesirable elements of their own societies.

The colonial experience of regular recruitment parties allows historians to understand why the British Army was viewed, at times, with such hostility in America; and why, in subsequent histories, it has been depicted in a negative, and deeply biased, light. It would be quite wrong to conclude, however, that such negative connotations are truly representative of the recruitment processes the army employed, or the corresponding caliber of the average British soldier. It is true that many enlistees in the British Army were hardly volunteers and it is clear that pressed men did constitute a considerable body within the service. The Press, implemented during times of emergency and designed to sweep up able-bodied men who did not follow a lawful calling or employment (or who did not have some other lawful and sufficient support and maintenance) is, in the modern age, a troubling feature of eighteenth-century martial culture. And yet even the Press was regulated by legislation which prevented it becoming perpetual or universal. Unlike the navy, the army Press was lifted by public announcements once a quota had been met.[45] Neither did pressed men always make bad soldiers. It is quite probable that, for many of those who entered the service in this way, the opportunities for food and clothing provided by the army were a welcome relief from the abject poverty that blighted their civilian lives. This is not to justify such measures in any way. Furthermore, even if a man was technically a "volunteer," he not infrequently belonged to the very bottom of the social ladder and had little to lose by embarking upon such a hazardous profession as the army. For such men, the benefits of hot meals, travel, shelter and clothing provided a strong incentive to join. In short, then, rather than being a force of coerced *de facto* slaves, the British Army of the eighteenth century reflected Georgian society as a whole, with all of its diversities, strengths and, of course, failings.

WEAPONRY AND TACTICS: EXPLAINING CONVENTIONAL EIGHTEENTH-CENTURY WARFARE

If the biased snapshot of the army so often conveyed by Whiggish (and neoprogressive) American literature is to be believed, the British army of the eighteenth century was an arcane, polarized and stratified society in which the rank and file were the very dregs of society pressed or cajoled into service. Paradoxically, the army's officers were the fops and failures of a corrupted aristocracy. The oppressed masses in the ranks, discontented by their bondage, were kept in line by a brutal regime of unrelenting punishment that was legitimized by a savage disciplinary code. Stuffed into their parade ground uniforms, the soldiers had no voice and no rights—they were automata whose duty was to serve their military machine without question. They were to live as they were told to live and to die as they were told to die. The officers cared little for these serfs in the ranks and concerned themselves only with self-advancement, utilizing any corrupt method that could be brought to bear as they strove for promotion. Officers, by extension of their class, were arrogant, condescending, incompetent and brutal but were able to disguise their shortcomings in the ritualistic protocols of eighteenth-century warfare. In such a mode of combat, initiative and intuition were hardly necessary and as such, the brutish incompetents of the officer corps could hide their shortcomings amidst the gentlemanly formalities of conventional battle. However, when removed from this comfortable paradigm and placed in an alien theater of operation, such as existed in America, these hapless halfwits would be exposed for all that they were, and would tragically lead their equally cumbersome subordinates to inevitable disaster.[46] Such is the myth. In the remainder of this chapter, it will be shown that this spurious position is built more on cultural prejudices, localized traditions and the need for a unique, exceptional "American identity" than it is on fact and careful analysis of the extensive historiography now available to modern military historians.

Admittedly, in many generalizations there is often a modicum of truth and the above is no exception. British discipline of the period was harsh, if not brutal, particularly if compared to the type of regulation (or, in British eyes lack of it) that many colonial units—particularly those of New England—were subjected to.[47] Furthermore, the traditional American image of the bungling redcoat, pathetically performing his deeply ingrained parade ground maneuvers while he and his comrades are picked off by canny enemies, is one that is based on the unquestionable difficulties of sending a European-style force to fight in the American backcountry. However, this image should not be taken out of context as the British Army of the eighteenth century was anything but an inherently inept, incompetent and unprofessional force. It had often proved that, when deployed against similarly trained and equipped European rivals, it was a very formidable fighting unit. One only has to reflect on the brilliant victories of talismanic generals such as the Duke of Marlborough for evidence of this prestigious legacy. Even when engaged in adverse and unfamiliar situations, the British Army proved itself to be a highly adaptable force. The soldiers and officers that crushed the Jacobite rebellion of

1745 had shown themselves (irrespective of their excessive brutality in the aftermath of the Battle of Culloden) remarkably resilient in the face of the stresses and strains of an irregular war.

Edward Braddock's regiments, the 44th and 48th, were, in their training and tactics, intended to be the epitome of a conventional European army. In such forces, tradition held that parade ground formations and rigorous drilling manoeuvers were essential if an army were to succeed in the environment for which it was raised and expected to fight.[48] Conventional European warfare at this time was, to all intents and purposes, a set-piece affair and consisted of two very similarly arrayed opponents engaging in formal battles fought on the cultivated plains of Germany, Flanders and Central Europe. To thrive in this open-field environment, a soldier had to be drilled in the art of loading and firing his cumbersome musket in a carefully defined sequence of moves. These were skills that needed to be driven home by hours of repetitious drill until they became second nature to the men in the ranks. The reason for such coordinated precision was quite simple—the weapons in service at this time were beset by an array of serious shortcomings that required a pattern of maneuvers that made the most of their limited capabilities.[49]

The musket issued to the British soldier from 1730 onwards, the venerable "Brown Bess," was quite an inaccurate weapon at distances over 50 yards. Estimates have suggested that even within this range, approximately one-in-ten musket balls fired from this weapon found its intended mark.[50] Therefore, in order to maximize the lethality of its weapon of choice, the British Army, like its fellow European counterparts, had to be trained to fire in coordinated blocks so that the number of musket balls in the air at any given time would be sufficient to offset the inaccuracy in the shots fired. Victory in the race to reload and fire often determined the outcome of battles: once a side had ground down its opponent with volleys of musketry, a similarly coordinated bayonet charge would follow. This would normally prove sufficient to drive an enemy from the field. Thus conventional military engagements were won.[51]

Repetitious drill in the art of massed musketry did more than just enable a man to fire off three or four shots a minute. The constant practicing of the intricate maneuvers which epitomized massed (or volley) fire also served to safeguard the wellbeing of individual soldiers. The Brown Bess, in the wrong hands, was a very dangerous weapon, and bad handling often caused terrible accidents. In the confusion of battle, for example, it was not unknown for soldiers in the front rank to be shot by careless comrades in the second, causing what today is known as "blue on blue" casualties. Furthermore, for poorly trained soldiers unaccustomed to the finer points of musket and bayonet maneuvers, the risk of being horrifically burned by cartridge boxes blowing up, eyes being poked out with bayonets wielded by ungainly comrades bungling drill movements, or ramrods being fired off carelessly after the process of re-loading, was a real one. Certainly, a soldier who fired off his ramrod in training would likely receive some form of corporal punishment as it would have resulted in a reduction in the all-important massed battlefield firepower a platoon could bring to bear.[52]

The movement of large bodies of men, so essential to warfare at this time, would have been acutely problematic without the use of drill and rigorous discipline. In today's armed forces, drill is normally associated with ceremonial duties or, in its elemental sense, is used to promote teamwork and discipline among raw recruits. In the eighteenth century, however, the coordinated movement of whole armies was central to success or failure in battle. The efficient movement of considerable bodies of soldiers across difficult terrain, often under fire, demanded that the soldiers in the ranks respond promptly and uniformly to the commands of their officers. Additionally, when battle was joined, it was important for commanders to be able to estimate when a body of troops ordered to change position would arrive at a certain point on the battlefield. Therefore, military drill required all units, from the platoon to whole regiments, to march in a regular manner, even to the point where the length of a soldier's paces was exact and their frequency precise.

Battle itself at this time required nerves of steel (the men were often required to march or maneuver to the very point that they could see the whites of their enemies eyes before giving, and receiving, fire) and individual fear, or a semblance of it, always risked provoking a wider panic—something that a watchful enemy would eagerly exploit. Officers attempted, therefore, to curtail the natural instincts of men confronted by hails of bullets, charging cavalry, death, mutilation and the screams of wounded and dying men and beasts by instilling an even greater fear of the consequences of what they considered "cowardice." This was reflected by James Wolfe's declaration in 1755 that:

> A soldier who quits his rank, or offers to flag, is instantly to be put to death by the officer who commands that platoon, or by the officer or sergeant in the rear of that platoon; a soldier does not deserve to live who won't fight for his king and country.[53]

This, too, could be applied to those who deserted, which is why this felony was also sanctioned with the harshest of punishments. There are, of course, many reasons why a man might desert; being drafted into unfamiliar surroundings, suffering poor conditions or a fear of being excessively punished for an offense were common, while some soldiers simply decided they were not cut out for military life and decided to quit the ranks at the earliest possibility. Such issues were exacerbated by the raising of recruits in America where many of the men, often settlers of mixed ancestry, felt no particular loyalty to either Britain or France and were happy to serve both. James Wolfe would himself encounter these difficulties in his campaign against Quebec in 1759; his Louisbourg Grenadiers for instance, included soldiers recruited into the British Army from French regiments captured at the siege of Louisbourg in 1758. Such practice was common, however, and not limited to the Americas. Many of the regiments deployed within the British Isles were in fact foreign in their origin; ultimately, Hanoverian troops would have been expected to serve alongside their English counterparts in the event of a French descent on the British mainland. What made this plural army gel was, in significant measure, the use of discipline. It was the army's codes in this regard that has, however, led to much criticism from historians writing from the vantage point of hindsight.

THE BRITISH ARMY AND DISCIPLINE: "THE TORTURE OF THE LOWER CLASSES"?

The contempt that many contemporary Americans developed for the soldiers of the regular army (and which has been used to create a negative stereotype of the common British soldier in subsequent histories), is quite evident in the rather derogatory nicknames they gave their redcoat counterparts: lobster and bloody back. The first was derived solely from the uniforms the British soldiers wore—their large coats appeared garishly red (at least when new) and hence evoked the image of a lobster.[54] The second, however, alludes to the brutal regime of discipline the Americans felt their Anglo counterparts were subjected to—something that deeply troubled the provincial soldiery. It was a code of discipline that, for the colonists, made British soldiers little more than slaves. Under such a regime, regular troops appeared to be at the mercy of the whims and fancies of brutal and contemptuous officers who held little regard for those they considered to be an inferior breed of humanity.

Historian Fred Anderson surmised the impact of this interaction between regular and New England soldiers when he stated that the latter came to believe that "a coercive disciplinary system was the engine that drove the British Army and the blood of common soldiers was its lubricant."[55] Anderson also correctly identified that the natural conclusion of the colonists was that "the mother country's interpretation of individual liberty differed markedly from their own."[56] In their zeal to criticize the decadence and oppression of the Old World in addition to the European military machines that conquered much of the New, many other historians have drawn on the numerous critical colonial accounts of the French and Indian War period to roundly condemn the British Army root and branch. Francis Jennings, for example, viewed the army through the prism of class struggle and oppression—themes which are recurrent in his work *Empire of Fortune*. Accordingly, he denounced the British Army as an institution in which the redcoats were literally whipped into shape under a code of discipline that passed for the torture of the lower-class soldiery by upper-class officers who commanded through fear as opposed to respect.[57] For Douglas Edward Leach, the redcoats were not led, but cowed into compliance by the Army's discipline. Whereas provincial soldiers enlisted on a contractual basis—which became null and void if breached by the imposition of unacceptable duties—"the repressive disciplinary system of the regular army" left its enlisted men powerless to protect their rights as Englishmen.[58]

No serious historian of the eighteenth-century British Army would deny that the methods it employed to maintain discipline and order were rigorous and harsh, if not brutal. This is particularly true if they are judged by twenty-first-century standards. Yet, among the officer corps of the period, such a stringent disciplinary code was widely deemed justifiable, and was epitomized by Bennett Cuthbertson's assertion that "Subordination, and strict Discipline, cannot (from the general depravity of the soldiery) be properly supported, without having recourse to the severest punishments."[59] This required that any soldier who infringed the "Articles of War" (which governed the expected conduct of the British Army) could expect some kind of corporal punishment. Rather than being arbitrary, however, this was discretionary and quite often liable to be waived or reduced in severity, depending on circumstances or a desire to create an effect on the malefactor's comrades. Punishment was also linked to the perceived severity of the offense and whether the perpetrator was a man of "good character" or a repeat offender.

The most common form of corporal punishment associated with the eighteenth-century army is, of course, flogging, which was normally applied by regimental drummers (paid extra for the service) armed with the notorious "Cat o' nine tails." For colonial soldiers, frequently raised on contractual terms and thus accustomed to much milder forms of martial governance, the seemingly unceasing use of flogging by regular officers caused revulsion and left them with a rather negative stereotype of British soldiers and their officers. This hostility towards regular discipline appears quite frequently in provincial soldier's diaries and journals from the French and Indian War. For example, Private Luke Gridley, a Connecticut soldier serving on the Lake George frontier (at Fort Edward) between May and November 1757 lamented that,

> Day 25th [May] thare was one Dannail Boake: one of Cap Gailaps men: Run the gandtelit thrugh 30 men for sleeping on gard which Cryed Lord god have mercy on me the B[l]ood flying every stroke this was a sorrowful sight: A[l]so one man was sintanced to ride the wooden ho[r]se for not turning out so soon as the Rest to train with 4 muskits tieed to his feet: But was reprieved.[60]

As Gridley's term of service progressed, his accounts of corporal punishment are less vividly written, suggesting that he, like his redcoat allies, was becoming accustomed to such sights and the disciplinary code that administered them. However, this is not to say that he become reconciled to such practices. Though lacking the detail of this preliminary observation, Gridley does document every flogging he witnessed or heard about from fellow soldiers. In all, his diary for this particular campaign notes 80 instances of flogging. In the month of September 1757, Gridley witnessed ten "severe floggings"—floggings of 100 lashes or more.

As has been stressed throughout this book, however, British North America was a diverse territory and evidence from other colonies does suggest that not all colonial soldiers (and officers) were as averse to regular discipline as those of New England appear to have been. In 1759, George Washington, lamenting his woes with the undisciplined Virginian recruits he was expected to defend the frontier with, would write that, "discipline is the soul of an army; it makes small numbers formidable, procures success to the weak and esteem to all."[61] He believed the use of regular discipline essential if his ragtag soldiers were to be transformed into an elite fighting force. Consequently, the young Washington would make very public displays of his determination to instill discipline into the Virginia Regiment, including the use of floggings and hangings. A letter written to Robert Dinwiddie following an execution provides some measure of Washington's resolve, with the future first president declaring that,

> Your Honor will, I hope, excuse my hanging instead of shooting them. It conveyed much more terror to the others and it was for example sake that we did it.[62]

Washington's task was made all the more difficult by the caliber of the men he was expected to lead—many of whom would have had the same qualities (or lack of them) as Braddock's raw recruits had exhibited upon their enlistment into that general's force. Likewise, a significant portion of those serving in the Virginia Regiment were foreigners, criminals or those from the bottom caste of Virginian society. Unlike many of the men raised for service in Massachusetts, for example, they had little stake in society and were scarcely motivated to fight a war whose premise and outcome had little effect on them.[63] Harsh discipline, rigorously enforced, was one of the few options available to Washington to compensate for these shortcomings.

These are just a few of the contrasting issues that undermine the deeply hostile reviews the British Army has received from many American scholars of the French and Indian War. Undeniably, the ability of British officers to inflict corporal and capital punishments upon their soldiers was a basic fact of eighteenth-century military life. Discipline was the means by which the army's leaders secured the obedience of their subordinates and, to some extent, rested on the belief that, however much the idea of battle may terrify a soldier, they had more to fear from their officers if they disobeyed orders. Nonetheless, despite the perceptions of provincial soldiers, and many subsequent historians, regular officers were no sadists and were governed by conventions. Indeed, the application of military law during the Seven Years War reflected the supposition that capital punishment was the mainstay of order and this, in turn, was a trend of English criminal law in general during the eighteenth century. As Douglas Hay has argued, English law was an ideological system that relied on the interaction of three basic precepts: justice, mercy and terror. The law was expected to be independent and above every interest and influence; it was, furthermore, to be incorruptible. When in action, it was to act impartially and blindly. In theory, irrespective of one's social status, wrongdoers were liable to the same penalties for transgressions of the law. When executed, the law's majesty was set in contrast to the criminal's helplessness and the terrible finality of judgments was particularly emphasized. Executions thus attracted huge crowds of spectators with the malefactor providing a pitiful example of the sinner's insignificance when compared to the justice and power of English law.[64]

Within this system, the criminal was expected to adopt the role of a tragic actor, upbraiding his own folly from the scaffold and warning others against similar transgressions. Their exclamations finished, the condemned then plummeted to their death, afterwards to be subjected to the post-mortem indignities of dissection or the public shame of hanging in chains—such was the extent of the law's terror. Despite the seemingly profound brutality of English law (at least, by twenty-first-century standards) there existed some scope for mercy. The crown, the ultimate force in the country, had the power to pardon, and the subsequent reality was that only half of the sentences handed down by eighteenth-century courts resulted in execution.[65] Quite often, sentences could, and were, commuted to transportation to the colonies or imprisonment.

It was historian E. P. Thompson who underscored the reasons for this legal pantomime. As Thompson suggested, the law had an important role in maintaining the governing class's control of England, and expressed through the drama of justice, mercy and terror, the very nature of English social relations. Because England's rulers believed the law had a life of its own, they never transformed the jurisprudential system into a vassal of their class interest. At the same time, they understood that the law perpetuated their influence and facilitated the task of governance.[66] This fundamental fact was essentially transposed into the justice system of the British Army, as many of its officers were drawn from the governing class. Within military law, property and life were safeguarded, just as they were in the civil system. In addition, the principles of justice, terror and mercy were also applicable to courts martial, and the anecdote of the criminal, tried for a capital transgression, only to be reprieved at the final moment and subjected to a lesser punishment (hence concurrently earning the hierarchy the loyalty of the pardoned and the esteem of the soldiery who were witnesses to these dramas), could be applied to numerous sentences handed down by military courts.

Therefore, though regular soldiers were accustomed to the terrifying ordeals of the Cat, riding the wooden horse and various other "corrective" measures the army brought to bear on condemned miscreants, it would be unfair to generalize this familiarity as unremitting acceptance or passive submission to the excessive application of force. The reality was that the soldiers of the British Army, though subjected to harsh methods of discipline, were protected from the excesses of an inherently strict justice system. This is further reinforced by the fact that evidence exists to show that soldiers knew when a punishment exceeded moral limits and actively stated so through whatever channels were available to them.

One such judgment is provided by Duncan Cameron, a Grenadier in the 44th Regiment of Foot, who served in Braddock's advanced guard at the Battle of the Monongahela. As the battered battalions recuperated at Wills Creek after this infamous rout, recriminations began and many soldiers were subjected to court-martial and punishment—on account of their perceived cowardice, disobedience of orders and so on. According to a disgruntled Cameron,

> ...there was Court-Marshall upon Court Marshall, and the most cruel Whippings succeeded them as I ever beheld...some where whipp'd for good reason, some for little, but, in general, they were too severe.[67]

If brutal, unrestrained and unaccountable punishment were truly the norm of army life, it is most unlikely that Cameron would have made this observation. That he did shows that there existed a military covenant that protected the limited rights men like himself enjoyed as professional soldiers.

There was one further element of military discipline that made unceasing and merciless punishment of the soldiers that much less likely. For, in reality, martial justice relied on the participation of the soldiers themselves in the grand dramas of justice, mercy and terror—if it were to stand any chance of being implemented.[68] Ultimately, enlisted men served as military police, witnesses, informants and executioners, and without their cooperation the whole system could not have functioned. The officer corps alone was too small to enforce the Mutiny Act and Rules and Articles of War, and their dependence on soldiers of good moral conduct to enforce this legislation gave the men some leeway to manipulate social dynamics and negotiate concessions that would have been impossible in an institution run solely by arbitrary power and terror. That is not to say that the army was never brutal or excessive in its application of justice and, of course, the temperament of individual officers should not be ignored. Furthermore, the nature and severity of punishments for offenses and crimes committed by serving soldiers depended upon whether the offender was a commissioned officer, non-commissioned officer, or man in the ranks; reflecting the fact that, ultimately, it was the commissioned ranks, utilizing the agency of NCOs (who were themselves exempted from floggings so as to reinforce their authority) who held the reins of power within the army.[69] Nonetheless, as the evidence adduced in the above section suggests, the reality of military justice does diverge significantly from established stereotypes of British soldiers as being the hapless victims of "a cruel and capricious court system that could hand out sentences of appalling magnitude" and, of course, unrelenting frequency.[70]

THE BRITISH ARMY AND IRREGULAR WARFARE: THE BACKGROUND OF AMERICAN MARTIAL TRADITION

Throughout the 1700s the British colonies and their French rivals based in Canada (New France) had engaged in low-intensity but extremely violent wars that were frequently sideshows to the greater dynastic conflicts that often erupted in Europe. In Britain's American colonies, such wars were named after the reigning monarch of the period; hence, in North America, King William's War, Queen Anne's War and King George's War ran parallel to wider European conflicts. Despite their undoubted ferocity, the said conflagrations were generally fought between the rival American colonists along the frontier territories of New York, New England, Pennsylvania, Virginia and Acadia (Nova Scotia) and did not see the deployment of "Old World" armies on the same scale witnessed during the later Seven Years War. Local experiences in these conflicts highlighted very quickly that to be successful in American warfare, it was essential to engage the aid of (and learn from) North America's native peoples, who buffered the respective colonies of the European antagonists. American-Indians had an unmatched knowledge of the continent's interior topography and their methods of war, based on the principles of hunting, and specifically adapted over many centuries to meet the rigors of pre-European America, made them indispensable allies to both European rivals.[71] Indeed, the arrival of advanced European weaponry had honed the lethality of these indigenous warriors, making their military value in the forests of America even more considerable. To harness the martial skills of native groups, both the French and British developed the previously discussed delicate web of Indian diplomacy that aimed to enlist the services of allies who could provide as vital a military service in the American hinterland as cavalry did on the plains of Europe.[72]

It was the French, superficially the weaker side, who often enjoyed greater success in establishing alliances with regional native tribes. A significant reason for this was the resentment caused by the Anglo-Iroquois pact, and the simple fact that sparsely settled New France did not provide the same level of threat as the land-hungry and demographically explosive British colonies. Correspondingly, manpower shortages meant that traditional set-piece battles with the British were unadvisable; thus native alliances were the bedrocks upon which the defense of New France was traditionally laid. Of course, the topography of frontier America made large-scale military engagements highly unlikely anyway; in no small measure a consequence of the daunting logistics involved in transporting armies, cannons and supply trains across virgin, primeval forests and landscapes. Even when significant numbers of European soldiers were dispatched to North America during the French and Indian War, the tactics of the Frederician military school were found to be largely incompatible with America's environment.[73] Consequently, New France's survival in the face of overwhelming numbers derived from a form of strategic defense—lightning strikes by relatively small parties of raiders that focused on vulnerable British outposts. These were complemented by the fortifying of key points along the strategic waterways of the St. Lawrence River and the Lake Champlain thoroughfare. Such outposts, utilizing the continent's terrain, made New France a virtual fortress-colony.

As a result of these tactical realities, what emerged in America was a localized development of *petite guerre* (as it was called by the French), or "guerilla warfare" as we would know it today.[74] This method of war would often involve the deployment of small groups of men who were frequently dispatched on spoiling raids that would involve the capture or killing of isolated colonists, the burning of individual farmsteads and even the annihilation of small settlements—as was exemplified by the destruction of Saratoga in 1745. Set-piece battles were very rare in the Americas; warfare, particularly when American-Indians served as allies, often consisted of a series of small-scale ambuscades which minimized the possibility of large-scale losses. Culturally, this pattern was very much derived from Native American traditions in which war was a means of replenishing a population debilitated by losses of various kinds, or proving one's martial prowess within a community. Heavy casualties akin to European pitched battles were simply not sustainable for American-Indian tribes whose demographic base had, in the sixteenth century, been severely reduced by European diseases and wars with foreign powers. Prolonged sieges and the storming of heavily fortified positions (at least along frontier territories) were also rare occurrences in North America; they simply involved too great a risk for natives asked to perform such missions alongside their European counterparts, while dragging cannons across the frontiers of European America was expensive, dangerous and impractical. Isolated settlements or other vulnerable outposts in which a garrison or community had failed to maintain sufficient diligence *were* vulnerable to French-Indian assault, however. Indeed, the possibility of acquiring scalps, booty and prisoners with minimum risk to life always appealed to indigenous warriors who, when serving alongside European forces, received no formal pay.

For the colonists of both sides, the possibility of capture by American-Indians was something that was dreaded as much as death itself (if not more). Since the very beginning of European settlement in America, many a lurid tale had been told of the gruesome fate that awaited any soldier or settler unfortunate enough to pass into native hands.[75] Though many of these tales did indeed have a foundation in truth, the reality was that, wherever possible, captured settlers were adopted into tribes to refurbish and renew a population that may have been depleted by war or a host of other natural exactions.[76] As an alternative to adoption, many British colonists were sold to the French in exchange for trade goods of various kinds. New France would often employ the hostages (who were released at the end of a conflict) in manual tasks such as domestic service or agricultural labor. Undoubtedly, this provided a welcome and cheap boost to Canada's stretched workforce in times of war.[77]

Within British America in particular, the death and destruction wrought by the French and their Indian allies was a constant grounds for trepidation, and every excess that was committed by these antagonists gave rise to a vitriolic hatred of the unseen foe. The Native Americans and their prowess in warfare generated widespread awe and fear as tales of rapacity spread along the frontier settlements, generating a level of hysteria that far outweighed the actual numbers of assailants and attacks involved.[78]

Compounding the military prowess of these French and Indian raiding parties was the intense political particularism that blighted Britain's North American Empire in which colonies failed to support one another unless doing so served parochial interests. This was, in fact, the situation the Newcastle ministry had faced in 1754 as it considered its options respective to French encroachments in North America. Essentially, with the exception of the Louisbourg expedition of 1745, the British colonies, divided, jealous, parochial and self-interested, had repeatedly proven that they could not be trusted to look after their own defense—forcing the ministry to send its soldiers to America to do a job the colonists simply could not, or would not, do for themselves. Whether the British Army itself was ready for an irregular war, however, was and is an issue of contention. In the following section of this chapter it will be shown that, even though many within the army's hierarchy possessed little appreciation, or experience of, the rigors of an American campaign, it would be very wrong to assume that the British Army had never faced the unique tactical challenges posed by a mode of warfare that, by definition and practical application, was the antithesis of its "regular" counterpart.

PETITE GUERRE IN EUROPE: THE EXPERIENCES OF THE BRITISH ARMY

When the British Army deployed to America in 1755 it did so with an ardent belief in the supremacy of the regular way of war that had led it to victory at iconic battles such as Blenheim, Dettingen and Culloden. The most enduring image of eighteenth-century European warfare is of two formally arrayed opponents fighting a chess-piece style battle that was epitomized by ordered volleys of musketry, intricate formations and cavalry charges that were carefully coordinated by the officers of each opposing army. It is this school of war that dominates contemporary paintings of the period and was supposedly intertwined with ideals of "chivalry and honor"; principles to which all armies were expected to adhere.[79] This meant that, in theory at least, the excesses of the horrific religious wars that blighted Europe in the seventeenth century could be curtailed.

This was always a rather romantic representation of eighteenth-century combat and is only part of the history of warfare during this period. Indeed, running parallel to this formal, official mode of war was a far nastier, brutal and indiscriminate strain. The French called this fighting style *petite guerre*, or small war, and it was something all European armies would have been familiar with at this time. For most, *petite guerre* was the antithesis of regular war. Unlike the parade-ground encounters of grand battles such as Fontenoy or Malplaquet, *petite guerre* focused on raids against enemy detachments, ambushes of isolated outposts, and the devastation of the infrastructure of one's enemy—fields, towns, villages and so on. It also included the use of terror tactics against civilians, and it was towards this most vulnerable segment of the population that the most barbaric excesses were often committed. The use of torture, rape and murder were the chilling by-products of *petite guerre*.

Despite the traditional notion of eighteenth-century warfare as a gentleman's pursuit, with *petite guerre* confined to the more criminal elements of opposing armies, the truth, by the middle of the 1700s, was that this particular brand of warfare had become central to the strategic thinking of nearly all major European armies. Indeed, some of Europe's most famous battles had already witnessed a growing role for irregular units whose worth had been proven to the commanders who often deployed them ahead of (and as auxiliaries to) large, regular armies. Prior to, and during, the epic battle of Fontenoy, for example, the fields and villages surrounding that battlefield were crammed with mercenary irregular troops—Pandurs, Grassins and the like. The latter, an important element within the French army, were instrumental in deciding the outcome of this engagement.[80]

Within most European armies, therefore, there existed, by the mid-1700s, specific doctrines concerned with the prosecution of irregular war. In France, notable figures such as the Marshal Saxe, Francois de la Croix and Thomas Auguste de Grandmaison had all contributed to the adaptation of irregular tactics into the French army. Saxe himself would, paradoxically, theorize about ways to counter such forces, having observed the confounding of Western forces by Polish irregulars on the vast plains that lay between the Russian and Austrian Empire.

Traditionally, therefore, much of the doctrinal approach to *petite guerre* developed by Western European armies in the eighteenth century evolved from the wars fought in Eastern Europe between the Austrian, Russian and Ottoman Empires. Eastern Europe became the classical region of guerrilla warfare and peasant risings. This was partly a consequence of the region's topography but also because "clashes between social strata were intensified by overlaying religious and ethnic tension."[81] This made Eastern Europe, such was its political condition at this time, the perfect breeding ground for a strain of conflict that would one day become known as "partisan war."

For the Comte de Saxe, the way to counter forces who, "made war in such a vague and irregular manner, that, if an enemy makes a point of pursuing them, he will thereby be presently rendered incapable of opposing their continual inroads," was to fight a war of posts.[82] Instead of vainly engaging irregular units in the mobile, hit-and-run style they so favored, a regular commander should strive to, "possess himself of certain posts upon the rivers, to fortify, to erect barracks for his troops, and to raise contributions throughout the provinces."[83] By these methods, Saxe believed the whole country surrounding such posts would be pacified.

Saxe's theories also suggested the creation of irregular units within the French Army. These "light companies," consisting of 70 men, all expert marksmen, conditioned to fight the rigors of *petite guerre*, were to accompany regular regiments, serving both regular and irregular functions with equal competency. For instance, they would patrol the countryside surrounding the *postes* Saxe advocated building in enemy territory; they would defend regular forces from partisan assaults while the latter were marching through hostile terrain, and they would serve as a tool to defeat regular armies either using conventional or unconventional means. Such sagacious observations soon became widely accepted among Western Europe's military hierarchy and Saxe's light companies became a standard feature of the armies of that often war-torn continent (with slight variations). The British Army was no exception and in 1741–1742, light infantry companies were attached to each of its battalions. Such men were expected to protect convoys and regular detachments from irregular assaults.

If such knowledge of irregular war was so widespread in eighteenth-century military circles, and overwhelming evidence suggests this was true, then the British Army's failure to successfully prosecute the war in America, against enemies who posed challenges not to dissimilar to the partisans of Eastern Europe, requires some explanation. Perhaps a major reason for this likely concerned the tactical traditions of the army, the leaders of which had never accepted the doctrines of *petite guerre* to the same extent their Continental counterparts had.[84] Even though "irregular wars" had been fought by the British Army, the colonization of Ireland and the suppression of Jacobitism in Scotland provide the most obvious examples, British officers failed to acknowledge *petite guerre* as an effective means to wage military campaigns against traditional, regular foes. Instead, it was considered a mode of war to be waged against rebellious populations and thus did not evolve a sanctioned doctrine (akin to French military theories of *petite guerre*) within the British Army. Indeed, English operations in Ireland, staged during the mid-to-late seventeenth century, were specifically designed to counter a campaign that was led by armed citizens; in other words, a war fought against a hostile civilian population. As such, they bore many parallels with the type of conflict that was to be fought against irregulars in America in 1755; an unlimited form of war in which the lines between combatant and non-combatant were blurred.

In short, accepted norms of behavior, in general, did not apply as a *guerre de postes*, the "feed fight" and transportation were brought to bear against a rebellious civilian population.[85]

The British Army's encounter with *petite guerre* in Scotland, most notably during the great Jacobite rebellion of 1745, afforded the institution a number of valuable lessons. As in Ireland, the Scottish war would see the army arrayed against an unconventional foe; one which was, just as the natives of America would be ten years later, dismissed as wild and barbarous savages by many contemporary Britons. Such overconfidence in the crown's regular soldiers soon proved to be woefully naïve as the so-called barbarous Highlanders, who formed the backbone of "Bonnie Prince Charlie's" force, wiped out government forces at Prestonpans; forcing a dramatic shift in the complacency that appeared to mar governmental attitudes towards this latest Stuart-inspired insurrection.

Prestonpans, like the small skirmishes that preceded it (which also highlighted the ineffectiveness of regular units and tactics against the unconventional Highlanders), did not, however, result in an overhaul of tactical practices within the British Army; most officers remained hostile to the evident advantages of *petite guerre*. Writing from Flanders shortly after word reached him of this infamous setback, Sir John Ligonier, one of Britain's most renowned soldiers in the eighteenth century, stated rather peevishly that eight regiments of regulars could, "put out this infernal flame [Jacobitism] at once."[86] Ligonier was not alone in this attestation. Many of his contemporary countrymen shared this belief in the inherent inferiority of irregular forces.

Nevertheless, eventual government victory over the forces of Charles Edward Stuart was in no small measure a consequence of raising and arming local, *irregular* units. These provided much-needed intelligence on Jacobite movements, forcing the latter onto the back foot by engaging them in the style of war they used against British regulars. With the Jacobites thus tied down, or hamstrung in their freedom of movement, the strengths of the regular army were brought to bear. The army consolidated its grip on government-controlled areas and rooted out suspected rebels. It was anything but the romantic, chivalric campaign that leaps from the canvases of those who depicted more conventional battles of the period. These were unlimited actions in which the families of suspected Jacobites were targeted and threatened with execution if they were found to have aided the insurrection. Fundamentally, British tactics were a fusion of regular and irregular forces and strategies; and it brought swathes of the Scottish countryside under control, paving the way for the Duke of Cumberland to quash the rebellion once and for all at Culloden in 1746. Cumberland's victory here was, essentially, a triumph for regular soldiers and the *traditional* European school of war. The battle showed that, just as professional soldiers could be unwieldy and clumsy when taken out of their preferred open field environment, so unconventional units would find themselves out of their depth when standing toe-to-toe with professional soldiers on open terrain. Indeed, Prince Charles Edward Stuart's pell-mell assault against well-trained, well-equipped and experienced veteran soldiers, across open and boggy terrain, could only ever have ended in disaster, the ramifications of which resounded in the Highlands for generations. The aftermath of the battle saw Cumberland and his army once more adopt unconventional strategies as they harried the Highlands and brutally eliminated those who had played an active role in the rebellion. For all its notoriety, it was a successful campaign, and the Highlanders never again rebelled against the British state.[87]

Despite the overwhelming evidence that suggested, rightly, that the marrying of conventional and unconventional forces had given the Hanoverian order ultimate victory against the Young Pretender, the British Army failed to acknowledge the key role *petite guerre* had played. For many, Culloden simply proved that regular units were superior to partisans, an opinion shared by the army's high command. Earlier Jacobite victories were not seen as evidence that irregular warfare was, given the right conditions, able to overcome conventional codes, but instead, excuses were found elsewhere. Blame for the loss at Prestonpans and other, lesser, setbacks was, for example, laid squarely at the feet of the indecisive Sir John Cope and the ineptitude of his inexperienced soldiers. If anything, one of the major lessons most drew from the debacle was that the army needed to retrench its conventional training. Good order, regularity of maneuver and discipline were considered the unequivocal means to defeat *any* adversary—conventional or not. Consequently, the adaptation of irregular tactics was deemed dangerous and, even if possessing certain benefits, impossible to implement. As one anonymous observer, writing in the *Gentleman's Magazine* wrote,

> It is particularly to be observed, that regular men can never fight well when reduced to the form of a mob, no more than a mob can fight like regular men. The former is a method of fighting which soldiers are not acquainted with, and the lesson and practice of their lives absolutely discharge it.[88]

It is therefore ironic that many of the skills developed and laid down in military manuals in widespread circulation among armies on the Continent, were so blatantly ignored by the very officers in Braddock's army who would have found them so useful in the war they were sent to fight in America in 1755. Just like the anonymous author of the above-mentioned *Essay on Regular and Irregular Forces*, who dismissed the real lessons of the army's encounter with the irregular Highlanders out of hand, most serving British officers continued to focus their studies and learning on regular war. Unlike the officers of France and other European armies, British officers had scarce little literature to inform them of the practices that needed to be mastered in the pursuit of irregular war. Even those works which had been translated into English were not widely read within the commissioned ranks; men like James Oglethorpe (a key figure in the tactical evolution of the campaign against the Highlanders) remained a scarcity within the British Army—until it was forced to adapt to *petite guerre* following the notable setbacks it suffered in the North American backcountry between 1755 and 1757.

Edward Braddock, sharing this entrenched attitude, would likewise learn the hard way that *petite guerre* was dismissed at one's peril. Braddock, epitomizing an ingrained British confidence in the supremacy of regular warfare and regularly trained soldiers would famously scold Benjamin Franklin with his infamous boast that, "These savages [Native Americans and French Canadian irregulars] may indeed be a formidable Enemy to your raw American militia; but, upon the King's regular & disciplined Troops, Sir, it is impossible they should make any Impression."[89] The tragedy of this attitude, despite Braddock's considerable attempts to incorporate indigenous warriors into his force, resonated on the banks of the Monongahela, and was felt by the officers and men of his army, being exemplified by the terrible casualties his soldiers suffered on 9 July, 1755.

A Tortured Mass Led by Colonel Blimps?

Essentially, the British Army of the eighteenth century was an army of paradoxes. It was undoubtedly forged in adversity, and not just the kind found on battlefields at home and abroad; it was frequently betrayed or manipulated by its government and was poorly treated by its countrymen. The men, a mixed cross-section of the lower orders (including those from non-British origins) with a fair sprinkling of recruits from more privileged backgrounds, drank too much and could be raucous in their behavior. The army's disciplinary code, by conventional standards intolerable, undoubtedly has cast a long shadow through the annals of history too.

Nevertheless, though the British Army lost battles, Braddock's defeat being a prime example in this epoch, it rarely lost a war. As an institution it was a typically British mixture of tradition and compromise and was fueled by the drive for place, honor, advancement and recognition. Irrespective of its commanders, the army always fought hard; that the soldiers of Braddock's force stood for three hours under withering French and Indian fire, while James Abercrombie's army would later hurl themselves fiercely into the Marquis de Montcalm's daunting *abbatis* and entrenchments at Ticonderoga, is testimony to the fighting qualities and motivation of the common soldier and, indeed, his officers. They were the real characteristics that defined the British Army throughout this period and give lie to the acutely negative stereotypes of the army as a force that consisted of a set of lumpish imbeciles led by incompetent, over-privileged sadists who undertook their duties without any sense of honor or human dignity. Ultimately, although discipline could be used to coerce obedience, such an explanation of the driving forces of the British soldier of the eighteenth century does not hold much weight. Something far more profound and deep-rooted operated within the organization and, indeed, among individual soldiers and officers.

Invariably, fear breeds fear and a man terrified of the lash behind the front line would likely carry his terror into battle. As Sylvia Frey has argued, a point is reached where fear of the enemy to the front is greater than that which lay behind, which is why, under the right level of duress, soldiers, at times in large numbers, broke and fled the battlefield.[90] What the British Army of the eighteenth century used to motivate its soldiers to confront what were, unquestionably, the face-to-face horrors of warfare at this time was, as James Hendrix argued, an *esprit de corps*.[91] It was a martial culture built on pride and honor that was cemented by a distinctive military style or "martial air"; one which was not adverse to the use corporal or capital punishment (at times excessively), but which nevertheless placed great emphasis on duty, honor and pride.

In an army yet to be exposed to nationalism or ideology, uniforms and drill, in other words the paraphernalia of martial enculturation, all served to build this spirit of belonging and a sense of duty and loyalty that cannot be explained by the application of the lash or fear of the hangman's noose. The latter were the stick to the carrot of the military spirit but, as I have demonstrated throughout this chapter, were regulated; not forgetting the fact that both were frequently commuted to build a sense of loyalty, gratitude, camaraderie and, ultimately, coherence and obedience. Military justice, at least within the British Army, reflected that of the society from which it originated and really was not that much harsher than its civilian counterpart in Britain at this time.

To conclude, when all factors are considered, it becomes apparent that, for all its faults (and there were many), the British Army of the eighteenth century was a very proficient fighting force; one which would prove itself, in conflicts across the globe, as being among the finest of its kind. When explaining the failure of the Edward Braddock, therefore, such an axiom emphasizes the importance of reassessing the impact shortcomings in the wider British Atlantic World played in the truncation of this campaign's (and certainly the wider Braddock Plan's) grandiose objectives. Allotting it to the failure of the British Army on the basis of ill-informed history is to miss the far wider weaknesses that were exposed as Britain and its colonies mobilized to fight North America's first truly large-scale and "Europeanized" war.

NOTES

1. Ian K. Steele, *Guerrillas and Grenadiers: The Struggle for Canada, 1689–1760* (Toronto: Ryerson Press, 1969), 132.
2. Stanley Pargellis, "Braddock's Defeat," *American Historical Review*, Vol. XLI (1936), 253.
3. Dallas Irvine, "The First British Regulars in North America," *Military Affairs*, Vol. 9 (Winter, 1945), 337–354.
4. Mel Gibson's *The Patriot* (2000) was particularly notable for playing on these stereotypes of the British Army of the eighteenth-century, as had been Robert Goldstein's earlier *Spirit of '76* (1917). See Frank Mancel, *Film Study: An Analytical Bibliography* (London: Associated University Presses, 1990), 223.
5. For a significant analysis of the evolution of "New Military History," see William P. Tatum III, "Challenging the New Military History: The Case of Eighteenth-Century British Army Studies," *History Compass 5.1* (2007), 72–84.
6. Again, Dallas Irvine's commentary, outlined earlier in this chapter, is a succinct summary of attitudes. Irvine, "Regulars in North America," 337–354.
7. See Benjamin Franklin, John Biglow (ed.), *The Autobiography of Benjamin Franklin* (Philadelphia, 1868), 311.

8. Harold Selesky, *War and Society in Colonial Connecticut* (New Haven, CT: Yale University Press, 1990), x.
9. See Glenn Steppler, "British Military Law, Discipline, and the Conduct of Regimental Courts Martial in the Later Eighteenth-century," *The English Historical Review*, Vol. 102, No. 405 (Oct., 1987), 859–886 and Stephen Brumwell, *Redcoat: The British Soldier and War in the Americas, 1755–1763* (Cambridge: Cambridge University Press, 2002).
10. "Wolfe to his Father, Southampton, 4th September, 1755" in Beckles Wilson (ed.), *The Life and Letters of James Wolfe* (London, 1909), 274.
11. Ibid., 351.
12. Ibid., 357.
13. Bennett Cuthbertson, *A System for the Compleat Interior Management and Economy of a Battalion of Infantry* (Dublin, 1768; corrected edition, Bristol, 1776), 111, 107, 163.
14. Ibid., 55, 59.
15. Stephen Brumwell *Redcoat: The British Soldier and War in the Americas, 1755–1763* (Cambridge: Cambridge University Press, 2002), 71.
16. Evidence from the Battle of the Monongahela reinforces this. Matthew Leslie, a Lieutenant in the 44th, remembered how enlisted men were willing to risk their lives for a good officer. Accordingly, "Our friend Captain John Conyngham is severely wounded, his horse fell on the first fire, and before he could be disengaged from the animal, which had fallen on him, received a wound on his arm; and his life was saved by the enthusiasm of his men, who seeing his danger rushed between the savages and him and carried him in triumph from the spot." See "Copy of a letter from Major Leslie to a respectable merchant of Philadelphia," in Paul E. Kopperman, *Braddock at the Monongahela* (Pittsburgh, PA: University of Pittsburgh Press, 1992), 204–205.
17. Humphrey Bland, *A Treatise of Military Discipline: In which is laid down and Explained the Duties of Officer and Soldier* (5th edition, Dublin, 1743), 143.
18. Historians are increasingly challenging even this assumption however. The great wars of the eighteenth century saw the British male population mobilized on a scale not yet seen in British history and many families would have known, or been related to, someone with some kind of service in the British Army. In addition, prior to 1750 Britain was, irrespective of the Union that existed between England and Scotland, a divided nation and the Jacobite rebellion of 1745 was the latest manifestation of this disunity. After the Seven Years War, however, those Jacobites who had raised their claymores against the state had actually served under its colors and in the process had won innumerable plaudits for their services and sacrifices. Such conduct was mirrored by the army's other regiments, and the glorious victories won on virtually every continent of the globe marked

the ascension of the army that had been instrumental in their achievement. As these victories were also considered British victories which benefited the British nation, by adding swathes of territories and resources to Britain's dominions—as opposed to continental European victories that were frequently offset by French counterstrokes or the sheer grinding bloodbaths that European conflicts often descended into—the Seven Years War and its outcome was, to all intents and purposes, a victory of British arms, and the army benefitted hugely from this. Though the American Revolution would provide a momentary blip in public enthusiasm for the army, patriotic fervor towards it re-emerged with the Napoleonic Wars.

19. See "English Bill of Rights, 1689: An Act Declaring the Rights and Liberties of the Subject and Settling the Succession of the Crown," [online] http://www.avalon.law.yale.edu/17th_century/England.asp accessed March 14, 2016.
20. Colonel H.C.B. Rogers, *The British Army of the Eighteenth Century* (London: George Allen & Unwin, 1977), 21.
21. Richard Holmes, *Redcoat: The British Soldier in the Age of Horse and Musket* (London: Harper Collins, 2001), 14–15.
22. Lord Loudoun would endure considerable difficulties when accommodating the army. He even felt compelled to threaten to billet his soldiers on private individuals if the colonists refused to acquire appropriate barracks for his beleaguered soldiers. See Stanley Pargellis, *Lord Loudon in North America* (New Haven, CT: Yale University Press, 1961), 187–210.
23. See J. A. Houlding, *Fit for Service: The Training of the British Army, 1715–1795* (Oxford: Clarendon Press, 1981), 57–74.
24. Sir John Fortesque *A History of the British Army: Volume II, First Part—to the close of the Seven Years War* (London, 1899), 24–26.
25. In truth, the military, economic, and political changes of the Military Revolution of the late Renaissance (and the Financial Revolution of the seventeenth century) meant that smaller maritime powers like Holland and England *had* to take stock of the transformation of warfare that had occurred in larger nations. That this process was slower in Britain was, as mentioned, in no small measure an effect of the waters of the English Channel protecting the nation from the ever-present reality of invasion faced by "landed" powers. See Geoffrey Parker, *The Military Revolution. Military Innovation and the Rise of the West, 1500–1800* (Cambridge: Cambridge University Press, 1988).
26. An excellent analysis of the 1745 rebellion is provided by Geoffrey Plank, *Rebellion and Savagery: The Jacobite Rising of 1745 and the British Empire* (Philadelphia: University of Pennsylvania Press, 2005).
27. H.C.B Rogers, *The British Army of the Eighteenth-century*, 23.

28. Brumwell, *Redcoats*, 66–68.
29. One of the many overlooked, or marginalized, causes of Braddock's defeat is the difficult task the general faced in welding a plethora of new recruits into an efficient fighting force.
30. Stanley Pargellis, *Lord Loudon in North America*, 105.
31. D. Hay and N. Rogers, *Eighteenth-century English Society* (Oxford: Oxford University Press, 1997), 19–20.
32. This particular soldier identifies himself as "Jonas," which is a pseudonym. See Anon, *A Soldier's Journal* (London, 1770).
33. See J. W. M. Hichberger, *Images of the Army: The Military in British Art, 1815–1914* (Manchester: Manchester University Press, 1988), 124.
34. George Farquhar, *The Recruiting Officer* (London, 1718), 36.
35. F. T. Nichols, "The Organization of Braddock's Army," in *William and Mary Quarterly*, IV (1947), 139.
36. Alfred Proctor James (ed.) *Writings of General John Forbes relating to his service in North America* (Menasha, WI: The Collegiate Press, 1938), 23.
37. See "Sharpe to Braddock, May 7 1755" in William Hand Browne (ed.), *Archives of Maryland: Volume VI, Correspondence of Governor Horatio Sharpe*, Vol. I: 1753–1757 (Baltimore: Maryland Historical Society, 1888), 204, 213.
38. Pargellis, *Loudoun in America*, 107.
39. Samuel Hazard (ed.), *Pennsylvania Archives: Commencing 1748*, Vol. II (12 vols. Philadelphia: Joseph Severns & Co., 1853), 578.
40. *Maryland Archives*, VI, 157, 165, 186, 189, 192, 208, 211; *Pennsylvania Archives*, II, 401, 412; *Rhode Island Colonial Records*, V, 409, 412; *Colonial Records of Connecticut*, X, 330–331.
41. Winthrop Sargent, *The History of an Expedition against Fort Duquesne in 1755: Under Major General Edward Braddock* (Philadelphia, 1855), 325.
42. See "Massachusetts General Court to William Bolland, Sept. 26, 1755" in, Charles Henry Lincoln (ed.), *The Correspondence of William Shirley, Governor of Massachusetts and Military Commander in America, 1731–1760*, Volume II (New York: 1912), 283–289.
43. Fundamentally, the colonists believed in "diffused sovereignty." See Steven Sarson, *British America 1500–1800: Creating Colonies, Imagining an Empire* (London: Hodder Arnold, 2005), 192.
44. At the time of Braddock's march, this was a view that was shared by, among others, Sir John St. Clair, Braddock's deputy quartermaster general, and Robert Orme, the general's aide de camp. See "Orme's Journal," in Sargent (ed.) *History of an Expedition*, 312.
45. See Brumwell, *Redcoats*, 63–66.
46. As mentioned previously, such opinions are synonymous with works such as Alan Rogers, *Empire and Liberty: American Resistance to British*

Authority, 1755–1763 (Los Angeles: University of California Press, 1974) and Douglas Edward Leach, *Roots of Conflict: British Armed Forces & Colonial Americans, 1677–1763* (Chapel Hill: University of North Carolina Press, 1986).
47. This is something covered extensively in Fred Anderson's *A People's Army: Massachusetts Soldiers & Society in the Seven Years' War* (Chapel Hill: University of North Carolina Press, 1984).
48. For Braddock the reality was somewhat different; his units consisted of large numbers of draftees and raw recruits, while training was limited, in America, to a mere 3 months due to delays of various kinds.
49. There were, in fact, an array of military manuals that officers could consult when training their men in the various forms of military practice. George Washington once told his Virginia Provincial Regiment subordinates that, "there ought to be a time appropriated to attain this knowledge; as well as to indulge pleasure. And as we now have no opportunities to improve from example; let us read, for this desirable end. There is Blands and other Treatises which will give the wished-for information." See "George Washington addressing his officers, 8 January 1756" in W. W. Abbot, et al., (eds.), *The Papers of George Washington: Colonial Service*, Volume II (10 vols. Charlottesville: University Press of Virginia, 1983–1995), 257.
50. Holmes, *Redcoat*, 32.
51. Indeed, before Braddock was deployed to America, the Duke of Cumberland would advise him that discipline and regularity of fire would overcome Native American and Canadian irregulars.
52. Holmes, *Redcoat*, 45.
53. "Instructions drawn up by the late Major General Wolfe for the 20th Regiment of Foot, then lying in Canterbury, in case of the French landing in 1755," *The Gentleman's Magazine*, Volume 29, 1759, 528.
54. Fortesque, *History of the British Army*, II, 582–583.
55. Fred Anderson, *The Crucible of War: The Seven Years War and the Fate of Empire in British North America, 1754–1766* (New York: Alfred A. Knopf, 2000), 286.
56. Ibid., 287–288.
57. Francis Jennings, *Empire of Fortune: Crowns, Colonies and Tribes in the Seven Years War in America* (New York: W.W. Norton, 1988), 208–10, 422.
58. Leach, *Roots of Conflict*, 123.
59. Bennett Cuthbertson, *A System for the Complete Interior Management and Oeconomy of a Battalion of Infantry* (London: Bolton Grierson, 1768), 119.
60. Luke Gridley, F.M., ed., *Luke Gridley's Diary of 1757 while in service in the French and Indian War.* (Hartford, CT, 1906), 30–31. According to the editor of this diary, Gridley was, "…a private in 'Captain Major' Payson's

company. He was from Farmington, of a numerous stock which also included a missionary, and members of which were on the committee to raise subscriptions for Boston after its closure by the Port Bill." See Ibid., 18.
61. George Washington, "Letter of Instructions to the Captains of the Virginia Regiments, 1759."
62. "Washington to Dinwiddie, 11 July, 1757," in Worthington Chauncey Ford (ed.), *The Writings of George Washington, Collected and Edited by Worthington Chauncey Ford* (New York: G. P. Putnam's Sons, 1889–1893). Vol. I (1748–1757), 411–414.
63. See Don Higginbotham, *George Washington and the American Military Tradition* (Athens: Georgia University Press, 1985), 53.
64. Douglas Hay, "Property, Authority and the Criminal Law," in Douglas Hay, Peter Linebaugh, John G. Rule, E.P. Thomson and Cal Winslow, *Albion's Fatal Tree: Crime and Society in Eighteenth-century England* (New York: Pantheon, 1975), 17–63.
65. Ibid., 43.
66. See E.P. Thompson, *Whigs and Hunters: The Origin of the Black Act* (New York: Pantheon, 1975), 258–269.
67. Duncan Cameron, *The Life, Adventures, and surprising Deliverances of Duncan Cameron, Private Soldier in the Regiment of Foot, late Sir Peter Halket's*, Third Edition (Philadelphia: 1756), 14.
68. Glenn Steppler, "British Military Law, Discipline, and the Conduct of Regimental Courts Martial in the Later Eighteenth-century," *The English Historical Review*, Vol. 102, No. 405 (Oct., 1987), 881.
69. Ibid., 880.
70. Albert N. Gilbert, "The Regimental Courts Martial in the Eighteenth-century British Army," *Albion 8*, No. 1 (Spring 1976).
71. An analysis of Indian Warfare can be found in, Armstrong Starkey, *European and Native American Warfare, 1675–1815* (London: University College Press, 1998), 17–35.
72. See Matthew C. Ward, "'Fighting Old Women': Indian strategy on the Virginian and Pennsylvanian frontier, 1754–1758," in *The Virginia Magazine of History and Biography*, Vol. 103, No. 3 (July, 1995), 297–320.
73. "Frederician military school" refers to the standard European practice of warfare at this time.
74. Louis Joseph de Montcalm-Gozon, Marquis de Saint Veran, Commander-in-chief of Canada's forces from 1756–1759, called this mode of war *La Guerre Sauvage*, a term which exemplified his developing hostility towards Canadians, Native Americans and their conduct during military campaigns. Just prior to his assault against Fort William-Henry (1757) he wrote that, "One needs the patience of an angel to get on with them. Ever since I have been here I have had nothing but visits, harangues and deputations of

these gentlemen. The Iroquois ladies did me the "honour" to bring me belts of wampum, which oblige me to go to their village and sing the war song. They make war with astounding cruelty, sparing neither women nor children."

75. Both English and French colonists had experienced the American Indians ferocity in cases where a torturous death was deemed a prisoner's fate. The reasons for the native employment of torture were several-fold: to exact revenge following a loss in battle; to serve as a sacrifice and to test the moral, spiritual and physical strength of the victim. Enemy combatants condemned to die this way were expected to withstand the rigors of torture with stoicism and courage. For a detailed summary of the means and usages of torture in North Eastern Indian tribes, I would recommend, as a classic, Nathaniel Knowles "The Torture of Captives by the Indians of Eastern North America," *Proceedings of the American Philosophical Society*, Vol. 82, No. 2 (Mar. 22, 1940), 151–225. For a more recent analysis of Iroquois warfare in particular see, Daniel K. Richter, "War and Culture: The Iroquois Experience" in Peter C. Mancall and James H. Merrell (eds.), *American Encounters: Natives and Newcomers from European Contact to Indian Removal*, 1500–1850 (New York: Routledge, 2000), 283–311.

76. See Matthew C. Ward, *Breaking the Backcountry*, 52–58.

77. An example of this can be found in the well-known experiences of a Susannah Johnson and her family, captured by French-Indian raiders near Charlestown, New Hampshire, August 30, 1754. For her full account see Susannah Johnson, *A narrative of the captivity of Mrs. Johnson: containing an account of her sufferings, during four years, with the Indians and French: together with an appendix, containing the sermons, preached at her funeral and that of her mother with sundry other interesting articles* (Vermont, 1814). Kidnapping was a common part of imperial conflict and was experienced by colonists all over the world; it certainly was not a localized phenomenon, even though American captivity narratives abound in historical literature. See Linda Colley, *Captives: Britain, Empire and the World 1600–1850* (New York: Pantheon, 2002).

78. Peter Silver, in his work *Our Savage Neighbors*, used a case study of Pennsylvania to show how the experience of fearing and fighting Indians bred a sense of unity among that colony's heterogeneous European communities. This, in turn, led to the emergence of what contemporaries considered a distinct "White People" that transcended religious and ethnic tensions and became the foundation of a future "American identity." See Peter Silver, *Our Savage Neighbors: How Indian War Transformed Early America* (New York: W. W. Norton, 2008).

79. One only has to examine Benjamin West's *The Death of General Wolfe* (1771) and Louis-Joseph Watteau's *Mort du Marquis de Montcalm-Gozon*

for evidence of how artists could romanticize conventional warfare at this time.
80. Fortesque, *British Army*, II, 110.
81. Lewis Gann, *Guerrillas in History* (Palo Alto, CA: Stanford University Press, 1971), 9.
82. Maurice Count de Saxe, *Reveries, or, Memoirs Concerning the Art of War* (Edinburgh: Alexander Donaldson, 1776), 134–137.
83. Ibid., 138.
84. John Grenier, *The First Way of War: American War Making on the Frontier, 1607–1814* (Cambridge: Cambridge University Press, 2005), 89. The fact that there was not a term in the English language for *petite guerre* is evidence that its concepts were not integrated well by the British army.
85. See Nicholas Canny, "The Martial Kingdom: Ireland as a Problem in the First British Empire," in Bernard Bailyn and Philip D. Morgan (eds.), *Strangers within the Realm: Cultural Margins of the First British Empire* (Chapel Hill: University of North Carolina Press, 1991), 35–67.
86. Quoted in Rex Whitworth, *Field Marshal Lord Ligonier: A story of the British Army, 1702–1770* (Oxford: Clarendon Press, 1950), 108.
87. As Geoffrey Plank (*Rebellion and Savagery*, 2005) has observed, the Jacobite Highlanders were denounced as rebels and savages, which helped to justify and legitimatize the violence of the government's campaign in the Highlands. Such terminology, and a fear of a wider conspiracy, was used to a similar effect against American-Indians, particularly during the French and Indian War.
88. Anon., "Essay on Regular and Irregular Forces," *Gentleman's Magazine*, 16 (1746), 30–32.
89. Benjamin Franklin, Charles, W. Eliot, (ed.), *The Autobiography of Benjamin Franklin* (Rockville, MD: Arc Manor, 2008), 120.
90. Frey, *British Soldier*, 129.
91. Hendrix, *Spirit of the Corps*, iv.

CHAPTER 5

Edward Braddock in America: Provincial Politics, Indian Alliances and the Prolonged and Arduous March to the Monongahela

The political and diplomatic weaknesses of the British Atlantic World were perhaps most evident in the lead-up to the military disaster Edward Braddock suffered on the banks of the Monongahela. Rather than treating Braddock's defeat (and hence the failure of the wider "Braddock Plan") as a purely martial setback, in this chapter it will be demonstrated that prevailing political and diplomatic conditions across British America did a great deal to hamper his advance to Fort Duquesne; delaying his arrival at the Monongahela by several weeks (at least), giving the French vital time in which they were able to hastily reinforce their position with allied Indian warriors. These political and constitutional failures included the fractious relationships that existed between governors and assemblies (or proprietors and people), and the fraternal infighting often evident between various factions of individual colonies. There also existed very real divisions between tidewater and frontier settlements, particularly in Pennsylvania and Virginia. Though these would be most evidently exemplified after Braddock's defeat, the fact remained that the pacifist Quakers refused to properly defend frontier communities (instead preferring to negotiate with the Indians), while the grandees of Virginia, perhaps distracted by the threat of a slave insurrection, were reluctant to spend significant sums of money on the defense of their distant frontier.[1] The diplomatic failings of the British Atlantic were also apparent during the build-up to the Battle of the Monongahela, specifically with regards to Braddock's attempts to engage native allies in his cause. In short, if, as has often been

© The Editor(s) (if applicable) and The Author(s) 2016
R. Hall, *Atlantic Politics, Military Strategy and the French and Indian War*, War, Culture and Society, 1750-1850,
DOI 10.1007/978-3-319-30665-0_5

suggested, Braddock squandered the possibility of forging alliances with the Ohio tribes, then Robert Dinwiddie (Governor of Virginia) and James Glen (Governor of South Carolina) were equally guilty of undermining the pivotal negotiations that would have seen Cherokee, Catawba and Iroquois warriors marching alongside Braddock's Anglo-American army. Unfortunately, personal rivalries and particularist jealousies squandered any hope of integrating such potentially vital native elements into his ill-fated force.

SETTING A RECURRENT TREND: BRADDOCK'S ARRIVAL IN AMERICA

Edward Braddock, when he arrived in British North America, was entering a world which lacked the formal and rigid command structures that he took for granted as a professional soldier. Through the neglect of various ministers and agencies in London over many decades, there had emerged in America a level of political autonomy that negated the importance of the colonial governors Braddock expected to command as martial subordinates—and whom he expected to behave as such—in the New World.[2] The fact that the British government was well aware of these failings was evidenced by the struggles that even that nation's most powerful ministers had suffered in their futile attempts to bring the colonists to heel. The Duke of Newcastle too, it will be remembered, had hardly facilitated the growth of metropolitan authority within the empire during his tenure as Secretary of State for the Southern Department (1724–1748). His predisposition to dispense patronage to allies in exchange for political favors did little to improve the cause of executive power and in actuality took away from colonial governors the ability to create their own power bases, creating what historian Steven Sarson has called, "political managers rather than executives or representatives of royal power."[3] In other words, Newcastle had inadvertently helped ensure that governors were "domesticated."[4]

It was this political backdrop that would so seriously hamper Edward Braddock's campaign of 1755, as was perhaps most strikingly evident in the way colonial assemblies interpreted the provisos of the Braddock Plan and its requests for a central fund, recruits and provisions. Indeed, when Braddock finally set foot on American soil in February 1755, it quickly became all too apparent that the American colonies had evolved a very different understanding of service and subordination from that to which he was accustomed.

Preliminary Political Problems

Soon after Braddock disembarked in Virginia on February 19, 1755, the colonists became aware of the tough, uncompromising and imperious characteristics that had made him such an appealing appointment for the Duke of Cumberland. The intelligence he had received of the dispositions of those he was sent to defend ensured that his first meeting with Robert Dinwiddie, on February 24, was characterized by complaints about the colonies' conduct and seeming indifference towards his forthcoming campaign. The pacifist Quakers, the dominant force in Pennsylvania's Assembly, irrespective of the fact that their colony was noted for its prosperity, had apparently refused to appropriate money for the campaign; and consequently, an acerbic communication to Governor Robert Hunter Morris was dispatched deploring the improper behavior of his assembly. Eager to press his authority, Braddock also threatened to billet his men on the province if they failed to provide the support they were required to.[5]

His rage against the Pennsylvanian lower house was no doubt stoked by the rather negative briefings he had received of their motivations and conduct from the manipulative Thomas Penn. Penn, who was the proprietor of the colony, was at this time embroiled in a power struggle with the assembly's Quaker majority. Indeed, despite his own Quaker roots, Penn, son of Pennsylvania's founder William, did not share the religious beliefs of the Society of Friends—having become an Anglican in 1751—and had, prior to Braddock's voyage to America, selectively fed the commander-in-chief "informations and advices" that, he claimed, would serve the good of what he defined as the "cause."[6] Unfortunately, the "cause" in question was principally focused upon his narrow proprietary interests rather than Braddock's eminently daunting task of capturing the remote Fort Duquesne.

The Anglican Robert Morris (deputy-governor of the colony) also shared Penn's dislike of Quaker control of the lower house and was a natural ally of the colony's proprietor.[7] Preferring a "high style" of governance, he further stoked Braddock's mistrust of the assembly with 'informations and advices' of his own. The root of the antipathy that existed between proprietor, governor and assembly at this time was a longstanding issue that revolved around the theme of taxation (notably proprietary exemption from it) and the challenges posed by the raising of capital to meet the threat posed by the French. Its central ideals were those common to many of Britain's American colonies in the mid-eighteenth century and reflected the significant influence held by colonial assemblies in the intracolonial balance of power (which, in theory, was supposed to be weighted in favor of executive authority). Penn, viewing this as a matter of hereditary privilege (his "rights" as proprietor of the colony), believed ardently that his own estates should be exempt from any form of taxation; the assembly, as Benjamin Franklin would later convey, vehemently disagreed. Rather, as yet another French war presented itself before the province, it was felt that all should share the burdens of wartime taxation:

> These public quarrels were all at bottom owing to the proprietaries our hereditary governors; who, when any expense was to be incurred for the defence of their province, with incredible meanness, instructed their deputies to pass no act for levying the necessary taxes, unless their vast estates were in the same act expressly exonerated.[8]

Difficulties may have been allayed if the colonies, Pennsylvania included, had been given more leeway to print their own monies to meet the added expenses wars always accrued. Certainly, earlier in its history the Pennsylvania Assembly, like the lower houses of other colonies, had, in times of emergency, printed paper money that offset the dearth of hard currency within British North America; these so-called "paper bills" being redeemed at a future date, sometimes up to 12 years after their initial issuance.[9]

The local creation of money by provincial governments had, however, naturally attracted the attention of the British Government, which was concerned by the potential for swift collapse in the value of fictitious currency that was insufficiently backed by an assured fund—leaving suppliers and merchants severely out of pocket if and when the value of local monies collapsed.[10] To allay this concern, a precedent had thus been set: in 1740 the then governor of Pennsylvania, George Thomas, had been instructed that Royal assent had to be acquired before any future "monetary prints" be established. This was, from the perspective of the metropolitan government, a sensible move that protected creditors from the kind of currency devaluation that had beset the paper monies of neighboring New England (and, indeed, the other middle colonies) following the conclusion of previous conflicts.[11]

Unfortunately, by denying the Pennsylvania Assembly the ability to meet its emergency fiscal obligations on a delayed, or promissory, basis, the British government ensured that the colony was now confronted with the prospect of meeting its financial compulsions through a heavy direct tax; something that it was not wealthy enough to do. Faced with another French crisis, which culminated in the ministry's request that the colonies contribute to a central fund for the Braddock Plan of 1755, the Pennsylvania Assembly's only recourse was to print paper bills which, even when legalized by metropolitan authorities, were required to be redeemed within five years of issue; a span too short for those in the assembly who represented local communities which would be very hard-pressed to meet this obligation. Such a policy thus exacerbated the great power struggle between the assembly and the colony's proprietor, the latter refused to acquiesce to the lower house's call for the proprietary estates to contribute to the tax burden now facing the colony. With Governor Morris bound by his duty to represent his government's (and indeed his proprietor's) interests, there was little room for maneuver in this deep-rooted constitutional conflict.[12]

To make Morris's position more difficult to sustain within this convulsive internal dispute and, it must be added, to score a victory in the war for British opinion (notably Braddock's), the assembly did vote to raise £40,000 in paper money for the forthcoming year; £20,000 of which was allocated to defense. This seemingly generous allocation, however, came with provisos attached; including the contentious conditions of making the paper bills redeemable after 12 years and omitting any mention of the usual suspension clause that was required by law to accompany the issue of local currency. Morris was now in a difficult position as he could not pass the bill without the assent of the Chief Justice of England, Dudley Ryder, who had unequivocally informed his predecessor, James Hamilton, that the printing of new currency was forbidden without the express permission of the government; in fact, it was made very clear that the terms concerning the printing of currency (redemption of paper money after five years and so on) could *never* be violated.[13] Morris was thus in a quandary which saw him having to maneuver between several intransigent positions. Unable to negotiate his way out of the situation, he had to endure an internal political war of attrition that was very soon presented before Sir John St. Clair—and later Edward Braddock himself—when they later quite legitimately enquired as to why Pennsylvania had seemingly done so little to support the British Army's crucial campaign in the Ohio Valley.

When eventually pressed upon this seeming failure to support a hugely important undertaking, Morris carefully spun his words, informing the irascible quartermaster-general St. Clair, that his assembly would not give money "upon any terms but such as were directly contrary to His Majesty's Instructions and inconsistent with their own dependence of the crown."[14] It was, unquestionably, a clever sleight of tongue. The assembly *had* granted monies for the campaign, but with certain conditions attached.[15] As such, Morris, unable to pass a currency bill without infringing upon the earlier advice of the still-incumbent Lord Chief Justice and, duty-bound not to undermine the position of his master, Thomas Penn, had vetoed the grant.

Morris retaliated by placing his antagonists in a tit-for-tat political headlock. Heaping pressure on his lower house through his carefully worded lamentations to Braddock, he hoped that the assembly would be forced to re-raise funds for the campaign without the usual awkward preconditions. Both sides knew that a victory in his dispute would have profound constitutional implications for the future. Certainly, if successful, the embattled governor (and indeed the colony's proprietor, Thomas Penn) would have wrested the right to raise and spend money without the usual provisos and conditions attached, shifting the political balance of power firmly towards the Royal (or proprietary) prerogative.

Fighting and funding America's first European-scale war, coupled with the deep-rooted legislative anomalies of the British Atlantic World—at a time when centralization was the pressing concern of the metropolitan government (and General Edward Braddock)—created enormous and complex difficulties for Cumberland's *generalissimo*, whose campaign became blighted by the emergent consequences of such ingrained disputes. These included delays in acquiring supplies, sustenance and recruits. Winthrop Sargent, whose iconic *History of an Expedition Against Fort Duquesne* is so frequently referenced in histories of Braddock's defeat, estimated that the delays the general endured as a result of this deeply ingrained factionalism (and the consequent stymying of his logistical efforts), in addition to French military assaults on the Virginian and Pennsylvanian frontiers (that also impacted upon the supplies colonists living in these areas could provide his army), checked the advance by *at least* two to four weeks.[16] Even this conservative estimate was, in hindsight, significant: it enabled the French to hastily reinforce their position in the Ohio Valley; most notably with American Indian allies who formed the major segment their army on July 9, 1755. It is reasonable to conclude, therefore, that the minimum two to four weeks Sargent estimated to have been lost to colonial politics (aside from contractor chicanery and other more unfortunate or circumstantial happenstances) was pivotal to the outcome of Braddock's campaign.

All of these factors were well beyond the control of Braddock, despite the vice-regal powers his commission granted him on paper. Though he may have been aware of these peculiarities before he arrived in America he, like the British government he represented, was ill-equipped (and ill-prepared) to deal with them. Unfortunately for the general, he was the hapless government agent expected to centralize the British war effort by resolving, through the force of his personality and the weight of his commission, innate constitutional dilemmas that were brought to a head by what would become a global war; one which, at least for Britain, would center on her American colonies. Ultimately, it was a charge too great for a man of Braddock's character and abilities. Indeed, only William Pitt's subsidies for colonial governments that raised troops to fight the French would provide short-term relief to this quandary and would, ultimately, help deliver victory in the Seven Years War.[17] However, the key issue of executive (and metropolitan) power that in the 1760s was defined by the Sugar Act, Stamp Act and a plethora of other imperial legislation (and the colonial resistance that ensued), would never be satisfactorily resolved. Consequently, British commanders like Edward Braddock, and later John Campbell, Fourth Earl of Loudoun, would find themselves engaged not only in military campaigns against the French, but also embroiled in domestic political disputes that reflected the very different emerging British-American understandings of liberty and "Britishness"; twenty years later, of course, this concept was supplanted by a wholly new "Americanness."

These complex internal legislative disputes were also compounded by more obvious, and highly questionable, economic practices within the British colonies at this time; traditions that urgently required Braddock's attention when he arrived in America. One such was the illicit trade that flourished between the merchants of Albany, Boston, New York and Philadelphia and the French at Montreal and Louisbourg.[18] The trade between Albany and Montreal in particular was a lucrative one that met the mutual economic needs of both towns. Canadian merchants always had a surplus of pelts, but were often short of trade goods which were in short supply at Montreal.[19] Albany's merchants, always in the market for furs, had a surplus of trade goods at prices the French could not hope to match. Each side sought what the other had, and thus smuggled, with the considerable help of the Jesuit Missionaries stationed at the strategic post of Caughnawaga, their respective wares along the waterways that linked both towns; it was a business that benefited everyone involved.[20]

Braddock, however, saw it another way. Quite naturally, he viewed this trade as a treasonous act that gave supplies to enemy forces who might otherwise suffer for their want.[21] Thus, to stymie this illegal and potentially detrimental traffic, in addition to addressing the myriad of other concerns he had with the colonists' conduct, he ordered a conference to be convened at Annapolis in early April of 1755 (it actually convened at Carlyle House, Alexandria). Here it was his intention to better instruct the colonists on their duties and how wars should really be fought. The pattern of Braddock's command was now being set. The early stages were to be dominated by a multitude of letters, commands and directives aimed at improving expediency and efficiency; in other words, getting things done. Quartering, provisioning, enlistments and a plethora of other concerns were all synonymous with a European-style campaign, the likes and intensity of which had never before been witnessed in North America. Braddock, the dutiful administrator, was determined to get the campaign moving.

The Congress of Alexandria

The Congress of Alexandria further highlights the difficulties General Edward Braddock, the professional soldier, faced when transposing himself into colonial civilian politics. Though his official orders granted him near vice-regal powers on paper, the reality was that his commission gave him little real influence on the ground. Braddock could never quite grasp that colonial politics rested on persuasion and compromise as opposed to obedience and subordination. Indeed, many of those governors he met at Alexandria and treated as military subordinates had themselves been, to borrow Jack P. Greene's terminology, "domesticated" by the nature of negotiated authority in Britain's American empire; and had to coexist among the carefully tiered structures of their colonies' bodies politic.[22] For Braddock, however, Alexandria was not a meeting of negotiated planning and compromise. He told the governors what was expected of them—money for the central fund, troops for the campaign—and expected his orders to be met. Each governor was held directly responsible for the fulfilment of his colony's obligations and failure to do so was considered as insufferable as the often treacherous Atlantic journey that brought him to America.

The governors were also acquainted with the campaign's plan of operations. They learned that Admiral Edward Boscawen was sailing off the Gulf of St. Lawrence to prevent French reinforcements reaching Canada. Meanwhile, Braddock's regiments, the 44th and 48th, were to march to

Wills Creek and would soon begin the campaign against Fort Duquesne. The recently re-raised 50th and 51st were to advance under the command of William Shirley and from Albany would strike at Fort Niagara on Lake Ontario. Having captured Fort Duquesne, Braddock and his British regiments would move north and roll up France's remaining forts in the Ohio Valley; he and Shirley would then unite their forces at Niagara in the autumn. Shirley himself was appointed second in command and given the rank of Major-General. Though talented enough for such a position, he had no experience or training for this level of martial authority. William Johnson, summoned from his home in the Mohawk Valley, was appointed superintendent of the Iroquois and all Northern Indians. In addition, he was informed that he was to command a joint army of Mohawk warriors (among whom he was particularly influential) and provincial soldiers from New England and New York in an assault on Fort St. Frederic, which sat on the southern end of Lake Champlain. Finally, the assembled governors were familiarized with a fourth expedition being fitted out in Boston, which was assigned for operations in Nova Scotia; commanded by Colonel Robert Monkton, its mission was to eradicate the troublesome French fortifications on the Chignecto Isthmus.[23] The logistical, political and military over-reach of the plan was not lost on the experienced Shirley and Johnson, who would later delicately express their concerns at the grandiosity of the campaign.[24] Braddock, resolute, determined and attached to his orders, would not heed their concerns; he would execute his instructions come what may.

The commander-in-chief was also becoming further acquainted with the major non-military flaw of the campaign he was to prosecute; the naivety of its expectations regarding the colonists' ability and willingness to coordinate their efforts. The central fund immediately became a contentious issue with the assembled governors, who informed Braddock that such a fund "can never be established in the Colonies without the aid of Parliament."[25] It was not that the governors, advocates of prerogative rights to a man, were unwilling to raise money on whatever terms the crown demanded. Likewise, it must be said, colonial assemblies were willing to provide revenue for Braddock's army. The problem, as always, was deciding how much, and by what means, each colony should be required to raise; and who was actually to decide any appropriation (not forgetting, of course, the nature of any subsequent disbursements). The assemblies, as was their guarded tradition, were not willing to raise an arbitrary sum of money and then hand it over to governor or commander-in-chief without specific limitations on its use. It was a point the governors themselves raised with Braddock but he, failing to appreciate the constitutional implications of his demands, remained insistent; the fund was ordered raised by his instructions so the governors must find the money. Braddock, a fine administrator and a good soldier, was no politician.

Today, the Congress of Alexandria is distinguished as being the harbinger of intercolony dialogue *and*, paradoxically, of political tensions between the colonies and Britain over the issue of taxation. Certainly, Braddock himself was left with a distinct opinion on how the problem of raising funds within the provinces could be resolved. His suggested solution, conveyed in a letter to the Secretary of State, Thomas Robinson, and which was so resonant of the policies of George Grenville in the 1760s, further highlighted the emerging divergences in British Atlantic interpretations of the legal and constitutional jurisdiction of the metropolitan government and the colonies' own provincial legislatures,

> ...You will be sufficiently informed, Sir, by the minutes of the Council... of the impossibility of obtaining from several colonies the establishment of a general fund agreeable to his Majesty's instructions... I cannot but take the liberty to represent to you the necessity of laying a tax upon all his Majesty's dominions in America, agreeably to the result of Council, for reimbursing the great sums that must be advanced for the service and interest of the colonies in the important crisis.[26]

Braddock's own inflexibility was also evidenced by his refusal to compromise his London-designed strategy, despite the sound advice of Shirley and Johnson that his campaign be modified to better expedite his advance against Fort Duquesne. Both men, possessing invaluable knowledge of French dispositions in the interior, urged Braddock to delay his advance to Fort Duquesne until Fort Niagara, the *entrepot* of all of New France's western forts, had fallen. Braddock, though acknowledging that this was a reasonable idea, lacked the will to adapt his orders (they came directly from the Duke of Cumberland, after all), demonstrating an intransigence that might have been offset by experience, had he commanded a large army previously. Stubbornly, he refused to deviate from his instructions as outlined by his patron and commander, and the Fort Duquesne expedition would thus take precedence.[27] His route to the Ohio also caused some concern among many of the governors who knew of the region's topography. They suggested that he modify his planned march so that it follow an approach through Pennsylvania, cutting a hundred miles off the journey. Privately, Virginia's neighbors also expressed a nagging belief that the route outlined in Braddock's instructions had been chosen on the back of extensive Virginian lobbying and was thus conducive to that colony's speculative interests in this most disputed of regions.[28] Braddock, no doubt seeing the logic of altering the planned route, nevertheless remained bound to his instructions which ordered him to advance "up the Potomach [sic] River, as high as Wills Creek"; and this is what he would do.[29]

From a historical perspective we should remember that Braddock, from George Anne Bellamy's recollection of his private thoughts about his mission, was never really confident of meeting success in this campaign (despite the bullish attitude he always exhibited outwardly during his time in command). Perhaps, therefore, he was ultimately concerned with the inevitable censure that would follow any failure on his account. If his mission did not meet its objectives, Braddock, at the very least, would not have wanted to have given his detractors additional ammunition to destroy his reputation. One wonders, therefore, whether his rigid adherence to his instructions was, in reality, a means of protecting himself from the fall-out of possible failure. This is certainly something that an officer, acquainting himself with the command of an army for the first time, would be inclined to do.[30]

Braddock undoubtedly exhibited some of his most intransigent characteristics at Alexandria, but it was the colonies, both during and after the council, that had allowed, and would continue to allow, their factional interests to dictate their commitments to the British war effort. Not only did they refuse to give guarantees for the raising of funds to support Braddock's operations, but through their posturing, habits and behavior demonstrated that even a British army led by a tough viceroy-general could not motivate them to serve a common cause. Indeed, immediately after the conference, William Shirley and Governor Morris of Pennsylvania (allies in the great colonial power struggle) travelled to New York to begin preparations for the Niagara campaign, ensuring that their "friends" were well looked after; and, by extension, their own private interests. With his connections to powerful merchants in Boston and Philadelphia, including the prominent Thomas Hutchinson—who enjoyed links to influential British merchant families—Shirley (second in command of the whole campaign) was able to award contracts for all of the supplies he needed both in America and England. This enabled him to strengthen his position by buying influence; indeed, his supply contracts made him powerful allies in New York, Pennsylvania and Massachusetts.

For Governor Robert De Lancey of New York, Shirley's appointment and the power he now wielded as a major-general and dispenser of contracts posed a threat almost as intolerable as that represented by the French. De Lancey's firm, frozen out by Shirley's longstanding antipathy towards New York's governor, had to bear the indignity of seeing major contracts awarded to mortal enemies—the Livingston–Morris faction. Shirley's brilliant short-term posturing ensured that though he made and cemented many influential friends, he also created powerful enemies, among whom would eventually be included the Irish-born Superintendent of Northern Indians, William Johnson.[31]

After Alexandria, Johnson, following a brief conference with De Lancey, hastened back to his estate on the Mohawk River, Mount Johnson. Here he would make preparations for the Crown Point expedition and begin engaging the Iroquois on behalf of the British cause; but to do this he would first need to hold a grand council with the natives. Following a period of hiatus during which Onondaga assembled the various representatives required, a conference attended by a thousand chiefs of the Six Nations was held at his estate on June 21. For Johnson himself, the gathering had several important aims. First, he hoped to acquire Six Nations aid for the Braddock campaign against Fort Duquesne, while also engaging Mohawk support for his Crown Point expedition; something vital if he were to reduce Fort St. Frederic. His last goal, however, was a purely political one aimed at undermining his staunch rival, William Shirley. In short, he sought to deny Shirley any Iroquois allies for the expedition against Fort Niagara.[32] A brilliant diplomat and politician, he achieved all of his initial goals. In exchange for London's repudiation of a land cession granted to the Susquehanna Company at the Albany Congress, in addition to a reduction in the size of a grant given to Conrad Weiser by Chief Hendrick, the Six Nations promised to support Braddock and provide allies for his Crown Point mission.[33] Unfortunately, the delay caused by gathering the conference's attendees ensured that any potential warriors for Braddock's command could not reach the commander-in-chief in time for his Ohio expedition. It was a disappointment that would have severe consequences for the campaign as it reduced Braddock's pool of already-depleted Indian warriors and thus intelligence-gathering abilities. Undoubtedly, native warriors could have provided his army with a vital screen of scouts who would have proven particularly useful as it drew nearer to Fort Duquesne.[34]

None of the above, of course, were problems of Braddock's making. Diplomatic failures both within the colonies and indeed the London ministry, which had belatedly thrown its weight behind a united Indian policy in 1754 in response to a crisis in Native American relations (manifest in growing Mohawk disaffection with their British allies), still did not resolve longstanding issues that had seen the Iroquois waver in their support for the British cause. These were failings representative of core weaknesses within the wider British Atlantic World which later impacted upon the 1755 campaign. Braddock, hardly helping matters when he himself delved into Native American diplomacy it must be said, was nonetheless left with a mere handful of Indian warriors as he made the treacherous march to Fort Duquesne.

Logistical Difficulties and Colonial Intransigencies

After departing Alexandria, Braddock journeyed to join Colonel Dunbar's column, meeting up with it at Frederick Town, Maryland, on April 22. It was here that he met two of America's most eminent future Founding Fathers, George Washington and Benjamin Franklin. Washington, for reasons pertaining to a 1754 War Office directive that made colonial officers of major downwards subordinate to British officers of the same rank, had earlier spurned an opportunity to command the Virginian provincials.[35] He therefore appeared before Braddock as a volunteer; serving without pay in a junior officer's capacity hoping that, in the future, his meritorious conduct would serve him well when he applied for the king's commission. Braddock, acknowledging the young Virginian's knowledge of the Ohio country, appointed him an aide-de-camp; the ambitious Washington was now a member of the general's "family."

Franklin, deputy postmaster general for the colonies had, at least ostensibly, been sent to Frederick Town to facilitate the exchange of dispatches between the army and coastal cities. This, however, was a secondary guise to cover his real objective, which essentially reflected the political schisms within Pennsylvanian politics at this time. The main purpose of his visit was actually to gather intelligence for the Pennsylvania Assembly, which was by now concerned that Braddock had conceived "violent prejudices against them."[36] These "prejudices," stoked by Governor Robert Morris and Thomas Penn, stemmed from the numerous obstacles the general and his quartermaster-general, Sir John St. Clair, had faced as they sought to organize the logistical operations of the British Army.

St. Clair, undoubtedly, had much to lament. From his first arrival in America, he had been frustrated by delays in establishing even the most basic requirements of the army. At Hampton, for instance, he had encountered difficulties in finding a suitable hospital for Braddock's force, the only buildings with any semblance of suitability being "two very small Ware Houses."[37] Intelligence of the terrain the army was to traverse was another vital element of the campaign and yet even acquiring maps to facilitate the movement of the army through the Virginia backcountry was a strenuous and patience-testing task. Those that did exist were sketchy and inaccurate, while a letter written to Governor Morris of Pennsylvania, requesting any available maps of that province, went a month without reply. A second letter received a similar silence. When Morris did respond, the map he sent was outdated, being first drawn in 1749, though it was grandiosely being revised under the title "A General Map of the Middle British Colonies." Alarmingly, it did not extend further west than the Conococheague and gave little indication of any viable routes that could be taken from Wills Creek (selected as the "base of operations" for the campaign) to Fort Duquesne—saving a rudimentary Indian path utilized by traders at Wills Creek, which stretched 106 miles to the contentious French fort. No other viable options being available, and Braddock insistent that he follow the route broadly outlined by his instructions, this path became the road the Anglo-American army would follow into the interior; twisting, rising and descending over the Allegheny mountains, traversing the Castleman and Youghiogheny rivers, before finally arriving at the Forks of the Ohio.

The fort at Wills Creek, assigned as a base of operations, offered scarce further encouragement. The position here was, in reality, "a small piece of Ground inclosed with a strong palisade joined pretty close." It was also, according to St. Clair, poorly located.[38] Dissatisfied, he protested to Governor Horatio Sharpe of Maryland who promised that a new position was being constructed on higher ground; one which was more appropriate to serve as a base of operations.

Transporting the troops from Winchester to Wills Creek, a stretch of 85 miles, also provided numerous difficulties. St. Clair, who had made the journey himself, lamented that the road he had to take was "the worst road I have ever travelled." To expedite the army's advance, he had considered sending the artillery and supplies by canoe down the Potomac River; though, having again made this trip in person, he soon realized that the falls and rapids of the unbridled Potomac made this virtually impossible. There was no other option—the army had to march.[39]

Unfortunately, even as late as April, the roads needed to enable the army to move in the backwoods had still not been fully constructed. St. Clair, embittered by what he saw as the intransigence and double standards of the frontier's inhabitants in aiding the logistical operations of the expedition, would let loose his anger in a tirade that shocked those unfortunate enough to be exposed to it. George Croghan, spokesman of a Pennsylvanian delegation sent to Wills Creek to meet the quartermaster general, received the full blast of his frustrations and growing contempt for the American colonists. In a letter to Governor Morris of Pennsylvania he recounted how St. Clair had threatened that,

> Instead of marching to the Ohio he would in nine days march his army into Cumberland county to cut the roads, press horses, wagons, that he would oblige the inhabitants to do it... that he would kill all kind of cattle and carry away the horses, burn the houses &c and that if the French defeated them by the delays of this province that he would with his sword drawn pass through the province and treat the inhabitants as a parcel of traitors...[40]

It was the failure of the provinces to properly supply the expedition with the necessary supplies and means of transporting them (horses and wagons) which had, in reality, drawn Benjamin Franklin to Frederick Town to meet Edward Braddock. It was this issue that, by early April, had driven Braddock to the point of despair. Despite the promises of Robert Dinwiddie, who had declared that 2500 horses and 200 wagons would be available for Braddock by May 10, as of April 10, none were available for hire. Dinwiddie's (and Virginia's) difficulties in acquiring wagons and supplies to support the expedition were reflective of poor strategic planning in London that had, in its infancy, been heavily influenced by the very persuasive pro-Virginia lobbying of that colony's governor (who also happened to be an Ohio Company investor). Dinwiddie had rather erroneously convinced first the ministry, and then Braddock, that he and his colony could meet the logistical challenges that a sizable army would place upon the province's resources. Unfortunately, because of the overarching nature of its core economic interests, Virginia was simply not equipped to meet the demands of a large-scale military campaign. The root of these weaknesses was clearly outlined by contemporary historian John Entick in his 1763 *History of the late War*, which explained that,

...Such is the attention of the Virginians towards their staple trade of tobacco, that they scarce raise as much corn, as is necessary for their own subsistence; and their country being well provided with water-carriage in great rivers, an army which requires a large supply of wheel-carriages and beasts of burden, could not expect to be furnished with them in a place, where they are not in general use.[41]

Poor strategic planning within the British administration, stoked by the applied vested interests of Ohio Company stakeholders, had dealt Edward Braddock the very worst of hands.[42] This, of course, was of no consolation to the hard-pressed general or his prickly quartermaster-general, St. Clair, who had been continually frustrated by the colonists' broken promises. From Braddock's (purely military) perspective, the problem he faced was perilously simple; without horses and wagons, he could not transport his artillery, tools for cutting roads and other vital supplies.

The inability of the British Army to quickly acquire martial essentials and indeed foodstuffs from among the inhabitants of the frontier, reflected, in considerable measure, the political and economic vulnerabilities that Braddock and colonial governors endured within provincial politics; mirroring one of the major anomalies of the British Atlantic World at this time.[43] Rather than being able to commandeer supplies for the army, or even galvanize the locals into supporting a common cause, men such as Robert Morris of Pennsylvania could only shrug their shoulders and advise the British commander-in-chief to try to purchase supplies from local farmers and, if necessary, impress wagons into service. Such advice was, in reality, all that could be afforded Braddock who, when attempting to directly purchase provisions from local colonists, also faced a plural population that, in the case of the German Dunkers who inhabited lands near the Conococheague, had conscientious objections to war and would not support any kind of military operation.[44]

There were other, equally deep-rooted constitutional issues also at play. Indeed, Braddock's campaign highlighted the difficulties of fighting a military campaign amidst what were still, even in the eyes of the colonists themselves, *British* communities. Britain itself had not seen a major invasion or conflict since the sixteenth century (though the Jacobite Highlanders who provided the backbone of the 1745 rebellion could still be defined as the "other" at this time) and the army therefore had no experience of campaigning within a host community comprised of its own countrymen. In England, troops could be barracked at ease and supplies and wagons could be obtained from contractors without conflict. In the sparsely settled Virginian and Pennsylvanian back country this was far from the case. By using military authority (or threatening to use it) to impress supply essentials for his army, Braddock alienated colonists who saw themselves as Britons and whom expected to be treated as British subjects; with all of the same rights and liberties enjoyed by their brethren across the vast Atlantic.[45]

By early April the general was, in view of these complex travails, reaching a point of despair. Despite the much-cited stereotype of him being a brute who dealt with the colonists in a high-handed and contemptuous manner, he had in reality been remarkably diligent in attempting to execute his orders, using only his authority—as expressed by his instructions—to press the colonists to act. Therefore, when he sent out staff officers to threaten, entreat and hire wagons for his army, these officers also carried with them peace copies of his orders that would be shown to county justices. Neither did he offer miserly rates to hire wagons; reflecting his desperation, he offered to pay fifteen shillings per day for a four-horse team and driver. His efforts proved futile and only 25 wagons were procured, some of which were in a deplorable condition.

Nevertheless, allocating responsibility for this particular shortfall to one group (or actor) would be unfair as it was the consequence of several distinct factors. In part, for instance, Braddock's difficulties in acquiring drivers, horses and wagons reflected the inability of the British Army and the provinces themselves to defend frontier communities; an issue that would be magnified as the campaign against Fort Duquesne advanced. Certainly, the backcountry settlers whom Braddock pressed and demanded supplies and transportation from were suffering the dangers and privations caused by the numerous raiding parties that the French had dispatched to scour the Virginian frontier as the British army advanced upon the Ohio. These raiding parties had their desired effect; settlers deserted the backcountry, which correspondingly affected the ability of Braddock's army to gather supplies. Colonists fleeing their homesteads also choked-up the road behind the British advance, hindering the army's communications. Those who stayed and could provide the army with wagons and supplies would not do so without an armed escort, forcing the British commander to divert men from his own force to provide a guard. These were issues, all synonymous with the perils of frontier warfare in eighteenth-century America, which would, in time, further slow Braddock's notoriously protracted, but pivotal, mission to reassert British sovereignty in the Ohio.[46]

Franklin Renews Hope

Benjamin Franklin's arrival at Frederick Town was then, a particularly timely one. A skilled diplomat and extremely able statesman, Franklin, though officially dispatched to Braddock in the capacity of postmaster general, was really sent to smooth relations between the British commander-in-chief and the Pennsylvanian Assembly. The assembly had certainly been stung by Braddock's earlier criticisms of their seeming indifference to his mission and by a warning from Admiral Augustus Keppel (initially commander of Britain's North American naval detachment) that all illicit trade with the French must cease. Reflecting Franklin's abilities as a negotiator and diplomat, throughout their meeting Braddock, thoroughly exasperated by those colonists he had encountered hitherto, was highly impressed by the astute statesman. Nevertheless, the latter's importance was not truly felt until he was about to take his leave of the commander-in-chief. It was at this point that Braddock learned first-hand of his officers" failure to acquire wagons for his mission. Bewailing that all was lost, as Franklin would later recount, the general declared that,

> ...the expedition was then at an end, being impossible, and exclaimed against the ministers for ignorantly landing them in a country destitute of the means of conveying their stores, baggage etc.[47]

Franklin, ever the shrewd analyst, now saw a chance to redeem Pennsylvania, suggesting, "it was a pity they had not landed rather in Pennsylvania, as in that country almost every farmer had his own wagon." It was a sentiment that John Entick in his 1763 publication, *History of the Late War* would echo, and Braddock, desperate for a glimmer of hope, took the bait, asking Franklin to procure wagons and horses from Pennsylvania's more prosperous inhabitants.[48] That colony's economy, based principally on food-crop agriculture, meant that the province possessed the wagons and horses so rare in neighboring tobacco-dominated Virginia. Braddock immediately provided the incisive Pennsylvanian with £800 that was to be disbursed in advanced payments. To further improve relations with the British Army, the latter also wrote a letter to the Pennsylvania Assembly Committee recommending that gifts be given to the junior officers of Braddock's force, who, struggling with the financial demands of their commissions, were unable to supply themselves with tea, sugar and wine in this most geographically remote of campaigns.[49] Such a gesture succeeded in winning him many friends, saving Sir John St. Clair, who was still irate with the failure of Robert Morris to oversee the building of a road to Wills Creek.

Franklin's endeavors, after many trials and travails, began to improve matters for the embattled general. He and his son William had firstly traveled to Lancaster where they ordered handbills printed addressed to the farmers of that country, as well as those of York and Cumberland counties. In these pamphlets, he expressed his desire to collect 150 wagons, "with four horses to each wagon" and "fifteen hundred saddle, or pack horses," for army use. The terms offered were very generous—15 shillings per day for each wagon with four good horses and a driver; two shillings per day for every able horse with a pack saddle. Franklin also gave his personal bond to underwrite those horses or wagons lost on the campaign. Payment would be made upon joining the army (before May 20), while seven days' pay in advance would close the deal at the time of contracting; the remainder would be provided by the army paymaster upon discharge.[50] This was the carrot Franklin offered. The stick was that the British Army, deprived of the necessaries it needed to fight the French, would resort to force to take what it needed,

> But if you do not this Service to your King and Country voluntarily, when such good pay and reasonable Terms are offered you... violent measures will probably be used; and you will seek recompense where you can find it, and your case perhaps little pitied or regarded.

Most menacingly of all, considering his reputation as someone who had developed a rather low opinion of provincials,

> If this method of obtaining the wagons and horses is not likely to succeed, I am obliged to send word to the general in fourteen days; and I suppose Sir John St. Clair, the hussar, with a body of soldiers, will immediately enter the province for that purpose.[51]

Evoking the visage of a marauding Hussar plundering his way through the Pennsylvanian countryside was a measured threat and one that had the desired effect on the Dutch and German farmers who inhabited the region. Many would, from recent memory, or memories handed down, have been all too familiar with the prowling Hungarian Hussars who terrorized Western Europe, bringing slaughter, pillage and cruelty in their wake. His threats, coupled with his immense political and negotiation abilities, enabled him to galvanize the colony's various factions and persuade many recalcitrant (or even hostile) locals to part with their wagons and horses.[52] Braddock, immeasurably grateful to the shrewd Pennsylvanian, declared him, "the only instance of ability and honesty I have known in these provinces." At the final moment, the army could march to its forward operating base at the newly christened Fort Cumberland at Wills Creek.

To Wills Creek

The march to Wills Creek is worthy of note because it epitomized the difficulties Braddock endured not only with nature, but with the colonies and their failure to meet the promises they made to provision his expedition.[53] Unquestionably, the British Army was rather rigid in its adherence to its traditions as it marched to the Ohio and would have benefited from instead travelling lightly through the American backcountry. However, army orderly books show that Braddock did, quite often, adapt to the unparalleled environmental conditions that existed in America, despite the fact that his regular forces were only in the New World three months before they engaged the French and Indians at the Battle of the Monongahela. On April 8th, for example, his orders stated that, "the Soldiers are to leave their Shoulder Belts, Waist Belts and hangers behind and only to take with them to the Field one spare shirt, one pair of Stockings, one spare pair of shoes and one pair of Brown Gaiter's."[54] As Braddock himself wrote, this was done because it was "often necessary to oblige the men to take with them seven or eight days provisions, it being frequently impossible to supply them by the great distance from one Magazine to another."[55] The logistics train, the heaviest element of the army, caused even further transportation difficulties. In addition to its artillery, some of which was hauled by a company of seamen provided by Commodore Keppel, the army possessed a sizable wagon train that included Braddock's own private coach. For Americans, such arrangements appeared ridiculous, but for the British Army they were normal; part and parcel of being a professional fighting force.

In view of the local environmental parameters and the challenges he knew the French and Indians posed, Braddock also adapted his soldier's training to counter his likely "irregular" foes. He drilled his men to form and fight in their companies, rather than platoons, where many of the men, told off, would not know their officers. Braddock's regiments also practiced an alternative fire using the 'senior battalion company in each regiment as a "Second Grenadier Company" upon the left, and leaving the other eight battalion-companies to form eight fire-divisions and sixteen platoons."[56] In the few weeks afforded him, his corps also exercised repeatedly. Eight weeks before the battle, for instance, while the army was stationed at Fort Cumberland, orderly books show that the 48th "had a Field day"; a week later the 44th had another.[57] All of the above were manifestations of Braddock's undoubted recognition of the necessity of preparing the troops for the challenges that could (and did) lie ahead.

Nevertheless, preparatory steps could only go so far. The army's difficulties on the march were magnified by the numerous natural obstacles that presented themselves on the virtually unbroken Virginian frontier, weakening the strength and resolve of the many inexperienced soldiers of Braddock's hybrid army. The men's exasperation was further compounded by the fact that any kind of relief in the guise of towns, taverns and other dens of entertainment was virtually non-existent.[58] There were other frustrations too. A planned-for meeting with potentially vital Indian allies at Winchester failed to transpire; Robert Dinwiddie had failed to inform Braddock of its cancellation, meaning that the general tarried for four days—all to no purpose. More seriously, Braddock received intelligence that the supplies promised to be waiting for him along the road to Wills Creek were in fact non-existent, forcing his commissary of stores to ask for three or four thousand pounds to buy these essential provisions—Braddock's own reserve again provided this. The microclimate of the backcountry also harried the march. His men were assailed by troublesome pests called "chiggers"; a type of mite that bit into the flesh of its victims, causing extreme irritation and discomfort. The threat posed by rattlesnakes was no less concerning for the men who heard of comrades falling sick and, in some cases, dying from their bites. Neither were the troops ignorant of the potential tactical perils of the topography over which they were now marching. One officer, fearing an ambuscade, declared,

> There is nothing round us but trees, swamps and thickets... I cannot conceive how war can be made in such a country... I cannot conceive how we must do if attacked, nor how we can get up to attack; but... His Excellency with great judiciousness says, that where the woods are too thick for us to hinder our coming at them, they will hinder them coming at us.[59]

When Braddock and his army finally reached Fort Cumberland, deflation again became the prevalent emotion. There was no well, no sutler, nor a cook-shop selling provisions. The fortification was, in essence, basic.

Charlotte Brown, an English widow and nurse who accompanied her brother (a commissary) on the expedition, lamented that Fort Cumberland was, in reality, "the most desolate" of places. Her quarters, provided by the "governor," were ramshackle, "I was put into A Hole that I could see daylight through every log, and a port hole for a window; which was as good a room as any in the fort."[60] Such was the state of the fort that was Braddock's base of operations.

At Wills Creek, however, the British Army did begin to take shape. Wagons arrived from Alexandria, companies of provincial troops from Maryland, Virginia and North Carolina awaited their commander, while the artillery and other stores had trundled into the camp over preceding weeks. All conceivable areas of military operation occupied the busy general, from inspecting the provincials to ordering medical examinations of those known as "camp followers"; specifically, in this instance, the army's women. In line with the army's strict regulation of camp followers, it was ordered, somewhat patronizingly from the latter's perspective, that they must be "clean and proper" if they were to follow the army on its march to Fort Duquesne. The issue of supply and the failure, particularly of Robert Dinwiddie of Virginia, to fulfil promises again reared its head. As more and more troops arrived at Wills Creek, what were needed were fresh supplies as the men had, while on the march, been subsisting on salted provisions. Matters were hardly helped by the refusal of many of the provincial teamsters who had transported supplies from Alexandria to Cumberland to remain with the army; having fulfilled their contracts, they went home. The 2500 horses and 200 wagons Dinwiddie promised were now desperately needed but such grand numbers were nowhere near being met by May 10.

When supplies did reach the army, they were frequently of poor quality and had to be disposed of. Twenty two casks of beef were condemned in one inspection. In another instance of supply malaise, a Virginian contractor failed to produce 500 beeves promised by Dinwiddie because the Virginia Assembly committee had failed to confirm his contract. Braddock, desperate for fresh provisions, told the contractor in question, a Mr. Hite, that he would pay for the cattle directly from his own reserve, upon which he was informed that the cattle could not be delivered to him before September, at a higher price, and in fewer numbers.[61] It was one of numerous instances of supply-line failure that forced Braddock to dip into his own funds (which the British ministry had sensibly provided) to meet the army's provisioning requirements. Having to do so, however, pushed Braddock's patience and, in one of his increasingly frequent outbursts against his provincial allies, he would tell George Washington that it "would be endless to particularize the number of instances of the want of public and private faith, and the most absolute disregard of all truth which I have met with."[62] Such delays no doubt sapped the morale of the men and, indeed, their physical condition. For those historians who see in Braddock's defeat the vindication of the old idiom that regular soldiers could not fight in the forests of America, it is perhaps worth remembering that, to quote Napoleon Bonaparte, "an army marches on its stomach." The failings of Braddock's supply chain at every stage of the army's march to the Ohio—a failure often bred of colonial legislative disputes and vested interests (in addition to local contractual misdemeanor)—had a very profound effect on the general's men; one highlighted by a post-battle enquiry into the defeat the British eventually suffered at the Battle of the Monongahela.[63]

The weeks the army spent at Fort Cumberland were thus frustrating and prolonged. The effects of inaction were becoming apparent among the men, too, as their morale dipped in the absence of fresh food. Gaming became a serious issue, and discipline was proving increasingly difficult to maintain as the soldiers grew more and more impatient with the conditions they were forced to endure. The perils of liquor and the presence of Indian women who had accompanied their husbands and had been awaiting the army at Wills Creek under the supervision of George Croghan, also undermined order. The quality of many of the American enlistees for the 44th and 48th—when they could be found—was also of concern. The independent American companies that had been raised were not much better; many, indeed, were scarcely fit for service. Of the New York Independent companies, Sir John St. Clair, who was given responsibility for overhauling them, scathingly observed that the men appeared "to be drafted out of Chelsea."[64] Robert Orme was equally scornful of what he saw as "Invalids [retired veterans] with the ignorance of militia."[65] As for the provincial units raised in Virginia, Maryland and North Carolina, Braddock remained skeptical of their worth, expressing a belief that "Scarce any military service can be expected of them" while also noting that it had cost "indefinite pains and labour to bring them to any sort of regularity and discipline." Orme shared his lack of enthusiasm, writing of the Virginians that,

> ...they performed their evolutions and firings as well as could be expected, but their languid, spiritless, and unsoldierlike appearance considered with

the lowness and ignorance of most of their Officers, gave little hopes of their future good behaviour.[66]

Though British prejudices may have been at play here, Braddock, St. Clair and Orme had a point—one borne out by the fact that when Braddock was eventually forced to split his army in two, many of those left in the reserve column were colonial soldiers. The evidence above once again suggests that those historians who in later years were so universal in their praise of the American contingent of Braddock's army were perhaps blinded by the "fervor of Americanism" that epitomized nineteenth-century (and, indeed, many later) interpretations of the Battle of the Monongahela. Ian K. Steele's suggestion that "in warfare, as in everything else, the men of the New World were better than the history-laden men of the Old" is a rather succinct reference point at this juncture.[67] The reality is that the failure of Braddock's mission against Fort Duquesne cannot be stereotyped in bland nationalisms but must be examined in a far wider context than a purely military history can perhaps permit.

Misgivings aside, Braddock was not, however, averse to using American units as supplements to, and for, his British regiments. He therefore formed his 850 Virginian recruits into nine companies, each being led by a captain after whom they were designated: "Poulson's" and "Mercer's" were companies of carpenters; "Stephens," "Waggoner's," "Peyronie's," "Hogg's," "Cocke's" and "Lewis's" were rangers, while "Stewart's" company was a screen of light horse.[68] Yet other soldiers raised by Virginia were drafted into the regular 44th and 48th.

Some of the colonial units were, in fact, quite promising. Maryland, for instance, had raised 100 men for the campaign and these had already seen service at Fort Cumberland, enlarging the fort and building barracks. Commanded by the veteran Captain Dagworthy, they were considered a good body of men by the uncompromising Sir John St. Clair. Eventually, 120 further Marylanders would join the army and were integrated into Braddock's regular regiments. Edward Dobbs's 84 North Carolinian rangers were the last element to join Braddock's force. In 1754, this unit, then commanded by Colonel James Innes at a supposed strength of 750 men (in reality only 350 were raised), had been disbanded prematurely when the colony's finances had been exhausted. They were supposed to have served with George Washington as he attempted to drive the French out of the Ohio and the unit's re-raising had no doubt been a face-saving effort on the part of North Carolina's assembly.

Supplies and indeed worsening discipline continually troubled Braddock's mind as he pondered the advancing season and growing disquiet among his troops.[69] Hamstrung by his provisioning and supply travails, he would remain at Cumberland until June 9, by which time he received intelligence that the French presence at Fort Duquesne was actually quite small. Skeptical that troops would reinforce the position on account of the French wanting their forces to be northward, Braddock, despite reservations over the treacherous road his army was to follow to Fort Duquesne, had become emboldened by news received from Robert Morris that forage, oxen and sheep were on their way to his army. A few more delays aside, he was now as ready to advance as he would ever be.

"He Looked Upon us as Dogs…" Contextualizing Braddock, Native American Alliances and the Ultimate Failure of Indian Diplomacy

As Braddock approached Fort Cumberland for the first time, he and his men would also have seen a group of Indian tribesman encamped on the edge of woods that sat a quarter of a mile from the fort.[70], [71] For redcoat and native alike, this early encounter between two distinct peoples was, to all intents and purposes, a meeting between alien worlds. The Indians stood mesmerized by the approach of the uniformly drilled and accoutered soldiers of the British Army. Likewise, the men of the British rank and file were intrigued by the tall, semi-clad, warpaint-besmirched warriors who had pitched their huts and lean-tos so close to the fort. Despite their previous orders not to engage the natives, the British soldiers found the allure of the Indians too great a temptation and began trading small trinkets, while others leered at the women who accompanied the warriors. The risk was that redcoat and Native American, crossing paths in significant numbers, would stumble into a confrontation exacerbated by the toxic mix of alcohol and exotic women.

On the grander scale of Indian diplomacy, however, Braddock would find that much damage had already been done to British standing in native eyes following years of ill-treatment at the hands of the American colonies. The fact that so few had followed George Croghan to meet him at Cumberland, despite his preceding requests, was testimony to the poor state of affairs that existed in this vital diplomatic field. Braddock, the sometimes tactless British general, now had to convince the suspicious natives of the Ohio (and beyond) that their interests would be best served by a British alliance. His fiery temperament and cultural naivety, coupled with the bungled promises of Robert Dinwiddie, who was in the midst of a feud with Governor James Glen of South Carolina, ultimately robbed him of any hope in this regard.

The natives assembled at Fort Cumberland with Croghan, who had in turn been ordered south by William Johnson, may not have appeared overwhelming in number, but their construct was of considerable significance. The original 50 or so Mingos Croghan had brought to Wills Creek were soon complemented by six hugely influential tribal chiefs, including Scarouady of the Oneida and Shingas, leading war chief of the resurgent Ohio Delaware. Contrary to popular belief, from a military perspective, Braddock knew the importance of Indian allies, which is why he placed great emphasis on ordering William Johnson to raise indigenous warriors to accompany his army to Fort Duquesne. Croghan himself would convey the pains his general took to engage Indian warriors as auxiliaries. While conferring with several chiefs, for instance, he "made them a handsome present, and behaved as kindly to them as he possibly could during their stay, ordering me [Croghan] to let them want for nothing."[72] Braddock undoubtedly saw native warriors as valuable scouts and skirmishers, very much a complement to his regular units. He did not, however, consider them an essential element within his distinctly European (or "Europeanized") force. His comment to Benjamin Franklin that, "upon the king's regular and disciplined troops...it is impossible they would make any impression" showed that he was supremely confident of his soldier's ability to defeat any irregular French-Indian force that might cross their path.[73] For Braddock, native allies were a useful screen of scouts, but it was the regular British Army that would, ultimately, bring victory in the Fort Duquesne expedition.

His early dealings with the Mingos also hinted at how his professional dispositions could alienate tribesmen whose martial, social and cultural norms were so very different from his own. Fearing that the women who had followed their husbands to Fort Cumberland would prove to be a disruptive influence on his soldiers, Braddock is said to have summarily ordered them to leave the camp, sending them back to George Croghan's trading post at Aughwick. As culturally insensitive as this may seem in hindsight, Braddock was likely using his soldierly instincts to preserve discipline among his own soldiers, removing what he felt to be the considerable temptation posed by such exotic followers. Although women (frequently the wives of serving soldiers) did follow the British Army into battle during the eighteenth century (serving as launderers of clothes, nurses and washerwomen among other roles), their character and numbers were carefully monitored by army regulations—in the case of Braddock's regiments at Wills Creek, "sixty to a regiment"—and they were expected to be of good reputation, often being inspected to insure they were indeed "clean and proper."[74] As many historical surveys of the army of this period have shown, there was good reason for this circumspection. Though in limited numbers of considerable use to regiments in the field, excessive numbers of women were often viewed as an irritant by officers of the Army's high command.[75] The threat posed by the spread of venereal disease as a result of acquaintances made by soldiers and female camp followers thought to be of unproven morality was a considerable concern for officers—particularly a commander like Edward Braddock serving on the remote borders of European America—who would have been well aware that men were a finite resource and had to be kept fit for service. Just as detrimental to regimental cohesion were the inevitable spats that often erupted between soldiers vying for the same female companion. Such conflicts could result in serious assaults or even murder, all of which was exacerbated by the prevalence of alcohol abuse (liquor was frequently sold to the men by soldier's wives) in the army at this time.[76]

For Braddock, therefore, removing the dangers posed by the Mingo women not only lessened the threat of diseases spreading among his troops, but also reduced the potential for infighting between British soldiers and the Mingo warriors who were the husbands of these females. It was perfectly logical reasoning, considering his martial and cultural origins, and was designed to protect his soldiers, his alliance with the Mingos and, fundamentally, his mission. Unfortunately, the Mingo, naturally, did not appreciate such European martial concerns. In native societies, women were considered the "other half" of their men and quite often enjoyed a level of equality and influence that would have been alien to Europeans at this time. Culturally, while Native American men were expected to maintain and protect their women, the latter had the no-less-valued responsibility of maintaining the household and, on a wider scale, upholding the values and bonds of Amerindian societies.[77] By sending the Mingo women away from his camp, therefore, Braddock had committed a serious cultural *faux pas*, ensuring that virtually all of the men—their husbands, brothers and sons—went with them.

Further problems beyond the general's control would also hinder his ability to deploy crucial native allies alongside his Anglo-American force.

Braddock could not have known, for instance, that as yet William Johnson had not even begun negotiations with the Six Nations, making the likelihood of Iroquois warriors joining his march remote (Johnson, after all, was in the process of organizing and assembling his conference at Mount Johnson). The general had also been led to believe that Robert Dinwiddie would provide him with fearsome Catawba and Cherokee allies who, with Johnson's Iroquois, would be more than sufficient to meet his Indian-auxiliary needs.

In view of the overarching Native American diplomatic norms at this time, this was a particularly forlorn hope. Indeed, one must question the motives of Dinwiddie who must surely have known that the Cherokee and Catawba would never have served alongside their inveterate enemies (the Iroquois) who Johnson was supposed to be concurrently raising. Neither did Virginia's lieutenant governor inform Braddock of a feud he was in the midst of with Governor James Glen of South Carolina. Again, particularism was to blame as both governors sought control of the Catawba and Cherokee who were so influential along the borders of the Middle and Southern colonies.[78] Furthermore, when the Iroquois heard of Cherokee and Catawba warriors joining Braddock's army, they refused to head south for fear, "Some Broils might arise, fatal to themselves, and very disserviceable to our cause."[79] These profound misfortunes, neither of which Braddock was to blame for (compounded by the poor advice of Colonel James Innes who had conducted Indian affairs at Fort Cumberland prior to his arrival), ensured that he would now have with him only seven Mingos and the Half King Scarouady as he marched on his fateful journey from Wills Creek to Fort Duquesne.[80] In practical terms, his army had also been deprived of formidable scouting units who could inform of French movements to reinforce that pivotal post.

THE FINAL MARCH TO THE MONONGAHELA BEGINS

Braddock had, however, succeeded in meshing together a force of British regulars and provincial units he believed more than able of capturing Fort Duquesne (and meeting his other objectives in the Ohio). As his colorful army, visually so distinct in the forested landscape it was to march, finally departed Fort Cumberland on May 29, it drew the slightly humorous observation from one commentator that it did so with "the Knight [Sir John St. Clair] swearing in the van, the General cursing & bullying in the centre & their whores bringing up the rear."[81] In front of Braddock's army 200 axmen, covered by 100 soldiers, began hacking a road out of the wilderness. It was slow and difficult work exacerbated by the nature of the terrain over which the Anglo-American force was to travel. To the frustration of all, the army was not so much marching, but crawling through the forest. In one day, eight hours of blasting and hacking carried the army eight miles, on another, sixteen hours labor saw it progress just three miles.

As had been anticipated by the army's high command, the journey from Cumberland to the Monongahela was a nightmare trek that tested, to their absolute limits, the endurance of man and beast. Braddock himself had always known that the most difficult aspect of his campaign was the long and arduous trial he would endure transporting the army's artillery, wagons and supplies through the forests of Western Virginia. For many historians, it was at this stage that Braddock made several serious errors. His failure to jettison some of this materiel, even much of his artillery train, so the theory goes, retarded his advance and exhausted his men to the point where they were in no fit state to engage the French and Indians when the two forces finally met in battle on July 9. Hindsight is a wonderful informant, but what is often overlooked is the reality that, for Braddock, treacherous march aside, the campaign against Fort Duquesne was always going to be conducted in a regular, European manner. It is evident that he never believed that France's Indian allies and irregular Canadian militia would pose a serious threat to his carefully coordinated British force; and the fact that so few of his men would be lost on the march (prior to July 9) is testimony to the precautions he took, and the rigidity with which he followed, the advice of conventional European military manuals; specifically Humphrey Bland's *Treatise of Military Discipline*, the soldier's gospel for British officers of the period.[82]

For Braddock, the main fighting, if there was any, would take place in the guise of siege warfare when he arrived outside the gates of Fort Duquesne. During a siege, if that were required, he would want hand grenades for the grenadiers, flints for muskets and spare swords with brass and iron hilts for his men. Just as essential were his army's axes, shovels, sand bags, tacks, spades, and nails; all needed to make the fascines, gabions and approach trenches that would zigzag their way, inch by inch, to a point at which the heavy siege artillery could open a hole in the fort's walls; most likely forcing a French capitulation.[83] None of this material could be left behind and, difficult though it would be, it had to be hauled to Fort Duquesne if the place was to fall to the British. The alternative, storming the work, would have cost many more lives than a formal siege; thus, from the perspective of a conventional British officer, the difficulties of dragging men, supplies and artillery to the Monongahela was the lesser of two evils.

Just 35 miles from Cumberland, however, the march began to take its toll as the army, men and horses alike, began to break down in alarming numbers. It was at this point that Braddock, following advice from 23-year-old George Washington, decided to divide his force in two. As Washington himself would later convey,

> I urged it in the warmest possible terms I was master of, to push on; if we even did it with a chosen detachment for that purpose, with the artillery and such things as were absolutely necessary; leaving the baggage and other convoys with the remainder of the army, to follow by slow and regular marches...[84]

The sick, unfit and idle, many of them Americans, therefore formed a support column which, under the command of Colonel Thomas Dunbar, would make its way as best it could behind Braddock's flying column. Sensibly, the general ordered much of the baggage and even some of the artillery to remain with the former and, as a result, his advanced column made good progress, sometimes as much as eight miles a day. Unfortunately, Dunbar's force fell further and further behind. Eventually, sixty miles separated the two British columns, but Braddock, emboldened by the lack of any real resistance to his march, and easily dispersing those French and Indians that did attempt to pick off stragglers, remained supremely confident.

What had been overlooked was the fact that a French-Indian ambuscade was unlikely to transpire so far from Fort Duquesne as the French would never engage the British on a lengthy supply line. Furthermore, any early setback would have likely resulted in the desertion of the French force's Indian allies, threatening Fort Duquesne, and perhaps all of France's sovereign claims in the Ohio, in one reckless gamble. The French commander, Claude-Pierre Pécaudy de Contrecœur, an experienced officer of the Troupes de la Marine, was wily enough to know that, considering the apparent disparity between Braddock's and his own force, he would have to fight on terms that suited the strengths of his largely Native American and Canadian militia force. Therefore, the French waited—for time, reinforcements and opportunity—knowing that a precipitate defeat would prove disastrous. In the interim, small parties picked off any stragglers in the British column while others raided the Pennsylvanian and Virginian frontiers which were particularly vulnerable now that Braddock's army was pressing deeper into Ohio territory.[85]

Those who criticize Braddock for being too rigid in his application of regular military doctrine would do well to remember that, throughout the march, he was willing, where possible, to adapt to the environment to facilitate the journey or to lighten the load of his men. Regardless, the soldiers and indeed camp followers of his army still had enormous travails to overcome even before they could consider the final approach to Fort Duquesne. Notwithstanding Braddock's diligence, many of his soldiers were apprehensive of ambush. Having been fed lurid tales of Indian barbarity by their provincial allies (and those civilians they had encountered since their arrival in North America), many of the regulars were unnerved by the scouting and scalping parties the French sent out to reconnoiter and pester the British advance. According to one officer,

> On our march our guides imagined they saw some Indians frequently lurking round our line which we had reason afterwards to think true. A wagoner going out next morning to bring back in his horses was surprised by a party of Indians who shot him 4 places in the belly & his horse in the neck, he made shift to return to camp, but after lingering some days he died; ye same morning 4 people more going out to look after their horses were killed and scalped.[86]

One of the more serious skirmishes involving French-Indian raiding parties resulted in the death of the son of one of Braddock's few remaining Indian allies. Led by George Croghan, a small party of British Indians had spotted a group of French-allied warriors whom had earlier waylaid and scalped three stragglers from Braddock's force. Entering the woods to ambush this party, Croghan's men soon opened fire on the assailants. Unfortunately, the Virginian rangers mistook this fire for that of the enemy and, consequently, unleashed their muskets on Croghan's men. In the melee that followed, the son of the Half-King Scarouady fell to so-called friendly fire. Knowing the damage that could be done as a result of this incident, Braddock buried the chief's son that evening with full military honors.[87] The Indians appeared pleased by this, though their anger was probably better sated by a scalp two of Croghan's scouts took from an unfortunate French officer caught off-guard while shooting game half a mile from Fort Duquesne.[88]

Irrespective of French-Indian harassment, the British column pressed on inexorably; blasting, hacking, toiling and no doubt swearing all the way to the banks of the Monongahela. But Braddock's column was now separated from Dunbar's by a considerable distance and swift reinforcement, unless a halt be made in the advanced division, was unlikely. George Washington, having been ill with the flux and forced to remain behind the main advance, summoned enough strength to rejoin the flying column and informed the general that it would be three weeks before they caught up, depending on the health of the horses—which was rather poor.[89] Equally debilitating was the bout of dysentery that had also broken out among the officers and men of Dunbar's units. Braddock, having recently received intelligence that French reinforcements were marching to Fort Duquesne, thus decided to press on without delay.[90] Dunbar's men would have to catch up as best they could.

Crossing the Monongahela was a risky business and posed the next significant problem. The general, at the advice of his guides (who included Christopher Gist) decided to ford the Monongahela in two separate places; thus avoiding the river's hazardous narrows and the potentially dangerous Turtle Creek ravine. A debate had also emerged among his staff regarding how it would be best to invest Fort Duquesne, particularly as many believed that the French would begin a withdrawal to Canada on news of the British Army's approach.[91] Sir John St. Clair, an officer who had by now developed a somewhat difficult relationship with his commander (on account of the latter's close relationship with Robert Orme) suggested privately (though not to Braddock, according to Orme) that a detachment be sent on a night-time march to invest the fort before the garrison had time to destroy their works. Consequently he had asked for 400 men to go ahead and "hinder any sortie to be made on the convoy." It would have been an audacious and risky mission, considering the fact that the army was still ten miles from Fort Duquesne, and St. Clair was persuaded to wait until the next camp was struck before the idea would be considered again.[92]

Sir Peter Halkett recommended that Braddock send his Indians to reconnoiter the fort in a night time mission. The commander-in-chief, no friend of Halkett, dismissed his suggestion. The ill-feeling between the two was partially based on Halkett's criticisms of the general's line-of-march, and reflected the schisms that ran through the British high command. Halkett, a very experienced officer, thought that the army should build blockhouses and stockades along the route they had constructed, while also expressing a belief that more men should be trained to operate the artillery. In hindsight, his reasoning was rather sound and was vindicated by Brigadier General John Forbes's campaign against Fort Duquesne in 1758. Forbes, of course, adopted a very similar strategy to Halkett's and delivered the French fort into British hands. Braddock, believing that his subordinate had overstepped the mark, saw his suggestions as unhelpful criticisms that undermined his own authority.[93]

Strategic considerations aside, finally, by the evening of July 8, Braddock's army was two miles from the Monongahela and was ready to begin its final march to Fort Duquesne. By now the men were in high spirits. Colonel Dunbar had sent a herd of oxen to the flying column (these reached Braddock's men on the 5th) and the soldiers had enjoyed, for the first time in many weeks, fresh beef. It seemed that the worst of the march was now over; the artillery had been dragged over the perilous mountains and swamps of the backcountry, while those French and Indians who had harassed the column had been disposed of without too much difficulty. For many of the soldiers, the following day would surely see them raise the Union Jack over Fort Duquesne where they would revel in the glory of a hard-earned victory. They had no inkling of the abject disaster that awaited them.

Notes

1. Matthew C. Ward, *Breaking the Backcountry: The Seven Years War in Virginia and Pennsylvania, 1754–1765* (Pittsburgh, PA: University of Pittsburgh Press, 2003).
2. Stanley Pargellis, *Lord Loudoun in North America* (New Haven, CT: Yale University Press, 1961), 32–39.
3. Steven Sarson, *British America 1500–1800: Creating Colonies, Imagining an Empire* (Oxford: Oxford University Press, 2005), 203.
4. See, See Jack P. Greene, *Negotiated Authorities: Essays in Colonial Political and Constitutional History* (Charlottesville: University of Virginia Press, 1994).
5. Lawrence Henry Gipson, *The British Empire before the American Revolution*, Vol. VI, *The Great War for the Empire: The Years of Defeat, 1754–1757* (New York: Alfred A. Knopf, 1946), 64–70.
6. Penn's "advices" had the desired effect. See, for example, "St. Clair to Morris, 14 January, 1755" in Samuel Hazard (ed.), *Minutes of the Provincial Council of Pennsylvania*, Volume VI (Harrisburg: Theo. Fenn & Co., 1851), 307–308.

7. Although often referred to as "Governor Morris" he was, in reality, a Deputy-Governor. Pennsylvania was, after all, a proprietary colony.
8. See Benjamin Franklin, *Memoirs of Benjamin Franklin*, Vol. 1 (2 Vols. New York: Harper & Brothers, 1839), 153.
9. Franklin was a great advocate of the issuing of paper money and his views were expressed unequivocally in *A Modest Enquiry into the Nature and Necessity of a Paper-Currency* (Philadelphia, 1729).
10. As a note, shortages in specie and the confusion over the value of colonial monies created considerable financial difficulties for the British Army in America throughout the French and Indian War.
11. Winthrop Sargent (ed.) *The History of an Expedition against Fort Duquesne in 1755, under Major General Edward Braddock* (Philadelphia, 1855), 147–150. Franklin, in his *Nature and Necessity of a Paper-Currency* argued that the value of paper money lay not in legal tender laws or fixed exchange rates between such a currency and gold and silver coins (he suggested that gold and silver were of no permanent value), but the quantity of paper money, as related to the volume of internal trade within the colony. As the sagacious Franklin recommended, it was land, not gold and silver, that would ultimately back Pennsylvania's currency.
12. See "Gov. Morris to Thomas Penn, April 9th, 1755" in Samuel Hazard (ed.) *Pennsylvania Archives. Commencing 1748*, Vol. II (12 vols. Philadelphia: Joseph Severns & Co. 1853), 286–288.
13. William S. Hanna, *Benjamin Franklin and Pennsylvania Politics* (Palo Alto, CA: Stanford University Press, 1964), 59.
14. This tit-for-tat war of words had indeed been on-going since Braddock's very arrival in America. On March 12th Morris had written that "The Conduct of the Assemblies upon the Continent almost without Exception had been so very absurd that they have suffered the French to take quiet Possession of the most advantageous Place…" See, "A Letter to General Braddock from Governor Morris, March 12, 1755" in Samuel Hazard (ed.) *Colonial Records of Pennsylvania*, Volume VI (Harrisburg, PA: Theo. Fenn & Co. 1851), 335–338.
15. See "Benjamin Franklin to John Ridout" in Alan Houston, "Benjamin Franklin and the 'Wagon Affair' of 1755," *The William and Mary Quarterly*, Third Series, Vol. 66, no. 2 (April, 2009), 235–286.
16. Sargent, *The History of an expedition against Fort Duquesne in 1755*, 179.
17. Pitt's reforms are discussed in significant detail in Julian S. Corbett's classic, *England in the Seven Years War: A Study in Combined Strategy*, Volume I (2 Vols. London: Longmans Green: 1907), 8–9, 28–29, 148, 150–152, 189–191, 374–376.
18. Such illegal operations were in fact common knowledge in America, the consequences of which were expressed by Robert Dinwiddie in a letter

Thomas Robinson on 20 January. "They carry large quantities of Flour, Bread, Pork, Beef etc. to Lewisbourg... where they sell it for Rum, Molasses, Sugar, the Produce of their Islands." All of which, of course, provided the French in the Ohio with much-needed supplies. Quoted in Gipson, *British Empire before the American Revolution*, VI, 65.
19. Long winter freezes on the St. Lawrence, wartime interception by British ships, monopolies and, of course, corruption, created high prices for trade goods in Canada.
20. Cadwallader Colden was one contemporary aware of the importance of this trade and thus documented its nature and importance. See Cadwallader Colden, "A Memorial Concerning the Fur Trade of the Province of New York, November 10, 1724" in *New York Colonial Documents*, Volume V, 732–733.
21. The illicit trade between colonists and French continued, despite Braddock's endeavors. On May 4th, he wrote "an open trade is carry'd on with the French at Reastown and Agwick, within your government, by means of the Indians in their Alliance; that they are thereby supply'd with powder and whatever they have occasion for..." See "Gen. Braddock to Gov. Morris, Winchester, May the 4th, 1755" in Samuel Hazard (ed.) *Pennsylvania Archives*, Vol. II, 299–300.
22. See, Greene, *Negotiated Authorities*. The attendees actually consisted of Braddock and five colonial governors: Robert Dinwiddie (Virginia), Horatio Sharpe (Maryland), Robert Morris (Pennsylvania), William Shirley (Massachusetts) and James De Lancey (New York). William Johnson, who was to be appointed Superintendent of all Northern Indians, also attended.
23. "Private instructions for Major-General Edward Braddock" in Stanley Pargellis (ed.), *Military affairs in North America, 1748–1765: Selected Documents from the Cumberland papers in Windsor Castle* (London, 1936), 53–54.
24. See "Johnson to Orme, May 19th, 1755" in James Sullivan (ed.) *The Papers of Sir William Johnson*, Vol. I (Albany, 1921), 521–522. Also, "Johnson to Shirley 19 June, 1755," Ibid., 614–618.
25. Concerning the difficulties of raising a central fund see Gipson, *The British Empire before the American Revolution*, VI, *Years of Defeat*, 71. Robert Orme would also allude to these difficulties. See "Journal of Robert Orme" in Sargent, *History of an expedition against Fort Duquesne in 1755*, 301.
26. Richard Henry Spencer, "The Carlyle House and is Associations—Braddock's Headquarters—Here the Colonial Governors met in Council, April, 1755," *The William and Mary Quarterly*, Vol. 18, No. 1 (July 1909), 1–17.

27. Douglas Edward Leach, *Arms for Empire: A Military History of the British Colonies in North America, 1607–1763* (New York: Macmillan, 1973), 355.
28. William Livingston, *A review of the military operations in North America: from the commencement of the French hostilities to the frontiers of Virginia in 1753, to the surrender of Oswego, on the 14th of August 1756; interspersed with various observations, characters and anecdotes; necessary to give light into the conduct of American transactions in general; and more especially into the political management of affairs in New York; in a letter to a nobleman; to which are added Col. Washington's journal of his expedition to the Ohio, in 1754, and several letters found in the cabinet of Major General Braddock, after his defeat near Fort Duquesne (1757)* (Dublin, 1757), 44–45.
29. A column led by Sir Peter Halkett of the 44th was sent through Virginia while the 48th, led by Colonel Thomas Dunbar, marched through Maryland. Braddock himself followed the latter route.
30. History is full of generals who, appointed primarily for political reasons, consequently lack the willingness to show initiative in the face of strategic and tactical realities "on the ground." Perhaps Braddock was wise to follow the course he did, as the British ministry could always find a scapegoat in the event of a military catastrophe. One only has to review the execution of Braddock's naval contemporary, Admiral John Byng, to see the lengths to which a chastened ministry would go to shift responsibility for a disaster that threatened its position.
31. John A. Schutz, *William Shirley: King's Governor of Massachusetts* (Chapel Hill: University of North Carolina Press, 1961, 197.
32. The prosecution of Indian affairs became a major thorn of contention between Johnson and Shirley, both of whom vied for influence among the Iroquois. The former's frustrations were made clear to the Board of Trade in a letter that bemoaned the 'scurrilous falsehoods," "base and insolent behaviour" and "destructive measures" emergent from Shirley's handling of Indian relations; needless to say, the letter also lays bare the antipathy existent between these two men. See "William Johnson to the Lords of Trade, Lake George, Sept. 3rd, 1755" in Charles Henry Lincoln (ed.) *Correspondence of William Shirley*, Vol. II (New York: Macmillan, 1912), 243–248.
33. The Albany Congress was convened to address the concerns the Iroquois had regarding British colonization of western lands in addition to providing a framework for a collective colonial defense. In terms of native diplomacy, the affair reflected the avarice, self-interest and factionalism that threatened to cost the British and their colonies their most important Indian allies in the Ohio.
34. "A return of His Majesty's Troops," in Pargellis, *Military Affairs*, 86–91.
35. The directive also made British Majors superior to the highest ranking American officers. See "George Washington to Robert Orme, Mount

Vernon, 15 March, 1755," in George Washington, Worthington Chauncey Ford (ed.), *The Writings of George Washington, collected and edited by Worthington Chauncey Ford* (New York: G.P. Putnam's Sons, 1889–1893), Vol. I (1748–1757), 141–144.
36. John Biglow (ed.) *The Autobiography of Benjamin Franklin* (Philadelphia, 1868), 302.
37. "Sir John St. Clair to Robert Napier, Williamsburg, Feb 10th, 1755" in Pargellis (ed.), *Military Affairs in North America*, 58–61.
38. "St. Clair to Braddock," Ibid., 61–64.
39. "St. Clair to Napier," Ibid., 60.
40. Hazard (ed.) *Minutes of the Provincial Council of Pennsylvania*, VI, 368–369.
41. John Entick, *The General History of the late War; Containing its Rise, Progress, and Event in Europe, Asia, Africa and America*, Volume I (5 Vols. London, 1763), 142.
42. Within the subject's historiography, it is accepted that Braddock's landing in Virginia (and not Pennsylvania), and the corresponding route he took to the Ohio, was a poor choice.
43. And, indeed, the premise of the "Braddock Plan" which assumed a British commander-in-chief could resolve such deep-rooted issues.
44. Lee McCardell, *Ill-Starred General: Braddock of the Coldstream Guards* (Pittsburgh: University of Pittsburgh Press, 1958), 172.
45. See Ward, *Breaking the Backcountry*, 82–83.
46. Ibid., 61–62.
47. McCardell, *Ill-Stared General*, 302–303.
48. See Entick, *History of the Late War*, Vol. I, 142.
49. Biglow (ed.) *Autobiography of Franklin*, 307–310.
50. "Advertisement of B. Franklin for "Wagons," Lancaster, April, 1755" in *Pennsylvania Archives*, Vol. II, 294–295.
51. See Franklin, Bigelow (ed.) *Autobiography of Benjamin Franklin*, 305–307.
52. As Alan Houston ascertains, Franklin also wanted to protect local inhabitants from increasingly frustrated soldiers who, perhaps following from Sir John St. Clair's belligerence, had begun commandeering horses—the latter frequently dying from neglect. See Alan Houston, "Benjamin Franklin and the 'Wagon Affair' of 1755" in *The William and Mary Quarterly*, Third Series, Vol. 66, No. 2 (April 2009) pp.235–286.
53. Regarding topography, Sir John St. Clair would write, "…from Winchester to this place [Little Meadows] is one continued track of Mountains…" As for intelligence regarding the terrain, "no one except a few Hunters knows it on the spot; and their Knowledge extends no further than in following their Game." See "St. Clair to Robert Napier" in Pargellis (ed.) *Military affairs in North America*, 94–95.

54. See William H. Lowdermilk, (ed.) *Major General Edward Braddock's Orderly Books, from February 26 to June 17, 1755* (Maryland, 1878), xix.
55. "Braddock to Napier" in Pargellis (ed.), *Military affairs in North America*, 81–84.
56. J. A. Houlding, *Fit for Service: The Training of the British Army 1715–1795* (Oxford: Clarendon Press, 1981), 356–357.
57. Charles Hamilton (ed.), *Braddock's Defeat: The Journal of Captain Robert Cholmley's Batman; The Journal of a British Officer; Halkett's Orderly Book* (Norman: University of Oklahoma Press, 1959), 61-127.
58. See, *The expedition of Major General Braddock to Virginia; with the two regiments of Hacket and Dunbar. Being extracts of letters from an officer in one of those regiments to his friend in London, describing the march and engagement in the woods*, London: H. Carpenter, 1755.. This letter is also available in Archer Butler Hulbert, *Braddock's Road and Three Relevant Papers, Historic Highways of America*, Volume IV (Cleveland: Arthur H. Clark Company, 1903), 137–165.
59. "Description of the Backwoods," Ibid., 150–151.
60. "Charlotte Browne, Maryland toward Fort Cumberland, June 13, 1755" in Andrew J. Wahll (ed.) *Braddock Road Chronicles, 1755* (Berwyn Heights, MD: Heritage Books, 1999), 275.
61. In late May, Thomas Cresap, a contractor at the storehouse at Conococheague, failed to ensure that a stock of beef supplied for the Maryland troops was properly salted. When the casks were opened, the meat was rancid, with the result that it was "condemned to be buried." See "Orme's Journal" in Sargent (ed.) *History of an Expedition*, 313.
62. McCardell, *Ill-Starred General*, 212.
63. This report, written by Thomas Gage and Thomas Dunbar stated that, "They [the men] were greatly Harrass'd by dutys unequal to their numbers; Dispirited by want of Sufficient Provisions, and not being allowed time to dress the little they had, with nothing to Drink but Water, and that Often Scarce and Bad."
64. "St. Clair to Braddock, February 9, 1755," in Pargellis (ed.) *Military affairs in North America*, 62.
65. "Orme's Journal," in Sargent (ed.) *History of an Expedition*, 284–286.
66. Ibid., 312.
67. Ian K. Steele, *Guerrillas and Grenadiers: The Struggle for Canada, 1689–1760* (Toronto: Ryerson Press, 1974), 132.
68. See "Robert Dinwiddie to Robinson, March 18, 1755" in *Dinwiddie Papers*, Volume I, 525. The ranger companies should not be confused with those of Robert Rogers, whose men proved effective in this role.
69. For punishments meted out to soldiers see, as an example, Lowdermilk (ed.) *Orderly Books*, xxxiv–xxxv and xxxiv–xxxv.

70. Quote of Scarouady, the Half King, in Kopperman, *Braddock at the Monongahela*, 99
71. A very typical impression of the natives assembled at Fort Cumberland is provided by the well-known contemporary "Seaman's Journal." "...The Indians were greatly surprised at the regular way of our Soldiers Marching and our Numbers." Likewise he noted that "[native] Men are tall, well made and active, but not strong; The Women not so tall yet well proportion'd & have many Children..." With the typical sweeping generalization of many contemporary European Christians, the author proclaimed, "These people have no Idea of a Superior Being or of Religion and I take them to be the most ignorant, as to the Knowledge of the World and things, of any Creatures living..." See "A Seaman's Journal" in Butler Hulbert (ed.), *Braddock's Road*, 90–93.
72. "George Croghan's Statement," in Sargent, *History of an Expedition*, 407–408.
73. Biglow, *Autobiography of Franklin*, 311.
74. See "Halkett's Orderly Book," in Hamilton (ed.) *Braddock's Defeat*, 89–90.
75. There is now a wide-ranging historiography relative to the role of women in the British Army. See, for example, Don N. Hagist, "The Women of The British Army in America," *The Brigade Dispatch*, 24/3 (1994): 2–10; 24/4 (1994): 9–17; 25/1 (1995): 8–14, http://www.revwar75.com/library/hagist/britwomen.htm accessed March 16, 2016.
76. The implications of such abuse have been discussed by Paul Kopperman in his article "The Cheapest Pay." See Paul E. Kopperman, "The Cheapest Pay:" Alcohol abuse in the Eighteenth-century British Army, *The Journal of Military History*, Vol. 60, No. 3 (July, 1996), 445–70.
77. Women were allowed to own property, land, housing, tools and other tangible items within American Indian societies. Within matrilineal societies, women had considerable influence in tribal governance too—one prime example being the Iroquois Confederacy.
78. Dinwiddie would later condemn Glen in the harshest possible tone for this conduct. He told South Carolina's governor and the British ministry that Glen was guilty of a gross negligence of duty. See John Richard Alden, *Robert Dinwiddie: Servant of the Crown* (Charlottesville: University Press of Virginia, 1973), 62.
79. See "Major-General Johnson to the Lords of Trade, Albany, 21st July, 1755," in E. B. O'Callaghan (ed.) *Documents Relative to the Colonial History of New York, Procured in Holland, England and France*, Volume VI (Albany: 1855), 961–963.
80. There were two Iroquois "Half King's," the other being Tanacharison.
81. Quoted in Fred Anderson, *The Crucible of War: The Seven Years War and the fate of Empire in British North America, 1754–1766* (New York, 2000), 96.

82. Again, I would draw the reader's attention to Humphrey Bland, *A Treatise of Military Discipline: In which is laid down and Explained the Duties of Officer and Soldier* (5th edition, Dublin, 1743); specifically pages 115–116.
83. Braddock's artillery included four 8-inch howitzers, four 12-pounders, six 6-pounders and 15 mortars. The 12-pounders required seven strong horses each to drag them, while the caissons (a two wheeled cart) filled with loads of considerable weight, required four horses each.
84. John Clement Fitzpatrick (ed.), *The Writings of George Washington from the Original Manuscript Sources, 1745–1799*, Vol. I, 1745–1756 (39 vols. United States Government Printing Office, 1931), 141–146.
85. Kopperman, *Braddock at the Monongahela*, 266 and Wahl (ed.) *Braddock Road Chronicles*, 333.
86. "Journal of a British officer" in Hamilton (ed.), *Braddock's Defeat*, 44–45.
87. Ibid., 47–48.
88. The unfortunate Frenchman could have been the "Peter Simard," an "unmarried inhabitant of the parish of Petit Riviere" who was aged "twenty-three or thereabout," referred to in the baptismal register of Fort Duquesne. See Rev. A. A. Lambing (ed.), *The Baptismal Register of Fort Duquesne (from June, 1754, to Dec., 1756) Translated, with an Introductory Essay and Notes* (Pittsburgh, PA: Myers, Shinkle & Co., 1885), 59.
89. See "Orme's Journal" in Sargent (ed.) *History of an Expedition*, 346–347.
90. See Charles Henry Lincoln (ed.) *The Correspondence of William Shirley, Governor of Massachusetts and Military Commander in America, 1731–1760*, Vol. II, (New York, 1912), 201–202.
91. Ibid., 181.
92. "Orme's Journal" in Sargent (ed.) *History of an Expedition*, 352.
93. Governor Sharpe of Maryland had also advised building a string of posts to secure the logistical concerns of the army. Orme, who was very influential with Braddock, advised otherwise, and this tactic was not employed. The fact that Halkett, Dunbar and St. Clair were Scottish officers may also explain Braddock's attitude towards these subordinates. Indeed, there also existed friction between the 44th and 48th regiments who comprised the regular element of Braddock's army. In the recent Jacobite uprising the 44th had, at the defeat at Prestonpans, been overwhelmed by rebel forces. The 48th meanwhile had been one of the few regiments to have stood their ground at the Battle of Falkirk.

CHAPTER 6

The Battle of the Monongahela: A Clash of Military Cultures

The fact that Edward Braddock, in the face of the multitude of challenges that had presented themselves before him on his arduous march to the Ohio, was now ready to strike against the principal objective of this long campaign was no small achievement. To borrow an old cliché, his bedraggled soldiers had, by their blood, sweat and tears, blasted and hacked their way to the banks of the Monongahela; and were now poised to claim the rightful victory that surely awaited them. As a consequence of the difficulties of advancing through remorselessly unforgiving terrain, particularly well-suited for a French ambush, Braddock, having finally reached the banks of the Monongahela, decided his army should ford the river in two separate places; it was a wise decision. The first ford was near Turtle Creek and here Braddock crossed the west bank of the Monongahela River. He then turned north, seeking to re-cross at a spot where his scouts had identified a second practicable ford. There were obstacles to be overcome here too, notably the sloping, sandy banks that had formed on the opposite side of the river—a troublesome, but not insurmountable inconvenience, though one which caused a degree of anxiety among the troops.[1]

If any major French resistance were to be encountered, then surely it would be at this point, as the position provided several obvious natural advantages for an ambuscade. Surprisingly, as the army approached this second crucial objective, no significant French presence was to be seen; and once again the principal difficulty the army faced was a topographical one. Commenting on the strenuous efforts required to cross the river at this ford, one participant recollected how,

> ... on the other side ye second crossing ye advanced party had halted at Frazier's House, close to ye Bank which was very steep and took us two hours to make it passable for ye carriages [sic].[2]

In a theme reminiscent throughout the campaign, it was the army's supply train and artillery that was causing the greatest difficulty. Nonetheless, having gained this ascendancy, the relief of the men at having surmounted such a daunting obstacle unopposed must have been palpable; one officer noted that as the army traversed the river it did so with, "Colours flying, drums beating and fifes playing the Grenadier's March." Harry Gordon, a Captain with the military engineers, would later relate how,

> Every one who saw these banks, being above 12 feet perpendicularly high Above the Shore, & the Course of the River 300 yards Broad. Hugg'd themselves with joy at our Good Luck in having surmounted our greatest Difficultys, & too hastily Concluded the Enemy never wou'd dare to Oppose us.[3]

Despite their exhaustion and a hunger that stemmed from the fact that many of the men had not eaten that day or 'had Nothing most of the day Before', Braddock's men were supremely confident of ultimate victory.[4]

The Battle of the Monongahela: A Historiographical Debate

For over 250 years, the events surrounding the infamous 'Battle of the Monongahela' have been the cause of intense levels of analysis, recrimination and censure. And yet a consensus regarding the ultimate cause of Braddock's defeat has never been reached; instead, historians have often found themselves aligning their conclusions along several discernable paradigms. The first, and one which was originally hinted at by contemporaries George Washington, Benjamin Franklin and, most vociferously, Adam Stephen (who served in the Virginian rearguard during the battle) was that Braddock's defeat was the result of his rigid adherence to European tactics and his soldiers' (and indeed, officers') unfamiliarity with the gritty realities of frontier warfare. Subscribers to this theory would argue that the British lost because their infantry became panic-stricken; a result of fighting an unfamiliar and seemingly invisible enemy in a country to which they were unaccustomed. Braddock's generalship was flawed because he failed to allow his colonial auxiliaries "to fight in their own mode," hence condemning the massed ranks of redcoats to ignominious death and defeat.[5] Daniel Boone (and, later, his biographer Lyman Copeland Draper), who served as a Wagoner on the Braddock expedition, was more critical of the commander-in-chief. Draper's claim that Braddock, though possessing "brutal courage" lost the battle because he rejected the "counsel of his Provincial and Indian allies" and adhered "with stubborn bigotry to a rigid system of tactics adapted only to the open plains of civilized Europe" is another argument that has found favor with many reflective American histories of the French and Indian War.[6]

Another explanation for the defeat, and one first expounded by Captain Robert Orme, Braddock's aide-de-camp, places the cause of the defeat on the army's vanguard (and its commander, Thomas Gage) who had fallen back on the advancing main body of Braddock's force after the initial volleys of the battle had been fired. Orme's numerous accounts of the battle, written for figures as notable as the Secretary of State, Henry Fox, colonial governors and the Duke of Cumberland, formed the basis for the many newspaper accounts that flowed from the aftermath of the engagement. In Orme's work, the rank-and-file in particular were also scolded in the harshest possible terms for their failure to follow orders as a result of the panic that he felt tore through the ranks; Orme would always maintain that the officers were heroes and the soldiers dastardly cowards.[7]

Completely contradictory to Orme's claims were those of George Croghan, the Irish-born Pennsylvanian fur trader and experienced frontiersman, who led a group of eight Indian scouts during the Braddock expedition. This account, contained in a letter from "Charles Swain to Richard Peters," was based on a conversation Croghan had with the former after the battle. Quite evidently, it argues that it was the officers in the British force that behaved poorly,

> It appears to me, that had there been any Officers to have rallied the men on retreating even at last the Enemy would not have got the six cannon and mortars, and perhaps they might have advanced toward the fort, for when the men were going off, many of the Officers called out Halt, Halt, which the men mostly did, but the Officers continued on and got the heels of them.[8]

For historians inclined to examine the reasons for the redcoats' supposed "dastardly behavior," the rawness of the troops was the contributory factor in the panic that swept through the ranks on July 9, resulting in a disastrous British defeat. Many of Braddock's men were indeed inexperienced draftees or American recruits with little combat experience and only minimal training. This was compounded by fluctuating morale levels that were, according to several post-battle accounts, in no small measure the consequence of British soldiers being fed (by American soldiers and civilians) lurid and barbaric stories of the horrible fate that awaited them if they were captured by French-allied Native Americans. These tales, on the day of battle, are said to have significantly contributed to the panic that gradually spread through the ranks when Braddock's army was eventually confronted by a largely irregular French-Indian force.

Yet another belief attributes the defeat to the determination of the French regulars who stoically held the ground in front of Braddock's army while the Canadians and Indians filtered into the forest along the British flanks. The latter, seeing the steadiness of their comrades and the devastating effect of their fire, were rallied by their example and subsequently routed the British force. Paradoxically, an alternative assumption (a very sound one, it must be added) declares the French victory a distinctively Native American success; one which highlighted their mastery of "wilderness warfare" (or *la guerre sauvage* as the Marquis de Montcalm would later call it) and indeed the qualities of the French officers assigned to them.[9]

In an interesting twist of interpretation, several notable scholars, including the much-esteemed Stanley Pargellis, have suggested that blame for the Monongahela debacle should, indeed, lay squarely with Braddock and his senior officers; but their assumption is based on a very different reading of the battle than was conveyed by men such as George Washington, Daniel Boone and, later, Lyman Copeland Draper.[10] For adherents of the Pargellis theory, the novelty of fighting Native Americans in their favored environment should not be discounted, and in this they stand with the school of thought epitomized by Washington, Adam Stephen and Benjamin Franklin. "Pargelianites," however, believe the cause of the disaster was Braddock's failure to properly implement, on the day of battle, the *European* tactics he had so staunchly adhered to previously on his campaign. By failing to follow the fundamental rules of war laid down in European military manuals—specifically that of Humphrey Bland—Braddock and his staff never properly established conventional battlefield formations. As a consequence, his soldiers simply did not have the chance to prove that Frederician methods, properly employed, could in fact triumph over hit-and-run tactics of the New World. In short, blame should be placed on the quality of the leadership, not the men.[11]

The debate highlighted above is central to this book which, after all, is concerned with outlining the reasons for the failure of the Braddock's campaign of 1755; therefore, any glossing over of this momentous event simply will not do. In truth, as a case-study Braddock's military catastrophe at the Monongahela is the perfect prism through which the difficulties the divergences in martial tradition between regular and American-origin forces (both enemy and friendly) can be examined. What will follow, therefore, is an analysis of the defeat that will tie together the narrative of the actual battle with an analysis of what the available evidence tells us. This will highlight, among other things, that Braddock's defeat can be partly characterized as the unauthorized, and ultimately failed, fusing of two distinct modes of war in a classic ambush environment.

The Battle Rejoined

The opening section of this chapter established the British Army on the other side of the Monongahela, ready to begin its final advance to Fort Duquesne; consequently, it was noted that many of the men felt that they would enjoy a clear march to their objective. In short, they were confident that little, if any, resistance would be met as they fulfilled their ultimate goal. What can initially be ascertained from the various maps and descriptions produced after the battle is that, having crossed the Monongahela for the second time and having commenced the final stage of their march, Braddock's army was drawn up in a typically conventional close-order column formation. This column consisted of around 1300 men, at the head of which was a vanguard of 300 regulars, divided into three groups, and accompanied by a small body of guides, a grenadier company and its reserve. Behind this vanguard advanced a road-making party of 200 regulars and Virginians, led by Sir John St. Clair, Braddock's quartermaster-general; a quarter of a mile to the rear of the van the main body, consisting of 750 men, marched. Fifty of these soldiers formed the general's guard and around 200 were detached in small flanking parties of 10–20 men each. These flanking units were to prevent a sudden surprise attack along the army's vulnerable flanks (they were posted 100 yards from each side of the main advancing column) and were a vital element in Braddock's defensive dispositions. The remainder of the regulars marched alongside the long column of wagons and artillery that would prove essential if Fort Duquesne had to be formally invested. The extensive supplies and artillery actually divided this section of Braddock's army in two, meaning that the soldiers here were split into two double columns; this was hardly ideal as the men were two abreast and separated in a way that meant the troops would have to march to the front or rear of the wagons if they were to join their adjacent comrades. Nevertheless, defense was essential for this logistical train and the soldiers expected to defend the wagons also had to be close enough to the working party to reinforce these men if they were suddenly engaged by an enemy force. Behind the van and main body marched a hundred Virginians, who were separated from the main column by a distance of around 20 yards and formed the army's rearguard. Noticeably absent from this force was any real discernible native presence—the vast majority of Braddock's American-Indian allies having deserted him earlier in the campaign.

For some in Braddock's army this formation was at least partly responsible for the disaster that was about to unfold. A historical source simply known to posterity as *The Journal of a British Officer*, whose author kept a detailed account during the campaign, gives us an insight into what he saw as the fundamental flaws in the dispositions of the army.[12] According to this officer, after the second ford was passed,

> The General now thinking ye dangerous passes were over, did not suffer ye Advanced Party to proceed any farther than ye Distance of a few yards from the main body. It was proposed to strengthen the flanks but this was rejected.[13]

From this it would seem that the tide of euphoria relayed by Gordon had in fact consumed Braddock as he too become overconfident of a victory he felt certain to be soon celebrating. It is also worth noting that this apparent complacency was in stark contrast to his earlier conduct which had placed great emphasis on securing the army from any possible ambuscade; the fact that so few men had been lost to skulking enemy parties is evidence of this resilience. It may be, however, that there was another reason for this overconfidence: it could have been a result of the more benign terrain that appeared to present itself before the army. Braddock's quartermaster-general, Sir John St. Clair, suggested the reasons for this:

After Colonel Gage and I had pass'd the river, we received orders from Cap: Morris Aid du Camp to march on; the underwood Continued very thick for about one quarter of a mile beyond the Monongahela then we came to an open wood free from underwood with some gradual riseings, this wood was so open the Carriages Could have been drove in any part of it...[14]

St. Clair's claim of "open woods" is not without dispute and runs contrary to observations made by Braddock's favorite, Robert Orme, who suggested the opposite was true. In this case however, it may well be that "openness" meant different things to different people. If St. Clair's observations were more accurate, however, then Braddock may well have felt more confident in this more "open" environment, which favored the tactical strengths of his largely regular force.[15] Regarding the charge of complacency that was made against Braddock, in actuality the general's martial dispositions on July 9 did conform to expected protocols outlined by Humphrey Bland and other leading military theorists.[16] He had protected his flanks with appropriate flanking parties, his vanguard was sufficiently numerous to protect the main body from a surprise attack and he did deploy a screen of horsemen to provide additional intelligence for this segment of his force. The charge, made by Stanley Pargellis among others, that his men were too compacted is also slightly misleading. As James Furnis, commissary of stores for the Ordinance Board (who, on July 9 was likely part of a line of wagons that advanced behind the working party) would attest, the distance between the van and main body was around a quarter of a mile—enough, in theory, to prevent a collision of units under conventional conditions but not too great a distance to prevent mutual reinforcement within a relatively short space of time.[17]

The French Move to Counter a Threat

While Braddock was advancing across the Pennsylvania backcountry, the French too had been considering the responses available to the threat posed by the seemingly inexorable British army. Hitherto, as the Anglo-American army pushed towards the Ohio, the French had deployed irregular raiding parties, consisting of mixed Franco-Ottawa, Potawatomi, Miami, Shawnee and Delaware units against the frontier communities left behind as their adversaries advanced. Settlements at Patterson's Creek (Virginia), and the wider counties of Frederick, Hampshire and Cumberland (the latter being a Pennsylvanian county, of course) were devastated by these raids which highlighted a lack of preparedness for the war in those regions; notwithstanding the limitations of the colonial militia who seemed powerless to stop these attacks.[18]

Such raids did not, however, halt Braddock's albeit slow advance to the Ohio. Constantly informed of British movements by scouts sent out for this purpose, as Braddock closed in on Fort Duquesne there were now two options available to the fort's commander, Captain Claude Pecaudy de Contrecoeur. The first was simply to blow up the fort and retreat; the second was to ambush the British before they could reach Duquesne. Simply retreating and destroying Fort Duquesne would have been considered a dishonorable action and one which would have seen the French surrender control of the Ohio to the British, perhaps indefinitely. Having boasted of their power and martial supremacy over the British, the loss of Fort Duquesne would also have undermined French power in the eyes of the Ohio's tribes, who would, for reasons of self-preservation, naturally ally themselves with the dominant European nation following the outcome of the impending clash. Out of the question was defending Fort Duquesne from its walls and bastions, as it simply was not strong enough to withstand a siege by an army as well-equipped with artillery as Braddock's was. Contrecoeur's best hope of stymying the British advance was thus to launch an ambuscade, an action that would utilize the martial strengths of the many native warriors who formed the bulk of his force; while exploiting the weaknesses of his adversaries in the forested terrain across which they marched.[19]

By July 8, Braddock's army was perilously close to Fort Duquesne and some response had to be made. Consequently, Contrecoeur, along with his subordinates, Captains Beaujeu, Courtemanche and Dumas, formulated a plan for meeting the British head-on, before they could invest their beleaguered position. Their initial strategy, advocated mainly by Beaujeu, would have seen the deployment of a force of *Troupes de la Marine*, Canadian militia and native allies (commanded by himself) in an ambush against the British at the very point where Braddock was to ford the Monongahela for the second time; it seems the French, too, appreciated the defensive advantages of this spot. This sandy, sloping ascent that stood before the path of Braddock's army was an extremely difficult pass and in a European military context would have been considered the perfect point from which a defensive action could be undertaken. However reasonable this idea may have appeared to Beaujeu, it first required the tacit approval of the numerous native warriors who had been reinforcing the French over the intervening days and who formed the greater part of their army. Frustratingly for the

Frenchman, the natives sought a period of deliberation before they would agree to his strategy—as was their custom—and, at least initially, refused to partake in the planned ambush. The effects of this discord were recounted by a "Monsieur Roucher," who claimed that,

> All the Indian Nations were called together, & invited to joyne & assist the French to repulse the English who came to drive them out of the land they were in possession of. Mr. Beaujeu began to Warsong & all the Indian Nations Immediately joined him except the Poutawatamis of the Narrows (Detroit), who were silent. Which occasioned all the other Nations to desire not to march till next day.[20]

For the American-Indians, many of whom had previously believed Braddock's army to be a small expedition, reports from scouts of the true scale of the British army arrayed against them probably caused them to think twice about unleashing an ambush that contained a real risk of large-scale losses. Such causalities, it must be remembered, were anathema to Indian tribes who frequently saw warfare as a means of *replenishing* a diminished population. There therefore followed a period of desperate negotiation in which the animated Beaujeu and other Canadians (including the influential Normanville brothers) cajoled and entreated the natives to fight alongside their "French father." At the very last minute, the hours of negotiation bore fruition and at 9 a.m. on July 9, 1755, Beaujeu, at the head of his small army of 108 officers and men of the *Marine*, 146 Canadian militiamen, allied to 650 Indians, headed east into the forest to intercept the Anglo-American army.[21]

According to the testimony of James Smith, one of Braddock's Virginian "road cutters," who had been captured while on the march to the Monongahela, the Native Americans in the French force now seemed confident of success. The young Virginian's story is a harrowing tale of capture, torture, imprisonment, adoption and eventual acceptance by his captors that bears striking similarities to many North American captivity tales. Upon reaching Fort Duquesne, Smith endured the torment of running the gauntlet and the mixed blessing of being ministered to by a French doctor, who bled the unfortunate youth. Following his interrogation, Smith had been allowed a degree of freedom by his assailants and as such had engaged in conversation with one of his native captors; a "Delaware Indian" as he referred to him. The young colonist, recalling his conversation with this warrior, later relayed how,

I asked him what news from Braddock's army. He said the Indians spied them every day, and he showed me, by making marks on the ground with a stick, that Braddock's army was advancing in very close order, and that the Indians would surround them, take trees, and (as he expressed it) shoot um down all one pigeon.[22]

This prognostication would prove very astute and, coupled with what could arguably be considered a purposeful recalcitrance (as conveyed by "Roucher"), also suggests that it was the French-allied Indians who significantly influenced the former's tactical response to the advancing British.

THE ARMIES COLLIDE

Having crossed the second ford of the Monongahela, the British Army, Colonel Thomas Gage's vanguard of 300 regulars and provincials leading the way, pushed into the forest towards Fort Duquesne. Unknown to the confident Anglo-American army, Daniel Beaujeu's two-column French detachment was concurrently advancing to contest the march, unaware that Braddock had stolen a lead on them and had already forded the Monongahela. About a mile from the river, Gage's units would have seen a hillock that rose to the right of their line of advance. It was one of the most notable features of the land's topography. An appreciation of the advantages such a position afforded surely could not have eluded the experienced Gage, who must have considered dispatching a strong detachment to occupy this strategic land feature. Standard military practice would have advised such a course of action but, with no enemy in sight and the most treacherous part of the advance already seemingly passed—the crossing of the second ford—Gage felt that such a measure would have unnecessarily retarded the advance of the army. Within a few minutes, therefore, this hill was bisecting his advance units as his men continued to push, unopposed, through the warm, tranquil forest. The soldiers were undoubtedly lulled by the serenity of the day and were secure in the knowledge that their weeks of heavy and excessive labor were soon to be broken by the triumphant accomplishment of this most arduous of missions. It was a brief illusion.

The complacency that may have lingered in Braddock's vanguard was very soon shattered by the approach of Gage's guides who came rushing towards his main force, having encountered Beaujeu's French-Indian detachment. Harry Gordon, who had ridden forward to meet the guides (possibly to discuss the nature of the terrain that lay in the army's advance), was able to confirm their startled reports that the French and Indians were at hand. It was a shock encounter and one which took the British completely by surprise. Gordon, reflecting the unexpectedness of the moment, would estimate this enemy force to be around 300 men strong. In reality, it was far larger.[23]

Beaujeu, an experienced bush fighter who had employed scouts in front of the French army, appears to have known exactly how to respond to the collision of the two armies (as did his native allies). He motioned his men to disperse into the woods and they quickly advanced along the British flanks. The British too had started to recover their poise and Gage's detachment began pouring several volleys into the French force (though whether they or the French fired first is still an issue of contention). In terms of casualties, this fire did little damage as the distance between the forces—200 yards—meant that the smooth-bore muskets of the redcoats were acting well beyond their useful range. One of those who did fall in this initial outpouring of fire was, ironically, the French commander Daniel de Beaujeu. With his death, command of the French army would pass to his second in command, Jean-Daniel Dumas.

Many historians have quoted the latter in their accounts of this initial encounter of the battle and as such have attributed the victory of the French and Indians to the leadership of this very capable officer. From Dumas, we are led to believe that,

> In the first moment of combat, one hundred militiamen—one half of the French forces—shamefully turned tail, shouting "Every man for himself!"... This retreat encouraged the enemy... On the enemy's third discharge of musketry, Monsieur de Beaujeu was killed... It was then Monseigneur, that by word and gesture I sought to rally the few soldiers who remained. I advanced, with an assurance born of despair. My platoon gave forth with a withering fire that astonished the enemy. It grew imperceptibly, and the Indians, seeing that my attack had caused the enemy to stop shouting, returned to me...[24]

Herein lays a quandary common to many histories. Men of power, influence or status frequently seek to glorify themselves and their actions in the pursuit of self-advancement. Unsurprisingly, therefore, British accounts of this initial engagement were rather different. The French-Indian force did not disperse pell-mell after the initial British volleys but instead, having immediately deployed along the army's flanks, began a withering fire upon the British van. This was corroborated by the post-battle accounts of Harry Gordon and the batman of Captain Robert Cholmley (who was deployed with the grenadiers of the advanced guard), the former stating that,

> As soon as the Indians perceived our Grenadiers, they Dispersed themselves & run along our right and left flanks. The Advanc'd party Coll: Gage ordered to form, which Most of them Did with the front rank upon the ground & Begun firing, which they continued for several minutes, Altho' the Indians very soon Dispers'd Before their front & fell upon the flank parties.[25]

Dumas's role, therefore, was to participate in, and at least *try* to exert some control over, an improvised plan that—in its implementation—rested on the forest-fighting acumen of the Native American element of the French force. Indeed, it is clear from Gordon's evidence that, from the outset, this was a distinctly American-Indian battle in which the tactical evolution of the encounter perfectly resembled indigenous practices of war. Perhaps in earlier delaying the French plan through negotiations and conferences, the Indian elements of the French army (its most numerous segment) were deliberately allowing the British time to cross the Monongahela and advance onto terrain that resembled, in many ways, traditional local hunting grounds.

The more conventional element of the Franco-Indian force played an important role too. Indeed, the deployment of the more conventional *Troupes de la Marine* in the path of the British advance likely did dispel any panic that may have engulfed some of the less experienced Canadians. It has been suggested that the colony regulars were deployed in a trench or ravine along the front of the British advance, though this, again, is a matter of conjecture. The disciplined counter-fire of these soldiers would have enabled the irregulars who filed along the flanks of Braddock's advanced guard to properly position themselves and take a careful aim at Gage's men from the relative safety provided by trees, fallen logs and other natural advantages. As Robert Cholmley's batman would lament, the British fought an enemy who was virtually invisible to the soldiers in the ranks, "If we saw five or six at one time [it] was a great sight."[26] Another eyewitness would later claim that, "the French and Indians crept about in small parties so that the Fire was quite around us, and in all the Time I never saw one, nor could I on Enquiry find any one who saw ten together."[27]

The fire of the French-Indian marksmen had a very tangible effect on the hard-pressed men of the advanced guard. Thomas Gage, its commander, would later claim, in an effort to alleviate the censure of his conduct emanating from the influential pen of Robert Orme, that the army began to disintegrate even before this firing began. According to Gage, on first hearing of the enemy's approach, "the guard in our van came to the right-about, but, by the activity of the officer who commanded them, were stopped from running in, and prevailed on to face again." It was at this point that he seems to have realized the importance of the hillock on the army's right, "The detachment was ordered to fix their bayonets with the intention of gaining a hill upon our right." Unfortunately, "not one platoon could be prevailed upon to stir from its line of march, and a visible terror and confusion appeared amongst the men." At the same time, the flanking parties were fired upon and the whole detachment "made ready, and notwithstanding the opposition made by the officers, they threw away their fire, when, I am certain, scarcely two of the men [French-Indians] could be seen by them."[28] Gage was clearly attempting to minimize his role in the defeat. Ultimately, however, it was his failure to properly secure the hillock before the chance encounter with Beaujeu's force that gave the French and Indians a distinctive tactical advantage over the British army. From this elevated position, the former were able to pour a withering fire down upon their adversaries. This was matched by the intensity and relative accuracy of the fire of those men posted along the army's flanks which crippled the British where they stood. Once this strategic linchpin had been lost, the nature of the French-Indian ambush made a concerted effort to regain the hill all but impossible, as officers were targeted and killed before they could rally sufficient men to launch any counterattack. Those men who were eventually deployed in attempts to wrest this elevation from the French were quickly forced to retreat from the galling fire that smashed their ranks from front, flank and rear.

Indeed, even at this early stage of the battle, officers were choice targets for the French-Indian force. Gage would claim that 15 out of 18 officers and 150 out of the 300 men who formed the vanguard would be killed or wounded in the preliminary stages of the engagement. Unsurprisingly therefore, within minutes of their chance encounter with the French and Indians, their numbers badly diminished and their enemies deployed in their favored arc formation around them, Gage's men began to retreat. As they did so, they quickly collided with the working party, commanded by Sir John St. Clair, that was advancing to their rear; the whole becoming intertwined and providing an even easier mass of targets for the French and Indians. This was the initial phase of the telescoping of Braddock's army that is so often described in histories of this battle. The mixing of these units would have done little to help Gage restore order to his battered troops and would have added to the confusion of the moment. Being further slaughtered by the murderous fire of the French and Indians as they stood huddled in a mass, the advanced guard was unable to hold its ground for long and retreated for a second time.

Braddock's reaction to this initial encounter was swift and matched the severity of the moment. He first sent a subordinate forward to gather intelligence on the commotion up-front. This was standard military procedure and was advised by Humphrey Bland in his manual-come-soldier's gospel, *A Treatise of Military Discipline*.[29] When this officer failed to return, Braddock took more direct action. According to Robert Orme, his aide de camp, the general decided to divide his army and launch a counterattack. Eight hundred men—three hundred from the main body (which was around five hundred strong) and the entire advance guard (which, unknown to Braddock, was already retreating)—were to march forward under the command of Colonel Burton and drive off the French. The remainder of the main body, including the flanking parties were, "to be left for the defence of the Artillery and baggage, posted in such a manner as to secure them from any attack or insults."[30]

It would have taken Burton some time to properly deploy these units but, upon doing so, he immediately moved forward to support the advance guard. Unfortunately, after advancing a quarter of a mile, Burton's men collided with Gage's retreating force. According to Orme, this fateful event occurred while Burton was deploying his troops in preparation for an attack on the hillock that Gage had earlier neglected. This was a wise move as the hill was already providing a source of fire that peppered Burton's advancing units. Additionally, had he captured the hill, Burton may well have been able to divide the French-Indian forces and throw them into confusion. Gage, however, contested Orme's charges; the latter was a friend of Burton and an antagonist of Gage; the vanguard's hapless commander suspected, with some reason, that Orme's testimony was driven as much by politics as it was by the pursuit of truth. For Gage, it was not just the vanguard that was in a state of confusion as it retreated, but the whole army had been thrown into disarray by the fire that now engaged them from all sides. In an advertisement in the *Pennsylvania*

Gazette, he would counter Orme's earlier report, written for the very same paper, which blamed the confusion of the vanguard for the army's eventual defeat,

> It is thought proper to inform the Publick, that in the Account given of the late Action on the 9th of July, wherin it is said, that the Detachment of Three Hundred (which was the Van Guard of the Army) fell back on the main Body, and put it in such Confusion that no military Expedient could retrieve, is a Mistake; the main Body being in Confusion before it joined the above Detachment.[31]

Irrespective of who was right and wrong on this manner, most officers, and latterly, historians, believe that this secondary phase of the telescoping of Braddock's army marks the point at which widespread panic began to spread through the rank and file. It is from this point that the circumspection of the regulars begins, reflected by numerous subsequent histories of the battle that depict the British soldier of the eighteenth century as the mindless automaton that was virtually incapable of adapting to the North American environment.

That the soldiers eventually did panic and flee the battlefield is beyond dispute but, contrary to the scathing denunciations of men such as Adam Stephen and even George Washington, considering the constitution of Braddock's army and the sheer happenstance of the battle of July 9, such a sentiment is unfair and is not wholly reflective of the reality of this typically North American (or American-Indian) engagement. The real issue that many have overlooked is whether this panic was symptomatic of an archaic military force encountering New World warfare that it simply could not match in a New World environment; or whether problems emergent from the integration of provincial soldiers and units into a British army needs to be reconsidered.

Certainly, it is evident that the onset of panic among the soldiers may not have been as instantaneous (or merely battle-related) as it is frequently depicted to have been; and that its roots were actually planted far earlier in the campaign. Indeed, a post-battle report written by Colonel Dunbar and Thomas Gates would help confirm this assertion. Dunbar's and Gage's report is also substantiated by two other accounts, written by non-commissioned participants (thus lacking the prejudices of the officer class), that suggest that many soldiers retained their composure for some time during the battle.[32]

The first of these was provided by Private Duncan Cameron, a veteran soldier who had previously served in Scotland against the forces of Bonnie Prince Charlie and who, on July 9, 1755, was stationed in the advance guard of Braddock's army; he was thus among the first British troops to encounter the French and Indian forces led by Daniel Beaujeu. Cameron's testimony, a very rare instance of a mid-eighteenth century private soldier documenting his experiences of war, is certainly not a complete account of the Battle of the Monongahela. In the first moments of the engagement he was wounded, rendered unconscious and, in the brief period during which the British retreated and the French advanced (leaving the wounded and dead where they lay), was able to regain his senses long enough to conceal himself in a hollow tree—from where he witnessed the remainder of the battle. Nonetheless, the evidence he does provide concerning the conduct of the regular troops would hardly suggest that, at least in the initial phases of the battle, the British soldiers were in any way panicked. From the experienced Cameron's perspective, on first encountering the French and Indians, "Our officers as well as Men generally behaved well; and all the Blame that can be properly laid, is in not having proper Scouts [by this he likely means Native American scouts] out to have prevented our falling into such an Ambush."[33] Cameron, however, would not have witnessed the telescoping of the army.

Robert Cholmley's batman *was* in possession of all of his faculties and was in a position to witness the infamous collision of the van and main body. His candid description highlighted how, "We was drawn up in large Bodies together, a ready mark." It is not certain whether he is describing troops in formation or a mass of bodies but he does later go on to claim that, "Having only death before us made the men fight almost longer than they was able." The general good behavior of at least some of the soldiers is also exemplified in his relation of the wounding of a Captain John Conyngham, after which his men "seeing his danger, rushed between the savages and him and carried him in triumph from the spot"; hardly an attitude associated with an "every man for himself" disregard for comrades.[34] As mentioned, as valuable as this testimony is, Cholmley's batman does not actually describe what "large bodies" of men actually means; he does not state whether the soldiers were a huddled mass or an ordered formation. Neither does he affirm whether the fire of the British was coordinated or whether the men were taking aimless, desperate, pot-shots at their unseen enemy. "Large bodies" would mean that the troops were huddled together in a dense body of soldiers which was a result of the telescoping of Gage's and Burton's men. These men may have fought on in this orderless mass but they were doing so from an instinct of self-preservation. From a textbook military perspective, the men were panicked; command and control had been lost. But this was not an immediate collapse; rather, it was a consequence of the unique circumstances that the men were forced to endure on that particular day.

Whether this was a peculiarity of sending regular soldiers to fight a distinctly irregular campaign is, as mentioned, highly questionable. There are, in fact, many other factors to consider which also suggest that non-battlefield failings significantly contributed to the army's collapse. The post-battle report of Thomas Gage and Colonel Dunbar, based on interviews with the men of the rank-and-file, supports this reasoning suggesting that,

> 1st: They [the men] were greatly Harrass'd by dutys unequal to their numbers; Dispirited by want of Sufficient Provisions, and not being allowed time to dress the little they had, with nothing to Drink but Water, and that Often Scarce and Bad
>
> 2nd: The frequent Conversations of the Provincial Troops and Country people was, that if they engaged the Indians in their European Manner of fighting, they would be Beat, and this some of their Officers Declared as their Opinion, and one of them to Coll Dunbar on the Retreat, for which he Severely Reprimanded him
>
> 3rd: The want of Indians or other irregulars to give timely Notice of the Enemy's Approach, having only three or four guides for Scouts.
>
> Lastly the Novelty of an invisible enemy and the Nature of the Country, which was entirely a forest.[35]

It is points 1 and 2 of this report that provide particularly interesting reading as they highlight notable accusations that are often marginalized or deliberately overlooked. The causes of point 1 have, in fact, been covered in the preceding chapter of this book, which highlighted the logistical challenges Braddock faced in the colonies. Though in some part a reflection of the challenges posed by European North America's natural frontiers, Braddock's supply headaches were in great measure the fault of provincial governors, assemblies, the British ministry, local contractors and, to some extent, local populations who jostled for influence, concession, fiscal advantage or conscience at a time when the common good should have been at the forefront of their concerns. That Braddock's campaign was severely slowed by the absence of a strong, central authority within the colonies at this time (exacerbated, it must be reiterated, by years of metropolitan neglect) also seems to have been lost on many historians who see this as a quintessential British military catastrophe. In truth, Braddock and his army were easy scapegoats. By apportioning virtually all blame to these men, the widespread failures of the colonists—and indeed the metropolitan government—whose factionalism and ignorance of North American affairs (in the case of the latter) did so much to hinder the unquestionably limited, yet conventionally competent, Edward Braddock, could be conveniently overlooked.

Point 2 of Dunbar and Gage's report is very telling and highlights something that really does demand greater credence than it is given by many histories of Braddock's defeat. This is particularly true of those American historians inclined, to return to Dallas Irving's famous quote, to depict Braddock's defeat as one of "Colonel Blimps and stupid brutes," getting their comeuppance in North America. What will now follow is an examination of the role provincial civilians and soldiers played in the battle on the banks of the Monongahela, and what is to be found are mixed results. This stands in contrast to many conventional American histories, which often lead one to believe that colonial soldiers were virtually blameless *victims* of the *British* defeat of July 9, 1755.

"THE STORYS THAT WERE HEARD..." FRONTIER TALES AND THE COLLAPSE OF BRITISH MORALE: "BLUE ON BLUE" PSYWAR

Contemporaneously, it was the staunchly parochial Adam Stephen who epitomized many colonial (and later American) interpretations of frontier warfare and the British Army's attempts to grapple with it in North America. For Stephen, as with many of his countrymen, the cause of Edward Braddock's disaster lay in one quarter. Accordingly,

> The British Troops were thunderstruck to feel the Effect of a Heavy Fire, & see no Enemy; they threw away their Fire in a most indiscriminate Manner, and shamefully turned their Backs on a few Savages and Canadeans... They kept in a mere huddle in spite of the most ardent Endeavours of many brave officers... Shame unto the infamous Dogs![36]

This was an opinion echoed, to some extent, by the legendary Daniel Boone who, in contrast to Stephen, was far more willing to condemn Braddock and his "Old World" tactics. Stephen's anti-British virulence, at least as applied to the rank-and-file redcoats, forms the basis of archetypal American exceptionalism. It disparages the regulars for their cowardice and places blame for the defeat squarely at the feet of Braddock's men. Stephen, however, was only a bit-part witness during the battle. His position in the rear of Braddock's force meant that he could not have seen the telescoping of Gage's and Burton's units, nor the unfolding events emergent from this misfortune. George Washington, who was at Braddock's side throughout the engagement, espoused views similar to Stephen. Washington did not claim that the panic of the soldiers was caused by the collision of Gages' and Burton's men (like Stephen, he could not have witnessed it) but did suggest that the soldiers themselves were to blame for the loss of the day. Accordingly, the regulars were eventually "struck with such a deadly Panick, that nothing but confusion and disobedience of order's prevail'd amoungst them." The American troops were said to have been praised by Braddock who, contemplating his defeat and impending death after the battle, apparently finally recognized the folly of engaging Indians in the European mode.[37] As mentioned, In many subsequent histories, this sentiment is echoed all too readily and the provincial allies of the redcoats are the few among Braddock's army who emerge from the battle with any real honor.

One detects the hand of self-interest in the ambitious young Washington's recollections, as he himself had sought a commission in the British Army—without success. In the months and years that followed the engagement, he also actively campaigned for the regiment he would later command, the Virginia Regiment, to be amalgamated into the regular army as a full-time British regiment—but again, was frustrated in this endeavor. Nevertheless, it is still, considering the credence given to such views, important to consider whether the sentiments of colonists like Washington and Stephen were sufficient to explain the root cause of Braddock's rout. Thus, to ascertain the accuracy of such claims, it is now appropriate to return to the evidence of Dunbar and Gage that, in addition to other accounts, came from the mouths of the British *rank-and-file*.

Indeed, these perspectives do make interesting reading as, from the viewpoint of the "British" element of Braddock's army, the behavior of the Americans (both martial auxiliaries and civilians) appears not to have been as free of fault as men such as Washington, Stephen, and those historians who adopt and utilize their evidence often suggest. Even before the battle had commenced, American civilians (and soldiers within Braddock's army) had fed the redcoats many a lurid campfire tale about the barbarity of Indians and the hellish torments that would be unleashed upon enemies who fell into their hands.[38] Though such stories could be dismissed as banter among allies, the post-battle report of Gage and Dunbar unequivocally indicates that this was an important factor in the army's defeat. When the soldiers found themselves surrounded in a large-scale classical Indian ambush and were exposed to the psychologically debilitating "infernal yell" of the Indians' war cries, in addition to the fact that so many were being cut down by the murderous fire of their enemy, such campfire gossip (and the images it evoked of the relatively few comrades who had earlier been captured, mutilated and left for all to see as the army advanced), virtually guaranteed that the British had, to all intents and purposes, lost the psychological phase of the Battle of the Monongahela.[39]

According to Robert Chomley's diligent batman, this fear of "Barbarous Usage" by the Indians made the men determined to fight to the bitter end, but such a resolve may not have been a good thing. The soldiers, eventually, began to fight on instinct and not in the way they had been trained, a factor that made their endeavors both futile and dangerous, undermining their officer's attempts to restore order amidst the chaos of the telescoping of the army. Tellingly, these conclusions were corroborated by another British witness who surmised the effect of American tales and stories on the morale of the redcoats: "The men from what *storys* they had heard of the Indians, in regard to their scalping; and mohawking, were so panick Struck, that their officers had little or no Command over them."[40] In layman's terms, the essential command structure that was so pivotal to armies of the eighteenth century broke down disastrously; the men, without clear orders, resorted to impulse and shot off their muskets in a loose and uncoordinated fashion. They were, as their formations disintegrated into a mass of tangled and terrified humanity, an armed mob firing blindly at unseen assailants who picked them off with seeming impunity. Yet, the cause of this was not simply British incompetence or even the unexpectedness of the collision with Beaujeu's force (not forgetting the fact that such an encounter favored the hit and run tactics of his largely Native American-Canadian command). Just as potently, propaganda and tales (merely banter to some) undermined British morale before battle had been joined and its devastating effects should not be understated.[41]

If we are to believe Gage and Dunbar, this was undoubtedly a critical factor in the collapse of morale. I would suggest that the campfire tales of the colonists who fed them to British soldiers in reality were little different to modern-day "psychological warfare." Indeed, even in the twenty-first century, battles are often preceded by psychological warfare (PSYWAR) that seeks to sap an enemy's will to fight. The effects of a successful PSYWAR operation will often result in an underlying fear of an opponent that can manifest itself in battlefield debilitation, paralysis and eventual flight; particularly when the unfamiliar or the subject of fear (American Indians in this case) is encountered at an inopportune and unexpected time, and in an environment which maximizes the advantages such an enemy possesses. Braddock's regular soldiers, exposed to tales of Native American barbarity (and their almost mystical forest-fighting capabilities) prior to the "Battle of the Wilderness," undoubtedly suffered from battlefield debilitation and the paralysis of command, which exacerbated, and ultimately resulted in their precipitous flight.

The Americans would later claim that their counseling was not intended to terrify the men but to educate and warn them of the fate they could expect if they tried fighting the Indians in the manner of the "Old World." In hindsight this was a calamitous underestimation of the impact of tales and stories that were, in reality, a case of blue on blue PSYWAR. Unfortunately, such advice was exacerbated by the reversal of American soldiers to a more familiar backcountry mode of war at a time of spreading bewilderment. According to the previously-cited anonymous British officer, upon commencement of the engagement, "ye American Troops, tho' without any orders run up immediately, some behind Trees, and others into ye Ranks, and put ye whole into confusion."[42] Those who threw themselves into the ranks seemed to have advised the regulars that their best hope of survival lay behind the trees that concealed the French and Indians. For the terrified soldiers of the 44th and 48th, this would have added to the confusion of the moment. Even though the trees provided potential cover, they were also the skulking places of their enemy and were the bastions of the death and destruction being unleashed upon them from all sides. The instinct of the British regulars was to obey orders and stay in line and yet, seeing comrades falling all around, and being urged on by their colonial allies, they would also have felt a compulsion to take cover. Obedience is certainly what their officers would have been expecting them to show and, as the battle progressed, Braddock himself was said to have beaten back into line those soldiers who attempted to follow the Americans' example by taking to the trees. Nevertheless, as units became intermingled and officers lost contact with men, or were killed and disabled in ever greater numbers, the resort to instinct must have been irresistible for many British soldiers—particularly those who had been recruited in America.

Panic, Command-Level Collapse and the Ultimate Effect of Friendly PSYWAR

With scenes of panic and terror now unfolding, reordering Burton's and Gage's men was a hugely important, though notably difficult, task. Many senior officers, such as Sir John St. Clair, who commanded the working party, had been disabled or killed and the men, in their confusion, "were sometimes 20 or 30 deep, and he thought himself securest, who was in the centre."[43] Perhaps many soldiers, seeing no relief amidst the trees surrounding them, had adapted to their American allies' advice and felt that the only option was to take cover behind their comrades.

It was now that Braddock himself attempted to exert some influence over the fray, first by ordering an aide to bring intelligence of the commotion up front and then by riding forward himself to take direct command of the battle; leaving Sir Peter Halkett in command of the baggage. According to Orme, when Braddock arrived on the scene, chaos was to be found everywhere, but the general had enough clarity of thought to try to separate the men—first into their proper regiments and then into platoons commanded by their own officers. As Orme related,

> The whole were now got together in great confusion. The colours were advanced in different places, to separate the men of the two regiments. The General ordered the officers to Endeavour to form the men, and to tell them off into small divisions and to advance with them; but neither entreaties nor threats could prevail.[44]

The general's bravery on the day of battle could never be questioned. He was constantly galloping along the perimeters of the mêlée giving orders with no concern for his own personal safety. Wearing a garish scarlet uniform, he was an easy target for Native American and French marksmen and the fact that he lost four horses during the battle, yet mounted a different steed each time, without hesitation, shows the very real strain of courage that, without question, he possessed. His tactical reasoning, from the perspective of a British officer, was also logical; it followed, as closely as was possible considering the environmental parameters of the landscape in which his army was engaged, the advice laid down by Humphrey Bland's *Treatise of Military Discipline*.

The general's industry was matched by the courage of the officers of his army who tried in vain to execute his orders. Many stepped out from among the huddled mass of soldiers in order to create rallying points for their men but, being so conspicuous in their bright scarlet coats, gold trimmed hats and silver gorgets, made easy and high-profile targets for the French and Indians. The fact that the army stood for over three hours under intense and debilitating fire is not only testimony to the desperation of the men who were fighting for their lives but is also a tribute to officers who remained overwhelmingly calm once battle commenced. If *they* had panicked and fled, one could only have expected the soldiers to follow.

Unfortunately, these efforts proved fruitless. The men had been reduced to such a state of terror that they would not be prevailed upon to attack— though they did remain on the battlefield for a little over three hours. Despite their clear contribution to the panic that gripped the regular rank and file, the behavior of many of the colonial soldiers who served in the provincial units had a notable effect on their enemy. This was particularly true of those who formed the rearguard under Sir Peter Halkett.[45] At first ordered to fight in a regular manner, after the death of the very popular Halkett, they soon reverted to fighting "Indian style" and enjoyed some success engaging the French and Indians in this mode. Unlike the Americans who had been left with Colonel Dunbar—the weaker elements of Braddock's American recruits—they were unquestionably of high caliber, as evinced by the tenacity with which they resisted the French-Indian ambuscade.

Nonetheless, for Braddock and his regular soldiers, the sight of the Americans supposedly fleeing (as they saw it) into the trees was a cause of grave concern. Considering American *petite guerre* unmilitary, Braddock reacted to their movements with virulent hostility. According to Colonel Thomas Dunbar who received, it must be added, his reports third-hand from eyewitnesses, many soldiers of all hues had, in fact, "insisted much to be allowed to take to the Trees, which the General denied and stormed much, calling them Cowards, and even went so far as to strike them with his own Sword for attempting the trees."[46] Braddock, rigidly attached to his own military schooling, felt the solution to the chaos was to detach the men into platoons commanded by their officers; something that needed a strong central order—impossible to enforce if the men were dispersed throughout the forest.

There were other concerns that a haphazard reaction to irregular warfare stoked. For instance, numerous eyewitnesses would later recall how the British regulars, seeing puffs of smoke from the surrounding forest, mistook this friendly fire for that of their enemy, unleashing devastating volleys upon their provincial allies, killing many in the process. In such an incident, "Capt. Waggoner, with 170 Virginians, went up to where the

Enemy was hid and routed them: But O unhappy! Our Infatuateds seeing a Smoke, fired and killed him with several of his Men."[47] It was not only the Virginians who were afflicted by "blue on blue" fire. According to one officer,

> The confusion and destruction was so great, that the men fired irregularly, one behind another, and by this way of proceeding many more of our men were killed by their own party than by the Enimy, as appeared afterwards by the bullets that the surgeons extracted from the wounded, they being distinguished from the French and Indian bullets by their size... Amoung the wounded men, there were two for one of these bullets extracted by the Surgeons, and the wounds were chiefly in the back parts of the body, so it must also been among the kill'd.[48]

Supporting this claim, a second officer would write that,

> If any got a shott at one [an Indian], the fire immediately ran through ye whole line, though they saw nothing butt trees; the whole Body was frequently divided into several parties, and then they were sure to fire on one another. The greatest part of the Men who were behind trees were either killed or wounded by our own people, even one or two officers were killed by their own Plattoon.[49]

Here it can be seen that all of the elements that contributed to Braddock's defeat had fallen into place. The environmental conditions for an ambush that maximized the advantages of *petite guerre* were encountered when the British army—many of whose soldiers had only received three months real training in America—were least expecting it. Concurrently, a seasoned officer, preferring haste and perhaps lulled into overconfidence (as indeed, the whole army appears to have been) had overlooked a pivotal tactical feature of the terrain. The psychological debilitations of campfire gossip (in reality friendly PSYWAR) conspired with prevailing topographical conditions, while the construct of the French army arrayed against the British maximized the impact these features had on the engagement. During the battle, the effects of such realities were felt very swiftly as the Native Americans and Canadians, the former clearly directing the engagement by this stage (but nonetheless aided by the stoicism of the *Troupes de la Marine*), dominated the tactical evolution of the encounter; in basic terms, ensuring the battle was fought on their conditions. The advance guard and main body of the British had collided. The rearguard, half a mile behind the main, was also being attacked and despite its fierce resistance, there were fears that the army would be surrounded, further undermining morale among a force that could not communicate sufficiently amidst the chaos. The troops were completely intermingled and had, in many cases, lost contact with their officers; with the result that unit cohesion, so central to *Frederician* armies, had broken down. The men were trapped in a murderous arc of fire that swept along their front, flank and rear. With their own flanking parties destroyed or driven in, the huddled mass of men was being incessantly raked by the fire of hidden foes that were virtually invisible in the forested environment. It was, in military terms, and to use a well-known cliché, a perfect storm compounded, at its core, by sheer bad luck.

Despite the efforts of officers such as Colonel Burton, the army could not rally in sufficient numbers to drive the French and Indians from the hillock that dominated much of the battlefield. Edward Braddock himself, though undoubtedly brave and indifferent to his own safety, was intent upon reinforcing martial order in the midst of chaos and chided, in the harshest possible terms, those who attempted to fight the enemy in their own manner and who were, ironically, enjoying the greatest success. Worse still, on the retreat of the van, the French had captured its two six-pounder cannon, which had proven useless against their intended targets but which could, if properly serviced, have wreaked havoc among Braddock's mass of tangled men.

Regardless of this awful situation, it seems that at various stages in the battle, small groups of men were prevailed upon to follow the orders of their officers; undermining somewhat the aspersions of cowardice so often leveled against the rank and file of the 44th and 48th. Braddock, acknowledging the importance of organizing a counterattack, was anything but timorous in the face of this deadly ambuscade and seems to have recognized the importance of the hillock to the right of the British column that Gage had earlier neglected.[50] Unfortunately, the attempts of his officers and soldiers to dislodge the French and Indians from this topographical linchpin, as well as their other positions around the army, met with little success. The core reasons for this were related by Colonel Gage,

> General Braddock tried all methods to draw the men out of this confusion, made several efforts to recover the cannon, as also to drive the enemy from our flanks, as likewise to gain possession of the hill already mentioned. Some few men were at times prevailed on to draw out for this purpose, but before

they had marched twenty yards, would fall back into a line of march by files, and proceed to attack in this manner, till an officer, or perhaps a man or two, should be struck down, and then the rest immediately gave way; the men would never make one bold attack, though encouraged to it by the enemy always giving way, whenever they advanced even on the most faint attack.[51]

Gage was describing the effects of a classic, well executed Indian ambush. Unwilling to face the redcoats muzzle to muzzle, the French and Indians merely melted away and returned to the offensive from different positions. The British, once casualties had been inflicted, were too demoralized to continue their attacks and returned to the ranks of huddled and battered comrades after numbers of them had been cut down by the unseen fire of their enemies.

As the battle wore on to its horrific conclusion, the French and Indians became increasingly emboldened and gradually began to enclose the British. Robert Cholmley's batman noted how, towards the end of the engagement, "They began to Inclose us more and more till they had Nigh Inclosed us in." Concurrently, he, reflecting the tales that originated among the Americans in the army "expected Nothing but death for Every One of us, for they had us surround[ed] all but a little in the Rear, which they strove for with all their Force."[52] By now the British position was, in reality, hopeless.

After three hours of fighting, the army's position was indeed desperate, if not mortal. Braddock, focusing on the tactical pivot of the battle, ordered one more attempt to be made against the hillock that had hitherto enabled French and Indian marksmen to unleash their debilitating fire upon his beleaguered army. It was to be his final command. Soon after issuing this order, he was shot from his horse and fatally wounded. According to Harry Gordon,

> The General Order'd the officers to Endeavor to tell off 150 men, & Advance up the hill to Dispossess the Enemy, & another party to Advance on the Left to support the two 12 pounders & Artillery people, who were in great Danger of Being Drove away By the Enemy, at that time in possession of the 2 field pieces of the Advanc'd party This was the Generals Last Order...[53]

Led by intrepid Colonel Burton, the assault was doomed to failure.

The officers leading the charge showed all of the determination they had displayed throughout the engagement. Through their industry the attacks were launched but, "the Enemy's fire at the time very much Encreasing, & a Number of officers who were Rushing on in the front to Encourage the men Being killed & wounded, there was Nothing to Be seen But the Utmost panick & Confusion amoungst the Men."[54]

This was to be the last offensive undertaken by the British on that day. Many of the soldiers had now fled, their terror heightened by the fact that Braddock himself had since been mortally wounded.[55] Their panic was matched by the wagoners of the supply train who 'unhitched' and fled on horseback, leaving crucial supplies marooned on the battlefield. With the army collapsing, a retreat was ordered. It quickly turned into a full-scale melee as the exhausted and terrified troops, fled for their lives striving for the sanctuary of the Monongahela River they had crossed so triumphantly just over three hours before. The descent from ordered retreat to absolute rout was unbridled and chaotic. It became virtually impossible for the surviving officers to exert any control over the broken remnants of the army. George Washington, who had served at Braddock's side during the engagement as an aide-de-camp, and who was, like his commander, exposed to all of the inherent dangers commensurate with this battle, vividly described this rout,

> At length, in despight of every effort to the contrary, [they] broke and run as Sheep before the Hounds, leav'g the Artillery, Ammunition, Provisions, and, every individual thing we had with us prey to the Enemy; and when we endeavour'd to rally them in hopes of regaining our invaluable loss, it was with as much success as if we had attempted to have stop'd the wild Bears of the Mountains.[56]

Colonel Burton, badly wounded during the final assault on the deadly hillock, would, along with the young Washington, try to rally some of the fleeing men on the far side of the Monongahela; some resistance was made, but it was a token gesture as any semblance of order had by now evaporated. The flight, continued by Colonel Dunbar who would, at Braddock's command, destroy the reminder of the army's stores at his encampment (near Jumonville's Glen) and continue the disorderly, and some may say precipitate retreat, would only halt when the remnants of the army reached Philadelphia.

For the British, the Battle of the Monongahela was a complete disaster. Out of the approximately 1300 men of the flying column who marched into battle with Braddock on July 9, 456 were killed and 422 wounded.

The officers suffered disproportionately high casualties in relation to their numbers, reflecting their courageous conduct throughout the engagement and the tactical pragmatism of the Canadians and Indians; 86 officers marched into battle on July 9–26 were killed, with 37 wounded.[57] Of the 54 women who followed the army into battle (serving as "washer women," nurses and cooks, among other roles), only four returned. Some of these captives would, however, be retrieved in Canada, being ransomed from the Indians by the French. Braddock would die five days into the retreat and was buried in the road that his army had constructed under so many debilitating strains. George Washington ordered the demoralized remnants of the Anglo-American expedition to march over his grave, effacing any sign of the tragic Braddock's final resting place. This was done to prevent the Indians exhuming and desecrating the general's body. Compared to the staggering British and American losses, French and Indian casualties were comparatively light. Eight Frenchmen were killed and four wounded. Their native allies lost 15 killed and 12 wounded.

The retreat itself was a hellish march that left a distinctive impression on those who witnessed it. For the soldiers left dying in the road as the army fled back to Dunbar's camp, the awful horrors of often mortal wounds must have been magnified by the fear of falling into the hands of vengeful Indians who, it was believed, showed little mercy to stricken enemies. As George Washington lamented, "The shocking Scenes which presented themselves in the Night's March are not to be described. The dead, dying, the groans, lamentation, and crys along the Road of the wounded for help... were enough to pierce a heart of adamant."[58]

The one mercy for the British was that the French and Indians did not pursue beyond the Monongahela River. Having driven their enemy from the battlefield, the Indians now sought their own "honors of war"—trophies, captives and scalps—all of which were powerful tokens of bravery and martial prowess that generated great esteem within their own communities. Having gained these testimonies of valor, the natives returned home to their tribal lands and, for many Frenchmen, this made the days following the battle particularly nerve-wracking; the question arose: What if the British returned? After all, there was still a very big and well supplied force under Colonel Thomas Dunbar out there that could rally and redeem their setback. Had they known their opponent's psyche they would have seen the folly of their fears.

For some of those Anglo-American survivors who did fall into native hands, there awaited, in a number of instances, a fate arguably far worse than an immediate death on the battlefield. James Smith, the young Virginian captured prior to the defeat on the Monongahela and held prisoner at Fort Duquesne, would recall the horrors he witnessed as the Indian allies of the French triumphantly paraded their spoils of war,

> About sundown I beheld a small part coming in with about a dozen prisoners, stripped naked, with their hands tied behind their backs, and their faces and parts of their bodies blacked; these prisoners they burned to death on the bank of the Allegheny river, opposite to the fort. I stood on the fort wall until I beheld them begin to burn one of these men; they tied him to a stake, and kept touching him with firebrands, red-hot irons &c., and he screamed in a most woeful manner; the Indians, in the meantime, yelling like infernal spirits.[59]

Beyond the terrible human cost of the campaign, the strategic and political implications of the defeat were very serious. On the battlefield lay a multitude of military supplies—cannon, powder and the like—some of which would be used by the French in subsequent years. Well over 500 horses and cattle, many slaughtered on the battlefield, as well as provisions and other valuable materials, were lost. Even more impressive were the munitions and supplies destroyed by Colonel Dunbar, at Braddock's behest it must be added, as he began his flight to Philadelphia. Most seriously of all were the contents of the thirty-odd wagons Braddock's army left to the French. In one of these was found the general's war chest, containing several thousand pounds. In another, the French retrieved Braddock's personal instructions from George II, the Duke of Cumberland and copies of his own papers. These provided a veritable intelligence bonanza as invaluable information about the campaigns of William Shirley and William Johnson in upper New York was gleaned from their contents. In addition, the French now had a spectacular propaganda coup that would prove to the world that the British, while espousing protestations of peace to the courts of Europe, were in fact preparing for war.[60]

WHY WAS BRADDOCK DEFEATED?

The conclusion to be drawn of Edward Braddock's defeat at the Battle of the Monongahela is that it had no single cause. Indeed, one could legitimately argue that its failure originated as much in the grandiose, but detached, strategic designs of the Duke of Cumberland, or the antipathy and political ambition of colonial governors and assemblies (who had hardly laid the ground for the huge logistical effort that was required to facilitate Braddock's exhausting advance across approximately 110 miles of mountainous and forested terrain), as it was on the military catastrophe that befell Braddock and his unfortunate soldiers.

The British *were* slower to evolve to the nature of the unfolding engagement; their tactics, at the point of conflict, were based on a rigid adherence to European formations and understandings of war but, at the end of July 9, 1755, such doctrines were beaten by irregular, very much Native American, principles of battle. Nonetheless, British defeat on the Monongahela was hardly an instance of wholly professional, well-trained, choice British regiments receiving an absolute drubbing at the hands of the French and Indians. Certainly, the 44th and 48th regiments were not the best of British and were in fact undermanned Irish regiments dispatched to America because George II would not allow mainland regiments to be sent to the New World. Braddock's British units were thus, considering the very nature of the Irish establishment, seriously under-strength and were only brought to their full capacity by draftees from other regiments and numerous *American* recruits—men who had, by any measure, little, if any experience of service in the British Army.[61]

Certainly, we can calculate the caliber of many of Braddock's American enlistees by considering the fact that those left with Colonel Dunbar at the Little Meadows, and who were considered of such insufficient quality that it was thought best to split the army and leave them behind, were mainly Americans. Neither were the men, both British and American, particularly well trained. The "Old World" soldiers, taken from peacetime Irish county cantonments were in need of considerable improvement, and the same was true of the draftees provided by donor regiments. Additionally, the colonial soldiers intended to fill regimental gaps were essentially raw recruits raised when Braddock arrived in America. Time limitations on the ground meant that Braddock did not have the scope he needed to properly bring the men up to scratch; despite the very evident efforts (some of which were successful) he made to improve their professionalism.[62] Through these factors alone we see that the traditional American depiction of Braddock's defeat as a bloody nose for conventional British martial tradition, does not match the real issues and complexities associated with this unique campaign.

Braddock's field dispositions clearly adhered to the expected military protocols of the period – both prior to, and during, July 9, 1755. Despite the claims of Stanley Pargellis and Peter Russell, his troops were not in any way bundled together; there was at least a quarter of a mile between the advanced guard and main body.[63] If anything, one could, if quoting Bland's rules in any denunciation of Braddock's tactical dispositions, argue that the general's main body was too distant from his advanced guard. This in itself, however, would be overly harsh and would show scant appreciation of the logistical challenges posed by a campaign in the American backcountry. Bland, after all, saw logistical operations from the perspective of a soldier who had served on mainland Europe, where there were cities, towns, roads and ports that were numerous and proximous to any army on the march. In the Ohio Valley in 1755, none of these existed and Braddock's division was forced to haul a significant supply train along a narrow road that his men had hacked through forests and over mountains and swamps to the banks of the Monongahela. This logistical element, which had to be defended, required that his tactical dispositions reflect a uniquely American environmental reality; one based on a necessity that few (if any) of his contemporaries would have encountered in more conventional military settings.

Returning to the charge that Braddock's defeat was caused by the appalling behavior of his British redcoats, this is also overstated and unfair for, undoubtedly, there were other, often overlooked factors at play too. Indeed, the conduct of the Americans who served within Braddock's ranks and, to some extent, in the independent provincial companies, contributed significantly to the demoralization of Braddock's "Old World" troops—both prior to and during the Battle of the Monongahela. A factor which is not given as much weight as it should in many analyses of the Monongahela defeat was the demoralizing effect of the lurid American-originated tales of Indian barbarity fed to the British by their colonial allies throughout the campaign. On July 9, 1755, such frontier tales, combined with the sudden collision of the British and Indian-French force, in addition to the environmental parameters of the battle, contributed to a unique storm of terror among the British rank-and-file; in short, every negative factor that could have befallen Braddock and his regulars fell into place at once. Fundamentally, even before a shot had been fired, the British Army had lost the psychological phase of the Battle of the Monongahela, though few in the ranks would have acknowledged this prior to the engagement. Such an assessment is based not only on the post-battle report of Thomas Gage and Colonel Dunbar who, it will be remembered, interviewed ordinary soldiers to ascertain the reasons for the collapse of morale among the men, but also on the testimony of men such as Robert Cholmley's batman, who, unprompted, alluded to the impact of campfire tales on the spirits of the men.[64]

Further corroborating this evidence was an unnamed British officer who wrote that, "The men from what *storys* they had heard of the Indians" were so "panick Struck" that their officers had "little or no command over them."[65] The effect of this pre-battle psychological barrage, unleashed by American soldiers and civilians, is all too apparent. Further, it can be argued that the negative consequences of American actions on July 9 did not end with Blue on Blue PSYWAR: the tactical variances between regular and colonial forces which emerged in the midst of battle created further problems for Braddock and his officers.

Again, we can here recall the testimony of serving soldiers who, in many cases, were less than impressed by the Americans' inclination to take to the trees in the face of the enemy. As our previously cited anonymous British officer would reflect, the effect of the colonial reversion to instinct—running "up immediately, some behind Trees, and others into the Ranks"—was to put the whole force into confusion. *Confusion* is the key word. Yes, the British regulars were already demoralized by their early encounters with the French and Indians. They had telescoped as a result of the surprise encounter with the Indians and French and had huddled together in ranks "20 to 30 deep."[66] However, this demoralization was clearly worsened by the irregular movements of colonial soldiers who undermined the instincts of subordination and discipline that characterized British martial tradition. They took away from officers, whose job it was to uphold these values, the ability to properly command and coordinate their men.

Likewise, it is easy to dismiss Braddock, who responded to such movements ruthlessly, as a wooden-headed martinet who refused, despite the expediency of doing so, to allow the Americans to fight in their own way. In reality, Braddock beat those he saw taking to the trees not because he was a stubborn and brutal disciplinarian, but because he feared the desertion of his army (desertion having been a problem throughout the campaign) and because such behavior ran contrary to everything he believed proper in a professional military force. For a 60-year-old eighteenth-century career British officer, the consequences of this "irregular behaviour," considering the education and advice he would have received from the manuals of men such as Humphrey Bland, was inevitable and shameful defeat. Ambushes and irregular foes were, as Bland himself had argued, best countered by professional, conventional and, most importantly, disciplined martial tactics.

Braddock, on the day of battle, followed as closely as circumstances allowed the doctrines of Bland's *Treatise on Military Discipline* (the gospel of all British officers at this time). Certainly, though Bland said nothing of Indian ambush, he would have stressed (by inference of his text) the importance of discipline and regularity against an enemy considered equally as "barbarous" as the Highlanders who had threatened the existence of the Hanoverian dynasty in 1746. The commander-in-chief, by following Bland's instructions, had done virtually everything that his profession required of him.

Ultimately, on July 9, 1755, Braddock was, quite frankly, unlucky. He was, as I have argued previously, a good conventional officer whose abilities were recognized by many of his contemporaries, including George Washington. As Charles Lee, one of the many participants in the future Revolutionary War who served with the general would attest,

> There will come a day (I hope) when justice will be done to this man's memory, who has left few behind him that are his Equals, in Courage, honesty and Zeal for the Publick, his death was a cruel stroke to us in particular, and a very unhappy stroke for the nation in general.[67]

The same circumspection applies to the belief that Braddock's Defeat was a *British* catastrophe. Braddock's defeat was far more complex than the outcome of a single engagement on a single day would suggest; it was, essentially, a British Atlantic one (that is not, however, to take anything away from the back country martial acumen of Native American warriors, Canadien officers and militia and the more regular Troupes de la Marine). Indeed, battles are essentially the culmination of many martial and non-martial factors; and overarching political norms, logistical delays and legislative deadlock can be as serious to an expedition's outcome as any battlefield foe. These elements, discussed in this and previous chapters, reinforce the premise of this work: the failure of Edward Braddock and the wider "Braddock Plan" represented core diplomatic, political and military failures, divergences and weaknesses within the British Atlantic World of the eighteenth century. It is an interpretation so often ignored or overlooked in many conventional military and general histories of the French and Indian War and, indeed, the Battle of the Monongahela itself.

NOTES

1. Thomas E. Crocker, *Braddock's March: How the Man Sent to Seize a Continent Changed American History* (Yardley, PA: Westholme Publishing, LLC, 2011), 207.

2. "The Journal of a British Officer," in Charles Hamilton (ed.). *Braddock's Defeat: The Journal of Captain Robert Cholmley's Batman; The Journal of a British Officer; Halkett's Orderly Book* (Norman: University of Oklahoma Press, 1959), 49.
3. Harry Gordon, "Journal of Proceedings from Will's Creek to the Monongahela River," Will's Creek, 23rd July 1755, in Stanley Pargellis (ed.) *Military Affairs in North America, 1748–1765: Selected Documents from the Cumberland Papers in Windsor Castle* (London, 1936), 106.
4. "The Journal of Captain Robert Cholmley's Batman" in Hamilton (ed.). *Braddock's Defeat*, 27.
5. Such subscribers include, Francis Parkman, *Montcalm and Wolfe: The French and Indian War* (Boston, MA: Da Capo Press, 1995); Guy Fregault, Margaret M Cameron (trans.) *Canada: The War of the Conquest* (Toronto: Oxford University Press, 1969); Douglas Edward Leach, *Arms for Empire: A Military History of the British Colonies in North America, 1607–1763* (New York: Macmillan, 1973) and J. H. Parry, *Trade and Dominion: The European Overseas Empires in the Eighteenth-century* (New York: Praeger, 1971).
6. Lyman Copeland Draper, Ted Franklin Belue (ed.), *The Life of Daniel Boone* (Mechanicsburg, PA: Stackpole Books, 1998), 133.
7. See "Captain Orme's Journal" in Winthrop Sargent (ed.) *The History of an expedition against Fort Duquesne in 1755, under Major General Edward Braddock* (Philadelphia, 1855), 281–358. For some, Orme was a man who through his influence could "justly be said to have commanded the expedition and the army." Apparently, he sought to keep the "lion's share" of the spoils of victory for his friends; notably "posts in a new regiment to be recommended for creation out of the seven independent companies in America." It was around Orme that a nucleus—or cabal—formed; one which excluded, among others, Sir John St. Clair, the second-most experienced officer in the army who "saw his advice and objections consistently overruled." See Stanley Pargellis, "Braddock's Defeat," *American Historical Review*, Vol. 41, No. 2, 266.
8. For letter see "Charles Swain to Richard Peters," August 5 1755, in Paul E. Kopperman, *Braddock at the Monongahela* (Pittsburgh: University of Pittsburgh Press, 1992), 184–186.
9. David L. Preston highlighted the fact that many of the Canadian militia who served with Beaujeu's detachment were "a youthful lot." It is clear that he believes the victory over Braddock's army was a Native one *and* a distinct triumph for those officers, such as Daniel Lienard de Beaujeu, Francois-Marie Le Marchand de Ligneris and Jean-Daniel Dumas, who were assigned to them. See David L. Preston, *Braddock's Defeat: The Battle of the Monongahela and the Road to Revolution* (New York: Oxford University Press, 2015), 225.

10. Peter Russell would follow this strain of argument in his article "Redcoats in the Wilderness: British Officers and Irregular Warfare in Europe and America, 1740–1760," *The William and Mary Quarterly*, 3rd Ser., Vol. 35 No. 4 (October, 1978), 629–652.
11. See Pargellis, "Braddock's Defeat."
12. We can ascertain with a degree of certainty that this man did indeed hold a commission as in an earlier contribution to his work he wrote "... the huntsman got us Venison every day but the Soldiers and Bast Men began to find themselves on short allowance." See "The Journal of a British Officer" in Hamilton (ed.), *Braddock's Defeat*, 39.
13. Ibid., 49.
14. "Sir John St. Clair to Sir Robert Napier, Will's Creek, 1755" in Andrew J. Wahll (ed.) *Braddock Road Chronicles, 1755* (Berwyn Heights, MD: Heritage Books, 1999), 405.
15. Considering the fact that, in 1755, the forest along Braddock's road was "virgin" (or unbroken), I believe St. Clair's observations to be more accurate—the canopy afforded by the trees would have been inhibitive to the development of "small growth."
16. Bland warned of the censure an officer who failed to secure his column against a sudden ambush could expect from contemporaries, "... if he [Commanding Officer] is surprised by neglecting the common Methods used to prevent it, his character is hardly retrievable, unless it proceeds from his Want of Experience; and even in that case he will find it very difficult." Braddock had certainly done everything in his power (environmental parameters considered) to properly secure his march. He had followed Bland's recommendation that advised that, "The common Method to prevent your being attacked on the March before you have time to make proper Defence, is, by having a Van and Rear-Guard, which Guards may be stronger or weaker, according to the danger you may apprehend from the enemy, or the Country you are to march through." See Humphrey Bland, *A Treatise of Military Discipline: In which is laid down and Explained the Duties of Officer and Soldier* (5th edition, Dublin, 1743), 115–116. Concurrently, an examination of Braddock's orderly book highlights the diligence with which he commanded his army on the march to Fort Duquesne. See Will H. Lowdermilk (ed.) *Major General Edward Braddock's Orderly Books, from February 26 to June 17, 1755* (Cumberland, MD, 1878).
17. In Furnis's own words, "On the 9th Instant the General at the Head of about 1200 Men—crossed the Monongahela near Fort DuQuesne. The rear of the Army had scarce forded the River before the advanced Party consisting of 250 Men Commanded by Lieutenant Colonel Gage received a smart fire from behind the trees which put them into some disorder,

upon which the General who was about a quarter of a mile distant immediately advanced with the troops..." For letter see "Furnis to the Board of Ordinance, July 23, 1755" in "Treasure Hunt in the forest," *Western Pennsylvania Historical Magazine*, 44 (1961), 388–389.
18. Matthew Ward, *Breaking the Backcountry: The Seven Years War in Virginia and Pennsylvania, 1754–1765* (Pittsburgh, PA: University of Pittsburgh Press, 2003), 60–61.
19. As David Preston has argued, French intelligence was itself quite imprecise. The fact that Contrecoeur and his officers were surprised by the proximity of Braddock's army as late as July 6 (three days before the Battle of the Monongahela) is testimony to this failing. See Preston, *Braddock's Defeat*, 193–194.
20. "Roucher," July 8th 1755, in Wahll, *Braddock Road Chronicles*, 345.
21. The diversity of the tribes Contrecoeur dispatched to attack the British reflects the numerous alliances the French had successfully harnessed in a plethora of different regions. The assembled native groups included Iroquois from Kahnawake and Kanasatake; Lorette Hurons; Abenakis of the St. Lawrence Valley; Odawas; Potawatomis; Wyandots; Miamis; Osages; Delawares; Shawnees and Senecas. Prior to July 9, Contrecoeur had deployed small raiding parties to harry the British advance, but Braddock's diligence in his defensive dispositions thwarted their chances of success. According to several reports, the Indians, in their frustration, resorted to carving insults and threats onto trees in a desperate attempt to demoralize Braddock's men. Some of these parties were quite considerable in their size. This suggests that Braddock's dispositions were worked. His army prior to July 9 was quite secure from sudden ambuscade and his force, regular and provincial alike, met the challenges posed by small raiding parties. For Contrecoeur's account see Pargellis, *Military Affairs*, 129–132.
22. James Smith, "Prisoner of the Caughnawagas," in Frederick Drimmer (ed.) *Captured by Indians: 15 Firsthand Accounts: 1750–1870* (New York: Dover Publications, 1985), 29.
23. "Roucher" claimed that the French army consisted of three Captains, four Lieutenants, six Ensigns, 23 Cadets, 112 Regular troops, 146 Militia and 637 Indians. See Wahll, *Braddock Road Chronicles*, 365.
24. "Dumas, July 24th, 1755," Ibid., 422–423.
25. Gordon, "Journal," in Pargellis (ed.), *Military Affairs*, 106.
26. "Journal of Chomley's Batman," in Hamilton (ed.), *Braddock's Defeat*, 29.
27. "Extract of a letter from Fort Cumberland, October 31, 1755," in Darnell N. Davis, "British Newspaper accounts of Braddock's Defeat," *The Pennsylvania Magazine of History and Biography*, Vol. 23, No. 3, (1899), 324.

28. See "Thomas Gage to the Earl of Albemarle," Fort Cumberland, July 24, 1755 in Thomas Keppel (ed.), *The Life of Augustus Viscount Keppel,* Volume I (London: Henry Colburn Publisher, 1842), 213–18.
29. Bland, *A Treatise of Military Discipline*. Chapter VIII of Bland's treatise specifically deals with the challenges posed by fighting on difficult terrain and includes instructions for the deployment of flanking parties, for instance (see page 123). With regards to a commanding officer's conduct during a sudden ambuscade or an encounter with an unknown force, Bland's instructions are unequivocal "… the Commanding Officer should immediately order the Whole to halt, and prepare for Action, and send the major, or an Officer that is well mounted, to Reconnoiter them near, in order to discover what he can of their numbers and quality, and whether they appear to be friends or foe…" (Page 125).
30. "Orme's Journal," in Sargent (ed.), *History of an Expedition,* 352–357.
31. Printed in Paul E. Kopperman, *Braddock at the Monongahela* (Pittsburgh: University of Pittsburgh Press, 1977), 65.
32. See Charles Henry Lincoln (ed.), "Thomas Dunbar and Thomas Gage to William Shirley: Behaviour of the Troops at the Monongahela," in *The Correspondence of William Shirley, Governor of Massachusetts and Military Commander in America, 1731–1760,* Volume II (New York: 1912), 311–313.
33. "Cameron" in Wahll, *Braddock Road Chronicles,* 354–355.
34. "Journal of Chomley's Batman" in Hamilton (ed.) *Braddock's Defeat,* 27–33. Thomas Mante in his *History of the Late War* recounted a similar anecdote. An engineer in Braddock's army, Lieutenant Treby of the 44th, had been wounded in both legs and lay helpless on the battlefield. Fortunately, a volunteer by the name of Mr Farrel, (when Mante wrote a serving officer in the 62nd regiment) "caught him on his back, and conveyed him, at the most immediate peril of his own life, to some distance from the field of battle, and then procured him such farther assistance, that, disabled as he was, he had the good fortune to reach Fort Cumberland with the other fugitives." See Thomas Mante, *The History of the Late War in North America and the Islands of the West Indies* (London, 1772), 28.
35. Lincoln (ed.), "Behaviour of the Troops at the Monongahela," *Correspondence of Shirley,* II, 311–313.
36. See Appendix D, "Adam Stephen," in Kopperman, *Braddock at the Monongahela,* 226–227.
37. See Edward G. Lengel, *General George Washington: A Military Life* (New York: Random House, 2005), 60.
38. We do not know precisely what these stories were but there are a several possibilities. A number of the Virginians and South Carolinians on Braddock's expedition would have served with George Washington at the Fort Necessity debacle—hence could have conveyed their experiences to

the regulars. More widely, stories, tales and narratives, in view of the fact that literature and indeed news spread throughout the colonies (and the Atlantic World) with impressive regularity, suggests that campfire gossip, fed to the regulars in its various guises, could have included those captivity tales (or legends based broadly upon them)—and other forms of Indian "horror stories"—that had proliferated across the American provinces for well over a century. Concerning the widespread circulation of captivity narratives, see Michelle Burnham, *Captivity and Sentiment: Cultural Exchange in American Literature, 1682–1861* (Hanover, NH: University Press of New England, 1997). Travelling agents and other methods of circulation (such as auctions) meant that exchanges of literature within the colonies also increased dramatically. Richard Van Der Beets, *Held Captive by Indians: Selected Narratives, 1642–1836*, Revised Edition (Knoxville: University of Tennessee Press, 1994), xxxiii.

39. The "war cries" of the Native Americans were, in isolation, a tool of psychological warfare that was used to intimidate and disorientate an enemy. Not that such behavior was unique to Native American societies, but its effect on men who had already been "conditioned" to fear a foe that had fallen upon them unexpectedly, in large numbers and at a time when the tired and hungry British were expecting a clear run to Fort Duquesne, must have magnified considerably the duress placed on Braddock's rank and file as the battle unfolded.
40. "Journal of a British Officer" in Hamilton (ed.) *Braddock's Defeat*, 50.
41. I have discussed this extensively in a recent article. Richard Hall, "'Storys, Scalping and Mohawking'. American Tales, Narratives and Stories—the 'Rhetoric of Fear'—and the Defeat of General Edward Braddock, July 9, 1755," *The Journal of Early American History*, Vol. 5, Issue 2 (2015), 158–186.
42. Ibid., 50.
43. Ibid., 50–51.
44. "Orme Journal" in Sargent (ed.) *History of an Expedition against Fort Duquesne*, 355.
45. Sir Peter Halkett was a Scotsman of considerable renown who was a respected, long-serving British officer. He had served with distinction against the Jacobites in the 1740s and on July 9 1755 was Colonel of the 44th, he being in command of the rear of Braddock's force. Very early in the engagement, Halkett was killed by enemy marksmen. His third son, Lieutenant James Halkett, serving alongside him, stooped to raise the body of his father and was cut down in turn. In 1758, British soldiers, having captured Fort Duquesne, recovered numerous bones belonging to the hundreds of soldiers who fell with Braddock in 1755. It is said that another of Halkett's sons, part of the successful "Forbes expedition," and with the help of an Indian, found two skeletons lying under a tree. By a peculiarity

of the teeth, he was able to identify his father and, consequently, his brother. See Parkman, *Montcalm and Wolfe*, 397.
46. Kopperman, *Braddock at the Monongahela*, 79.
47. Although a credible eyewitness, this chronicler was wrong to state that the unfortunate Captain was Thomas Wagoner. We cannot be certain who the ill-fated officer was but two names are possibilities: Captain William de Peyronie or Lieutenant Edmund Waggoner, who were both fatalities on that day. Lists of casualties appear in many correspondences written after the battle, though they only refer to the officers by their actual names. See, for example, "Alexander Hamilton to his brother, August, 1755," in Wahll (ed.) *Braddock Road Chronicles*, 458–459.
48. See "British Officer B" in Kopperman, *Braddock at the Monongahela*, 166–173.
49. "Journal of a British Officer," in Hamilton (ed.) *Braddock's defeat*, 50.
50. Ibid., 51.
51. "Gage to Albemarle" in Keppel, *Life of Augustus Keppel*, 213–18.
52. "Journal of Chomley's batman" in Hamilton (ed.), *Braddock's Defeat*, 28–30.
53. Harry Gordon, "Journal of proceedings from Wills Creek," in Pargellis (ed.) *Military affairs*, 107.
54. Ibid., 107.
55. Interestingly, a Virginian by the name of Thomas Fossit of Shippensburg, Pennsylvania, would claim to have deliberately killed Braddock after the former had "run through" his brother. This however, remains an unproven claim and one which is most likely based on bravado than fact.
56. During the engagement Washington would urge Braddock to allow the Virginians to take to the trees to fight in the Indian mode; to no avail. Fortunately for the future President of the United States of America, he was not wounded (despite his clothing being torn by enemy fire) and survived the battle. For quote see "George Washington to Mrs Mary Washington, July 18th, 1755," in John Clement Fitzpatrick (ed.) *The Writings of George Washington from the Original Manuscript Sources, 1749–1799*, Vol. I (39 vols. United States Government Printing Office, 1931), 150–152.
57. Sources abound with regards the casualties of the day. See, for instance, "Journal of a British Officer," in Hamilton (ed.) *Braddock's Defeat*, 54–58 or "Copy of a Document given by Captain Hewitt R. N. to his friend Captain Henry Gage Morris," in Sargent (ed.), *History of an Expedition*, 359–365. These are in addition to official lists drawn up by Orme, for instance.
58. Cholmley's batman elaborated on the horrors of the retreat and the terrible sufferings endured by the wounded. On July 13th he noted that, "The wether being very hot Caused a great many magets in the men's wounds

when they were drest." On July 25th he noted how the men were "Dying so fast that they [the survivors] dig holes and throw them in without Reading any service Over them, Altho we having two Ministers with us." Finally, on the following day, "There was a Wounded Soldier Came up who says there was seven more Came from the place of Ingagement together but they all dyed on the Roade and he says there was several dead as he marched along, he not being Able when he Ariv'd here hardly to speake for want of Nurishment, he living on Raw Flower and water when he Came to it, which was left for them [the abandoned wounded] and directions wrighting to follow and the [y] should find more at such and such places till the Join'd us." See Hamilton (ed.), *Braddock's Defeat*, 32, 34.

59. James Smith, "Prisoner of the Caughnawagas" in Drimmer (ed.) *Captured by Indians*, 30.
60. Indeed, it was an opportunity the French did not miss. See, for example, _____, *The Conduct of the Late Ministry or a Memorial; Containing A Summary of Facts with their Vouchers, in Answer to The Observations, sent by the English Ministry, to the Courts of Europe. Wherein (among many curious and interesting Pieces, which may serve as Authentic Memoirs towards a History of the present Quarrel between Great-Britain and France) several Papers are to be seen at full Length; Extracts of which lie now, under the Consideration of P_____T* (London: Golden-Ball, 1757), 25–54.
61. See Colonel H. C. B. Rogers, *The British Army of the Eighteenth-century* (London: Hippocrene Books, 1977), 23.
62. On May 20th 1755, Robert Orme would likewise highlight the inadequacies of the men of the Virginia Regiment who were to serve with the 44th and 48th. In his entry for that day he wrote, "The General had now frequent opportunities of seeing and hearing of the appearance and disposition of the Virginia Recruits and companies. Mr Allen had taken the greatest pains with them, and they performed their evolutions and firings as well as could be expected, but their languid, spiritless, and 'unsoldier-like' appearance considered with the lowness of their officers, gave little hopes of their future good behaviour." A document of typical British prejudice? Certainly so. However, Orme was merely highlighting the fact that, compared to regular regiments, these recruits were poorly trained and unaccustomed to the rigors of military service. Despite their effectiveness on July 9, the fact remains that their irregular movements on the day of battle (a consequence of their lack of schooling in European warfare) added to the disorientation and panic that eventually swept through Braddock's army. See "The Journal of Captain Robert Orme" in Winthrop Sargent (ed.) *The History of an expedition against Fort Duquesne in 1755, under Major General Edward Braddock* (Philadelphia, 1855), 312.
63. These maps can be found in Sargent, *History of an Expedition against Fort Duquesne*, 218 & 352 and Pargellis, *Military Affairs*, 114–115.

64. See Charles Henry Lincoln (ed.), "Thomas Dunbar and Thomas Gage to William Shirley: Behaviour of the Troops at the Monongahela," in *The Correspondence of William Shirley, Governor of Massachusetts and Military Commander in America, 1731–1760*, Volume II (New York: 1912), 311–313.
65. See Hamilton (ed.) *Braddock's Defeat*, 40–58.
66. Ibid., 40–58.
67. Kopperman, *Braddock at the Monongahela*, 95.

Conclusion: Braddock's Defeat and Its Legacy

Reflecting the core themes and factors outlined hitherto in this book, the other prongs of the grand Braddock Plan of 1755, with the exception of the Acadian mission of Robert Monkton, were failures in their own right; despite William Johnson's pyrrhic tactical victory at the so-called Battle of Lake George. Indeed, the missions of William Johnson and William Shirley are noteworthy principally for the fact that they were American campaigns that relied almost exclusively on provincial soldiers raised in the colonies; and were dominated by two central figures of regional politics, Shirley and Johnson. Shirley's own campaign had been belatedly adopted by Braddock when he arrived in America, though this mission was not, at least initially, a priority for the ministry in London. Johnson's task was one that would, it was felt, secure the New York frontier and, perhaps more significantly, Britain's increasingly tentative alliance with the Iroquois. It was the lobbying of Massachusetts's governor, who had been convinced, ironically, by William Johnson, of the merits of a campaign against Fort Niagara, that had seen that vital French post become an objective of the campaign. Unfortunately, the folly of creating a split command in New York—one that was magnified by the intensively ambitious nature of these soon-to-be jostling rivals—was not a factor that ever seemed to have been considered by Braddock when he was presented with this plan at Alexandria.[1]

Ultimately, both missions witnessed the age-old colonial bane of weak executive authority—transcolonial jealousies and individual vested political and economic interests hamstringing key strategic objectives. Indeed, an

© The Editor(s) (if applicable) and The Author(s) 2016
R. Hall, *Atlantic Politics, Military Strategy and the French and Indian War*, War, Culture and Society, 1750-1850,
DOI 10.1007/978-3-319-30665-0

227

in-depth analysis of the Shirley and Johnson campaigns would exemplify poor British planning (at the governmental and indeed colonial levels); transcolony and personal rivalries and the martial shortcomings of colonial soldiers operating virtually independently of British command and support (despite the aforementioned Lake George success of Johnson). When combined, these led to logistical and political deadlocks, enormous expenditure outlays and two painstakingly slow campaigns.[2] Indeed, William Shirley's military career was destroyed by the recriminations that followed from the 1755 campaigns in New York.

As for Robert Monkton's Acadia campaign, the reason why this was successful was because the British descent upon the peninsula maximized the localized seaborne advantages the Royal Navy could bring to bear (even in 1755), while the army would fight a conventional, as opposed to backcountry, campaign. In addition, the crown promised to defray the costs of the mission, negating the constitutional deadlocks and quarrels associated with the expeditions of Johnson, Shirley and Braddock.[3] In short, it was organized in the way the wider Braddock Plan should have been, and in many regards bears parallels the objectives, priorities and strategic acumen of the Pitt ministry from 1756.

Edward Braddock's own mission to Fort Duquesne, by comparison, with all of its political, diplomatic, economic and martial travails perhaps demonstrates the latent divergence of empire that, in the longer term, would see the Thirteen Colonies split from Great Britain. These fractures, of course, had existed before 1755 and it would be quite wrong to suggest that the Braddock campaign (and wider Braddock Plan) was *the* definitive point at which the road to American Revolution began. Other underlying factors associated with imperial administration in the late 1740s and 1750s had portended a schism of empire too (at least in hindsight), not the least of which was the rise of one of the great advocates of legislative and territorial expansionism, the Earl of Halifax, to the position of President of the Board of Trade in 1748.

Braddock's defeat provided an *indicator* of future imperial divergences, however. In Braddock we see a commander in chief who had been sent to North America as a *de facto* viceroy; his orders, superficially, allowed him to demand appropriations from assemblies that he anticipated would meet his requests with little objection or resistance. Failing to comprehend how passionately the colonists would cling to the idea of diffused sovereignty—one in which representative local assemblies were seen as the equivalents of parliament in their own jurisdictions—it was inevitable that abrasions and conflicts of interest would emerge. In the 1760s British officials would again evoke the kind of resistance to imperial authority that Braddock's tenure as commander in chief unleashed in 1755 (this was also true of John Campbell, Fourth Earl of Loudon's tenure in this position from 1756 to 1758); and here again an overarching theme can be drawn. Britain, to pay for a war (as opposed to a campaign) fought, from its perspective, to defend the colonists, demanded, in return for its manpower and treasure, contributions from colonial authorities. Little scope was given for negotiation in obtaining these requisitions and, in an empire in which negotiation was, and always had been (particularly in view of Britain's largely *laissez faire* attitude towards its American possessions) a *modus operandi*, such intransigence could only spell trouble. Yet, whereas the turmoil of the 1760s would lead to cries of tyranny and theft of liberty (resulting in resistance and revolution in the 1770s), in the aftermath of the Braddock campaign such profound differences, though indeed a source of great tension and resentment, were offset by the necessity of defending the backcountry, defeating the French and securing national and local interests in coveted, contested regions.[4]

As for Edward Braddock the man and general, he came, in the wider scope of nineteenth and twentieth-century historiography (most notably in its "Whig" and neoprogressive manifestations) to represent the very worst failings of Britain as a "mother country"—one increasingly inclined towards oppression of traditional liberties as its power and empire grew on the back of its colonial expansion. Braddock's apparent haughtiness, contempt for American traditions and customs (indeed his supposed disdain for the colonists per se), when coupled with his demands and attempts to enforce imperial legislation (for that is what many of his orders amounted to) came to exemplify Britain's heavy-handed and oppressive approach to its colonies; and hence, ultimately, its violation of colonists' rights as freeborn Englishmen. The contempt we see for Britain's conduct in "Whiggish" histories of the American Revolution is evident in their interpretive line of Edward Braddock and his defeat at the Monongahela. Braddock, and to an extent his subordinates, through their haughty, supercilious, condescending and downright aggressive attitudes and actions mirrored in many ways those policies which would force Americans to unite in the defense of their liberties 20 years later.[5]

This somewhat denigratory caricature of Braddock did emerge rather swiftly after the Monongahela debacle and was not limited to the American side of the Atlantic. In an age where military commanders were frequently lauded or condemned on the strength of their virtues as officers and gentlemen, Braddock's difficulties in leading a campaign in the midst of what was a pseudo-autonomous segment of the British Atlantic World ensured that his memory would be tarnished by the slurs—and indeed lies—that were spread after his demise in battle. Certainly, in comparison to subsequent "victorious" British commanders such as John Forbes and James Wolfe, Braddock emerges in many works as one of history's greatest blunderers; something profoundly unfair.

Indeed, to compare Edward Braddock to General John Forbes, who led a successful assault against Fort Duquesne in 1758, is to overlook the fact that Forbes had benefited from three years of British lesson-learning in American warfare and American politics and Indian diplomacy. In the latter case, he enjoyed considerable autonomy in forging alliances with the Ohio's indigenous groups and was able to streamline the archaic processes that had epitomized British Indian diplomacy in previous years. Furthermore, French policy towards Native Americans, hampered by the growing hostility of the Marquis de Montcalm towards Indian warfare (particularly after the capture and "massacre" of Fort William-Henry in 1757) had alienated many of that nation's traditional American-Indian allies. Hyperinflation, caused by monopoly, corrupt practices within Canada's body politic and thus the increasing difficulties that the French faced in supplying their frontier posts (and hence native allies) with trade goods and presents also impacted upon indigenous diplomacy at this time; meaning that many of the Ohio's native groups were better-disposed towards a British alliance. This was something that, despite the significant defeat of Major James Grant in September 1758 outside the very walls of Fort Duquesne, was cleverly exploited by Forbes at the crucial Treaty of Easton.

General Forbes' campaign also demonstrated that the logistical tribulations that Edward Braddock had faced had, to a great extent, been learned from. Quickly realizing that Braddock's old road to the Ohio was a perilous one to say the least, Forbes, despite intense protestations from Virginians such as George Washington, significantly shortened his march by taking an alternative route through Pennsylvania. By proceeding in measured stages, and by fortifying his advance with a series of storage posts and blockhouses, he also ensured that the perils associated with long, winding logistical trains and over-extended supply lines were reduced (even though the establishment of his posts was a time-consuming process).

CONCLUSION: BRADDOCK'S DEFEAT AND ITS LEGACY 231

Finally, Forbes' mission of 1758 was undoubtedly conducted in a period of greater collaboration across the British Atlantic World; another contributory factor in his success. The priorities of war for the British government following the rise of William Pitt had seen the American colonies become a major theater of what had by then become the Seven Years War. No longer were strategic objectives limited by purely European concerns; the weight of the British nation was behind a principally colonial conflict that, at least for that country, had an air of totality about it. Provincial assemblies, promised significant reimbursement for their expenditures, were far more willing to support major expeditions than they had been during the Braddock Plan. That is not to say that Forbes did not endure frustrations and delays when dealing with the colonists, but these were not on the same scale as those Braddock (and indeed William Shirley and William Johnson) had suffered in 1755.

Many of the charges laid against the ill-starred Braddock in the wake of the Monongahela defeat were not then fairly attributed to him. From the decision to use the resource-light Virginia as the launch-pad for the expedition into the Ohio Valley, to squandering native alliances and to more minute campaign-related decisions, such as carrying an excessive baggage train resplendent with vast numbers of burdensome (and resource-draining) camp followers, the deceased Braddock had a plethora of poor decisions laid at his feet. In many ways too the caricatures that had circulated of Braddock before his deployment to America—ones which portrayed a profane, bigoted and brutal "Iroquois"—fed into the prejudices of his post-battle detractors, who have seen in the memory created of him the essence, and underlying causes, of his subsequent failure as a commander. As has been argued in this work repeatedly, however, if we examine Braddock's campaign-related trials it is soon evident that they were ones which, for the most part, had their origins in far deeper-rooted failings, weaknesses and divergences within the British Atlantic World of the eighteenth century. As for the slurs against his character, these too have to be reviewed carefully and measured against other evidence (outlined earlier in this book) which tells us that Braddock, as a conventional European officer at least, was in reality very competent (if deeply conservative) indeed.

None of this, however, can change the fact that the rout of the Anglo-American army on the banks of the Monongahela was deeply significant in defining an American identity; one clearly *separate* from that of the mother country. It was, through the benefit of hindsight at least, part of a process which saw, in North America, "Britishness" become replaced by a new "Americanness."[6] The friction that had existed between the professional regulars of the 44th and 48th and their colonial comrades during the 1755 campaign brought to the fore, and provided a prism-view into, the wider underlying schisms that had been growing between Old and New World Britons whose experiences of environment, war, diplomacy and indeed more widely held "visions of empire" varied so drastically by the mid-eighteenth century.[7]

This was revealed most obviously in the different approach to war the provincials and British adopted on July 9, 1755; the consequences of which, if more favorable (in terms of memory) for the American contingent of Braddock's force, nevertheless contributed to the catastrophe that befell the long, winding Anglo-American column. As has been suggested previously in this work, the Anglo-American response to the Battle of the Monongahela also demonstrated the perils of attempting to fuse two contrasting martial traditions in an overwhelmingly conventional force; and one that was not properly accustomed to the doctrines of *petite guerre*. Braddock's defeat therefore exemplified a clash of military cultures not just between regular soldiers and their largely irregular Indian and Canadien foes, but also between redcoat and locally raised provincial soldiers—many of whom were evidently more inclined to fight according to North American martial practices.

Braddock's defeat, as it is remembered, also fitted on to a neat timeline of humiliating failures that included defeats at Oswego, Fort William-Henry, Fort Ticonderoga and Major James Grant's rout before the very gates of Fort Duquesne in 1758. These were, conveniently, also viewed as distinctly *British* catastrophes and contrasted starkly to the few victories Britain and her colonies enjoyed during the "nadir" years of the French and Indian (later Seven Years) War; the latter were, it must be outlined, unequivocally portrayed as profoundly *provincial* successes. In September of 1755, William Johnson, leading a force of *American* soldiers, had resoundingly defeated a fearsome Franco-Indian division in upper New York—all without the aid of clumsy and cumbersome redcoats. Likewise, in 1758, it was another almost uniquely colonial army (out of a force of 3000 men, only 150 were regulars) that captured the strategically pivotal Fort Frontenac, cutting a major communication link between Quebec and Montreal.

All of these successes had sown a belief in the colonial mind that they could defend themselves and that they could, certainly by the early 1770s, take up arms against a professional European army—in this case, ironically, the British Army. The long shadow of Braddock's defeat in particular gave the Americans significant confidence that they had the wherewithal necessary to exploit the weaknesses of their former fellow-countrymen who had shown that they could, given the right conditions, be defeated by a distinctly irregular foe. As Benjamin Franklin would assert 30 years after the Monongahela catastrophe, the disaster had served to undermine the colonists' previous "exalted ideas of the prowess of British Regulars" which, he believed, had not been "well founded." During the War of Independence, Charles Lee, a former British officer turned revolutionary, shared this sentiment as he encouraged colonial militias to hold no fear of supposed redcoat supremacy. Citing again the catastrophe at the Monongahela, the acerbic Lee pointed out that "It may be very possible for men to be dressed in red, to be expert in all the tricks of the parade... be smartly dressed, keep their arms bright...be expert in all the anticks of a review" and yet still be "very unfit" for what he called "real action."[8]

Perhaps most profoundly, however, Edward Braddock's campaign of 1755 (and indeed the more extensive Braddock Plan) signifies, in the context of imperial history, the strength of an "Americanness" that was notably different to post-Glorious Revolution "Britishness." Frequently discussed in the context of the American Revolution, this can be described, on the imperial scale, as the conflict between parliamentary (or executive) and diffused sovereignty; and internal legislative dysfunction, between governor and assembly, in the local political sphere. In 1755, Braddock essentially represented a new British colonial imperative that sought to change what was considered an insubordinate segment of that nation's empire; reasserting executive power and setting a precedent for future reforms that the Earl of Halifax in particular had long been advocating as President of the Board of Trade. Colonial resistance to Braddock's attempts to wield his authority (as outlined in his instructions) ultimately mirrored their historic attitudes towards metropolitan interference in their internal affairs. For the colonists, the empire was a partnership in which local assemblies enjoyed considerable autonomy, even to the extent that they were equal to Britain's parliament. This stood in stark contrast to the British vision of that body's almost sacrosanct role in the maintaining of British liberties *everywhere* (not just the mother country). For mainland Britons, this constitutional question had been settled way back in 1688–1689 when the supremacy of parliament, and the operation of sovereignty through the king in parliament—the principle of co-ordination as it was sometimes called—essentially brought constitutional turmoil to an end.

No such thing had happened in the colonies. Governors, who before 1688–89 decided if and when legislatures would meet, who prorogued and dissolved legislative assemblies, who vetoed legislation, created courts, and dismissed judges still did so in the eighteenth century. Governors-in-assembly akin to the crown-in-parliament in England had not emerged in America, neither did the principle of co-ordination—to mediate imperial politics—exist. Assemblies wielded the all-important power of the purse, with the result that executive power, and the ability of London governments to influence and exert authority over local affairs, was truncated. The *laissez faire* attitude of British ministries before 1748 (and certainly before 1755) meant that colonial abrasions had been minimized—particularly as the colonists were adept at circumventing imperial legislation, like the Navigation Acts, that did exist (in turn, governors were unable to enforce executive orders because of their "domestication"). Edward Braddock's arrival in America temporarily changed this dynamic. He was, in retrospect, the vanguard of British reforms that were to be pushed through during his, and indeed his successor's (Lord Loudon's), tenures as commanders in chief. These reforms, perhaps inevitably, proved unsuccessful as colonial assemblies resisted any measures that represented trespasses upon what they saw as English liberties. This included freedom from arbitrary appropriation and the quartering of soldiers on private properties and individuals—both of which Braddock and Loudon were permitted, or were compelled, to do as they battled to prosecute large-scale, Europeanized military campaigns in the ill-equipped colonies.

All of these factors are divergences and schisms of the British Atlantic World that the mission of Edward Braddock to Fort Duquesne exemplified; and thus place this event firmly on the road to the American Revolution. William Pitt's interlude would, as outlined previously, temporarily slow this momentum, with his polices of subsidies and reimbursements placating the fears of local assemblies and galvanizing the colonists behind a war effort that was now focused on imperial expansion—as opposed to the *containment* of France in Europe and America. However, when Britain again attempted to compel its colonies to contribute directly to the costs of war and administering a vast empire in the 1760s and 1770s (following the almost ruinously expensive Seven Years War), the divergence of Anglo-American visions of empire—ones that had done so much to frustrate Braddock in 1755—reared again. This time, in the absence of a French threat in Canada and with both sides obstinate in their defense of their visions of ancient British rights and liberties, the consequences were a fratricidal conflict and the birth of the United States of America.

NOTES

1. For historian Patricia Bonomi, New York was *the* most "factious" of Britain's Thirteen Colonies. See Patricia Bonomi, *A Factious People: Politics and Society in Colonial New York* (New York: Columbia University Press, 1971).
2. See Cynthia A. Kierner, *Traders and Gentlefolk: The Livingstons of New York, 1675–1790* (Ithaca, NY: Cornell University Press, 1992).
3. For an account of this particular campaign see, John Grenier, *The Far Reaches of Empire: War in Nova Scotia, 1710–1760* (Norman: University of Oklahoma Press, 2008).
4. The colonists saw things rather differently. From their perspective, they had contributed greatly—in men, materiel and money—to the war effort; and at considerable cost to themselves.
5. Edward E. Curtis in his classic study of the administration of the British Army during the American War of Independence exemplifies the attitude of traditional scholarship towards the institution in this later conflict. For Curtis, poor administration and the ineptitude of an arcane officer corps represented far deeper failings in British society and its Empire; "a long-standing evil" as he suggested. See Edward E. Curtis, *The Organization of the British Army in the American Revolution* (New Haven, CT: Yale University Press, 1926; reprint, New York: AMS Press, 1969), 50 & 149.
6. Although it is true that British America and the mother country saw scenes of nationalistic euphoria following the great victories Britain enjoyed after 1758 in the Seven Years War, it is apparent that this sense of patriotic devotion was a temporary aberration in the process of colony–metropolis divergence that had been significantly accelerated during the period 1748–1760.
7. Richard L. Merritt, who, through the quantification of symbols of American identity in the colonial press, noticed a surge in such sentiment after the Braddock Defeat. In his own words, "The curve remained low until the outbreak of the French and Indian War in 1754. The highest point of the ensuing cycle occurred in the year of Braddock's Defeat." Richard L. Merritt, *Symbols of American Community, 1735–1775* (New Haven, CT: Yale University Press, 1966), 61.

8. Charles Lee, *Memoirs of the Life of the Late Charles Lee, Esq. Second in Command in the Service of the United States of America during the Revolution* (London: 1792), 148–149. In this diatribe Lee referred to Braddock's regular units as "some of the most esteemed." This, as has been shown previously in this work, was far from the case in reality.

BIBLIOGRAPHY

PRIMARY SOURCES

Anon, *A Letter from a gentleman in London to his friend in the country: concerning the treaty at Aix-la-Chapelle, concluded on the 8th of October, 1748* (London, 1748)

Anon, *A Letter to His Grace the Duke of Newcastle on the Present Crisis in the Affairs of Great Britain. Containing Reflections on a later Resignation* (London: R.Griffiths, 1761)

Anon, *A Soldier's Journal* (London, 1770)

Anon, 'Essay on Regular and Irregular Forces', *Gentleman's Magazine*, Volume 16, (1746)

Anon, *Reasons Humbly Offered to Prove that the Letter Printed at the End of the French Memorial of Justification is a French Forgery and Falsely ascribed to His Royal Highness* (London: Royal Exchange, 1756)

Anon, *The Conduct of the Late Ministry or a Memorial; Containing A Summary of Facts with their Vouchers, in Answer to The Observations, sent by the English Ministry, to the Courts of Europe. Wherein (among many curious and interesting Pieces, which may serve as Authentic Memoirs towards a History of the present Quarrel between Great-Britain and France) several Papers are to be seen at full Length; Extracts of which lie now, under the Consideration of P_____T* (London: Golden-Ball, 1757)

Bates, Albert Carlos (ed.), *The Fitch Papers: Correspondence and Documents during Thomas Fitch's Governorship of the Colony of Connecticut 1754–1766*, Vol. XVIII (Hartford: Connecticut Historical Society, 1920)

Bellamy, George Anne, *An Apology for the life of George Anne Bellamy, late of Covent Garden Theatre*, Volume II (3 vols. London, 1786)
_____, *An Apology for the life of George Anne Bellamy, late of Covent Garden Theatre*, Volume III (3 vols. London, 1786)
Blakeney, Col. William, *The New Manual Exercise, by General Blakeney. To which is added the Evolutions of the Foot, by General Bland* (Philadelphia, 1746)
Bonin, 'Jolicoeur' Charles, Andrew Garrup, (ed.), *Memoir of a French and Indian War Soldier* (Maryland, 1993)
Bland, Humphrey, *A Treatise of Military Discipline: In which is laid down and Explained the Duties of Officer and Soldier* (5th edition, Dublin, 1743)
Bougainville, Louis Antoine de, Edward P. Hamilton, (ed. & trans.), *Adventure in the Wilderness: The American Journals of Louis Antoine de Bougainville, 1756–1760* (Oklahoma, 1990)
Brock, Robert Alonzo (ed.), *The Official Records of Robert Dinwiddie: Lieutenant-Governor of the Colony of Virginia, 1751–1758,* Volume III (Richmond, Virginia, 1883)
_____, *The Official Records of Robert Dinwiddie: Lieutenant-Governor of the Colony of Virginia, 1751–1758,* Volume IV (Richmond, Virginia, 1883)
Browne, William Hand (ed.), *Archives of Maryland:* Volume VI, *Correspondence of Governor Horatio Sharpe*, Vol. I: 1753–1757 (Baltimore: Maryland Historical Society, 1888)
Burke, Edmund, Paul Lankford (ed.), *The Writings and Speeches of Edmund Burke*, Volume II: *Party, Parliament and the American Crisis, 1766–1774* (Clarendon Press, 1981)
Burnaby, Rev. Andrew, *Travels through the middle settlements in North America in the years 1759 and 1760 with observations on the state of the Colonies* (Dublin, 1775)
Cameron, Duncan, *The Life, Adventures, and surprising Deliverances of Duncan Cameron, Private Soldier in the Regiment of Foot, late Sir Peter Halket's*, Third Edition (Philadelphia: 1756)
Carson, Ritchie I. A. (ed.), *General Braddock's Expedition* (Woolwich, 1962)
Chauncey, Charles, *A letter to a friend : giving a concise, but just, account, according to the advices hitherto received, of the Ohio-defeat ; and pointing out also the many good ends, this inglorious event is naturally adapted to promote ; or, shewing wherein it is fitted to advance the interest of all the American British colonies, to which is added, some general account of the New-England forces, with what they have already done, counter-balancing the above loss* (Boston: Edes and Gill, 1755)
Clarke, William, *Observations on the Late and Present Conduct of the French with regard their Encroachments upon the British Colonies in North America. Together with Remarks on the Importance of these Colonies to Great Britain* (Boston Printed: London Re-Printed: Royal Exchange, Cornhill, 1755)

Colden, Cadwallader, *Cadwallader Colden Papers:* Volume V *(1755–1760)* (New York Historical Society, 1921)
Cuthbertson, Bennett, *A System for the Complete Interior Management and Oeconomy of a Battalion of Infantry* (London: Bolton Grierson, 1768)
Drimmer, Frederick (ed.), *Captured by Indians: 15 Firsthand Accounts: 1750–1870* (New York: Dover Publications, 1985)
Entick, John, *The General History of the late War; Containing its Rise, Progress, and Event in Europe, Asia, Africa and America*, Volume I (5 vols. London, 1763)
Farquhar, George, *The Recruiting Officer* (London, 1718)
Fitzpatrick, John Clement (ed.), *The Writings of George Washington from the Original Manuscript Sources. 1745–1799*, Vol. I, 1745–1756 (39 vols. United States Government Printing Office, 1931)
Flick, Alexander C. (ed.), *The Papers of Sir William Johnson*, Volume IX (Albany, 1939)
Franklin, Benjamin, John Bigelow (ed.), *Memoirs of Benjamin Franklin*, Vol. 1 (2 Vols. New York: Harper & Brothers, 1839)
_____, *The Autobiography of Benjamin Franklin* (Philadelphia, 1868)
Franklin, Benjamin, Carl Van Doren, (Introduction), Julian P. Boyd, (Historical & Biographical notes), *Indian Treaties printed by Benjamin Franklin* (Philadelphia, 1938)
Galissioniere, Marquis de la, 'Memoir on the French Colonies in North America, 1750', *American History from Revolution to Reconstruction and Beyond*, <http://www.let.rug.nl/usa/documents/1701-1750/marquis-de-la-galissoniere-memoir-on-the-french-colonies-in-north-america-december-1750.php>
Gridley, Luke, F.M. (ed.), *Luke Gridley's Diary of 1757 while in service in the French and Indian War*. (Hartford, Connecticut, 1906)
Hall, Dennis Jay (ed.), *The Journals of Sir William Johnson's Scouts, 1755 & 1756* (Panton: Essence of Vermont, 1999)
Hamilton, Charles (ed.), *Braddock's Defeat: The Journal of Captain Robert Cholmley's Batman; The Journal of a British Officer; Halkett's Orderly Book* (University of Oklahoma Press, 1959)
Hazard, Samuel (ed.), *Colonial Records of Pennsylvania*, Volume VI (16 Vols. Harrisburg: Theo. Fenn & Co. 1851)
_____, *Minutes of the Provincial Council of Pennsylvania*, Volume IV (16 vols. Harrisburg: Theo. Fenn & Co., 1851–53)
_____, *Minutes of the Provincial Council of Pennsylvania*, Volume VI, (16 vols. Harrisburg: Theo. Fenn & Co., 1851–53)
Hazard, Samuel (ed.), *Pennsylvania Archives. Commencing 1748*, Vol. II (12 vols. Philadelphia: Joseph Severns & Co. 1853)
Hopkins, Stephen, *The Rights of the Colonies Examined* (Providence, Rhode Island, 1762)

Huske, John, *The Present State of North America* (Boston, 1755)
James, Alfred Proctor, *Writings of General John Forbes relating to his service in North America* (Wisconsin: The Collegiate Press, 1938)
Johnson, Samuel, *The Works of Samuel Johnson, LL.D.*, Volume XIII (13 vols. London: John Stockdale, 1777)
Johnson, Susannah, *A narrative of the captivity of Mrs. Johnson: containing an account of her sufferings, during four years, with the Indians and French: together with an appendix, containing the sermons, preached at her funeral and that of her mother with sundry other interesting articles* (Vermont, 1814)
Kemp, Peter (ed.), 'Boscawen's Letters to His Wife, 1755-1756', *The Naval Miscellany* (Greenwich: The Navy Records Society, 1952)
Keppel, Thomas (ed.), *The Life of Augustus Viscount Keppel*, Volume I (London: Henry Colburn Publisher, 1842)
Lambing, Rev. A. A., *The Baptismal Register of Fort Duquesne (from June, 1754, to Dec., 1756) Translated, with an Introductory Essay and Notes* (Pittsburg: Myers, Shinkle A & Co., 1885)
Laslett, Peter (ed.), *Locke: Two Treatises of Government* (Cambridge: Cambridge University Press, 2003)
Lincoln, Charles, Henry (ed.), *The Correspondence of William Shirley, Governor of Massachusetts and Military Commander in America, 1731-1760*, Volume I (New York: 1912)
_____, *The Correspondence of William Shirley, Governor of Massachusetts and Military Commander in America, 1731-1760*, Volume II (New York: 1912)
Linn, John B. and William H. Egle, *Pennsylvanian Archives: Second Series*, Vol. VI, 'Relating to the French Occupation of Western Pennsylvania, 1631-1764' (Harrisburg, 1891)
Livingstone, William, Smith, William, Alexander, William, *A review of the military operations in North America: from the commencement of the French hostilities to the frontiers of Virginia in 1753, to the surrender of Oswego, on the 14th of August 1756; interspersed with various observations, characters and anecdotes; necessary to give light into the conduct of American transactions in general; and more especially into the political management of affairs in New York; in a letter to a nobleman; to which are added Col. Washington's journal of his expedition to the Ohio, in 1754, and several letters found in the cabinet of Major General Braddock, after his defeat near Fort Duquesne (1757)* (Dublin, 1757)
Lowdermilk, Will H. (ed.), *Major General Edward Braddock's Orderly Books, from February 26 to June 17, 1755* (Maryland, 1878)
Lucier, Armand Francis (ed.), *French and Indian War notices abstracted from Colonial Newspapers, Volume 1: 1754-1755* (Maryland, 2007)
_____, *French and Indian War notices abstracted from Colonial Newspapers, Volume II: 1756-1760* (Maryland, 2007)
Mante, Thomas, *The History of the Late War in North America and the Islands of the West Indies* (London, 1772)

Mitchell, John, *The Contest in America Between Britain and France* (London, 1757)
O'Callaghan E.B., Berthold Fernow (eds.), *Documents Relative to the Colonial History of New York, Procured in Holland, England and France*, Volume VI (15 vols. Albany: 1855)
_____, *Documents Relative to the Colonial History of New York, Procured in Holland, England and France*, Volume X (15 vols. Albany: 1855)
Pargellis, Stanley (ed.), *Military affairs in North America, 1748–1765: Selected documents from the Cumberland papers in Windsor Castle* (London, 1936)
Pouchot, Pierre, Cardy, Michael (translator), Dunnigan, Brian Leigh (ed. and annotator), *Memoirs on the late war in North America between France and England* (New York: Old Fort Niagara Association, 1994)
Pownall, Thomas, *Principles of Polity, being the Grounds and Reasons of Civil Empire* (London, 1752)
_____, *The Administration of the Colonies*, 4th Edition (London: J. Walker, 1768)
Putnam, Rufus, E.C. Dawes (ed.), *Journal of Gen. Rufus Putnam kept in Northern New York during Four Campaigns of the Old French and Indian War, 1757–1760* (Albany, 1886)
Raymond, Chevalier de, Joseph L. Peyser, (ed. & trans.), *On the Eve of Conquest: The Chevalier de Raymond's Critique of New France in 1754* (Michigan, 1997)
Sargent, Winthrop (ed.), *The History of an expedition against Fort Duquesne in 1755, under Major General Edward Braddock* (Philadelphia, 1855)
Saunders, William L. (ed.), *The Colonial Records of North Carolina*, Vol. V (10 Vols. Raleigh: Josephus Daniels, 1887)
Saxe, Maurice Count de, *Reveries, or, Memoirs Concerning the Art of War* (Edinburgh: Alexander Donalson, 1776)
Sedgwick, Romney (ed.), *Letters from George III to Lord Bute. 1756–1766* (London: Macmillan and Company, 1939)
Seven Years' War Journal of the Proceedings of the 35th Regiment of Foot (1757)
Smyth, Albert H. (ed.), *The Writings of Benjamin Franklin*, Volume I (10 vols. New York: The Macmillan Company, 1907)
Shebbeare, John, *A Second Letter to the People of England. On Foreign Subsidies, Subsidiary Allies, and their Consequences to this Nation* (4th edn., London, 1756)
Shirley, William, *A Journal of the proceedings at two conferences: begun to be held at Falmouth in Casco-Bay, in the county of York, within the province of the Massachusetts-Bay in New-England, on the twenty-eighth day of June, 1754, between His Excellency William Shirley, Esq., captain-general, governour and commander in chief, in and over the province aforesaid, and the chiefs of the Norridgwalk Indians, and on the fifth day of July following, between His said Excellency and the chiefs of the Penobscot Indians* (Boston, 1754)

Simmons, R. C. and P. D. G. Thomas, *Proceedings and Debates of the British Parliaments respecting North America 1754–1783* (6 vols. New York: Millward, 1983)

Smith, William, *A Brief View of the Conduct of Pennsylvania for the Year 1755; So far as it affected the General Service of the British Colonies, particularly the Expedition under the late General Braddock. With an Account of the Shocking Inhumanities, committed by Incursions of the Indians upon the province in October and November; which occasioned a Body of the Inhabitants to come down, while the Assembly were sitting, and to insist upon an immediate Suspension of all Disputes, and the Passing of a Law for the Defence of the Country. Interspersed with several interesting Anecdotes and original papers, relating to the Politics and Principles of the people called Quakers: Being a Sequel to a late well-known Pamphlet Intitled, 'A Brief State of Pennsylvania'* (London, 1756)

Sparks, Jared, *The Writings of George Washington*, Volume II (12 vols. London, 1838)

Stewart, Irene (ed.), *Letters of General John Forbes relating to the Expedition against Fort Duquesne in 1758* (Pittsburgh, 1927)

Sullivan, James (ed.), *The Papers of Sir William Johnson*, Vol. I (Albany, 1921)

Sullivan, James (ed.), *The Papers of Sir William Johnson*, Vol. II (Albany, 1922)

The London Magazine, November, 1755

Thorner, Thomas & Thor Frohn-Nielsen, (eds.), *A Few Acres of Snow: Documents in Pre-Confederation Canadian History* (Toronto: Toronto Press Incorporated, 2009)

Thomas, John, *Diary of John Thomas, Surgeon in Winslow's Expedition of 1755 against the Acadians* (Boston, Press of D. Clapp & Sons, 1878)

Timberlake, Lieutenant Henry, *The Memoirs of Lieut. Henry Timberlake* (London: 1765)

Trent, Captain William, *Journal of Captain William Trent from Logstown to Pickawillany, A.D. 1752: now published from a copy in the archives of the Western Reserve Historical Society, Cleveland, Ohio, together with letters of Governor Robert Dinwiddie; and historical notice of the Miami Confederacy of Indians; a sketch of the English post at Pickawillany, with a short biography of Captain Trent and other papers never before printed* (Pittsburgh, 1871)

Tucker, Josiah, *A Brief Essay on the Advantages and Disadvantages which Respectively Attend France and Great Britain, with Regard to Trade. With Some Proposals for Removing the Principal Disadvantages of Great Britain. In a New Method* (3rd edn. London, 1753)

Wahll, Andrew J. (ed.), *Braddock Road Chronicles, 1755* (Maryland, 1999)

Walpole, Horace, W.S. Lewis, Warren Hunting Smith, George L. Lam (eds.), *Horace Walpole's Correspondence with Sir Horace Mann: Volume IV 15 November 1748 NS 18 September 1756* (Oxford, 1960)

Walker, Lewis Burd (ed.), Edward Shippen, et al. *The Burd Papers: The Settlement of the Waggoner's Accounts Relating to General Braddock's Expedition towards Fort Duquesne* (1899)
Walpole, Horace, John Brooke (ed.), *Memoirs of King George II, January 1751-March 1754* (Yale, 1985)
_____, *Memoirs of King George II, March 1754–1757* (Yale, 1985)
_____, *Memoirs of King George II, 1758–1760, Appendices and Index* (Yale, 1985)
Washington, George, *The Journal of Major George Washington, sent by the Hon. Robert Dinwiddie, Esq; His Majesty's Lieutenant Governor, and Commander in Chief of Virginia, to the Commandant of the French forces on Ohio, To which are added the Governor's letter and a translation of the French Officer's answer* (Colonial Williamsburg, 1959)
Washington, George, Fred Anderson (ed.), *George Washington Remembers: Reflections on the French and Indian War* (Maryland, 2004)
Washington, George, Worthington Chauncey Ford (ed.), *The Writings of George Washington, Collected and Edited by Worthington Chauncey Ford* (New York and London: G. P. Putnam's Sons, 1889–1893). Vol. I (1748–1757).
Wilson, Beckles (ed.), *The Life and Letters of James Wolfe* (London, 1909)
Winter, Richard, *The Importance and Necessity of His Majesty's Declaration of War with France Considered and Improved, in a Sermon Preached, May 23, 1756, at the Meeting-House in Moorfields and to the Congregation of Protestant Dissenters at Islington* (London, 1756)
Wolfe, James, 'Instructions drawn up by the late Major General Wolfe for the 20th Regiment of Foot, then lying in Canterbury, in case of the French landing in 1755', in *The Gentleman's Magazine*, Volume 29, 1759.
Wright Louis B. & Elaine W. Fowler, *English Colonisation of North America: Documents of Modern History* (London 1968)
Young, Arthur, *Political Essays concerning the Present State of the British Empire* (London, 1772)

PhD Theses

Bannerman, Gordon Elder, *British Army Contracts and Domestic Supply, 1739–1764* (PhD Thesis, University of London, 2005)
Bassett, J. H., *The Purchase System in the British Army, 1660–1871* (PhD thesis, Boston University, 1969)
Hendrix, James N., *The Spirit of the Corps: The British Army and the Pre-National Pan-European Military World and the origins of American Martial Culture, 1754–1783* (PhD Thesis, University of Pittsburgh, 2005)

Wood, Andrew B., *The Limits of Social Mobility: Social Origins and Career Patterns of British Generals, 1688–1815* (PhD Thesis, London School of Economics and Political Science, 2011)

Yagi, George, *A Study of Britain's Military Failure During the Initial Stages of the Seven Years' War in North America, 1754–1758* (PhD thesis, Exeter University, 2007)

SECONDARY SOURCES

Alden, John Richard, *Robert Dinwiddie: Servant of the Crown* (Charlottesville: University Press of Virginia, 1973)

Anderson, Fred, *A People's Army: Massachusetts Soldiers & Society in the Seven Years' War* (Virginia: The University of North Carolina Press, 1984)

_____, *The Crucible of War: The Seven Years War and the fate of Empire in British North America, 1754–1766* (New York, 2000)

_____, *The War that made America: A Short History of the French and Indian War* (Penguin Books, 2005)

Armitage, David, Michael J. Braddick (eds.), *The British Atlantic World, 1500–1800* (New York: Palgrave McMillan, 2002)

_____, *The Ideological Origins of the British Empire* (Cambridge: Cambridge University Press, 2000)

Arneil, Barbara, *John Locke and America: The Defence of English Colonialism* (Oxford, 1996)

Axtell, James, *Beyond 1492: Encounters in Colonial North America* (New York: Oxford University Press, 1992)

Axtell, James, *European and Indian: Essays in the Ethnohistory of Colonial America* (New York: Oxford University Press, 1981)

_____, *The Invasion Within: The Contest of Cultures in Colonial America* (New York: Oxford University Press, 1985)

Ayling, Stanley, *The Elder Pitt: Earl of Chatham* (New York: David McKay Company Inc. 1976)

Baily, Bernard and Philip D. Morgan (eds.), *Strangers within the Realm: Cultural Margins of the First British Empire* (North Carolina: University of North Carolina Press, 1991)

Bancroft, George, *History of the United States of America, from the Discovery of the American Continent*, Vol. IV (10 vols. Boston: Little, Brown and Company, 1942)

Barker, A. J., *Redcoats* (London. Gordon Cremonesi Ltd. 1976)

Bartlett, T. and K. Jeffrey (eds.), *A Military History of Ireland* (Cambridge: Cambridge University Press, 1996)

Baugh, Daniel A., *The Global Seven Years War, 1754–1763: Britain and France in a Great Power Contest* (Harlow: Longman, 2011)

Bickham, Troy O., *Savages within the Empire: Representations of American Indians in Eighteenth-Century Britain* (Oxford: Oxford University Press, 2005)
Black, Jeremy, *America or Europe? British Foreign Policy, 1739–63* (London: UCL Press, 1998)
_____, *Debating Foreign Policy in Eighteenth-Century Britain* (Surrey: Ashgate Publishing Limited, 2011)
_____, *Robert Walpole & the Nature of Politics in Early Eighteenth-century England* (Singapore, 1990)
_____, *The British Seaborne Empire* (New Haven: Yale University Press, 2004)
_____, *The Continental Commitment: Britain, Hanover and Interventionism, 1714–1793* (Oxon: Routledge, 2005)
Bonomi, Patricia, *A Factious People: Politics and Society in Colonial New York* (New York: Columbia University Press, 1971)
Boorstin, Daniel J., *The Colonial Experience* (London, 2000)
Borneman, Walter R., *The French and Indian War: Deciding the Fate of North America* (New York: Harper Collins, 2006)
Brereton, J. M., *The British Soldier: A Social History from 1661 to the Present Day* (London: The Bodley Head, 1986)
Brewer, John, *Sinews of Power: War, Money, and the British State, 1688–1783* (New York: Alfred A. Knopf, 1988)
Brown, Gillian, *The Consent of the Governed: The Lockean Legacy in Early American Culture* (Cambridge, MA, 2001)
Browning, Reed, *The Duke of Newcastle* (London, 1975)
Bruce, Anthony, *The Purchase System in the British Army, 1660 – 1871* (London: Royal Historical Society, 1980)
Brumwell, Stephen, *George Washington: Gentleman Warrior* (London: Quercus, 2012)
_____, *Redcoat: The British Soldier and War in the Americas, 1755–1763* (Cambridge: Cambridge University Press, 2002)
_____, *White Devil: An epic story of revenge from the savage war that inspired The Last of the Mohicans* (London: Orion Publishing Group, 2004)
Calhoon, Robert M., *Dominion and Liberty: Ideology in the Anglo-American World* (Illinois: Arlington Heights, 1994)
Calloway, Colin, *New Worlds for All: Indians, Europeans, and the Remaking of Early America* (Baltimore: Johns Hopkins University Press, 1997)
_____, *The Scratch of a Pen: 1763 and the Transformation of North America* (New York: Oxford University Press, 2006)
_____, *The Western Abenaki of Vermont, 1600–1800: War, Migration and Survival of an Indian People* (Oklahoma: University of Oklahoma Press, 1991)
Carbone, Gerald M., *Washington: Lessons in Leadership* (New York: Palgrave MacMillan, 2010)

Cardy, Michael, *The Iroquois in the Eighteenth Century: A Neglected Source* (Personal collection)
Carswell, John, *From Revolution to Revolution: England, 1688–1776* (London: Routledge and Kegan Paul, 1973)
Charteris, Hon. Evan, *William Augustus, Duke of Cumberland: His Early Life and Times (1721–1748)* (London, 1913)
_____, *William Augustus, Duke of Cumberland and the Seven Years War* (London, 1925)
Chet, Guy, *Conquering the American Wilderness: The Triumph of European Warfare in the Colonial Northeast* (Boston: University of Massachusetts Press, 2003)
Clary, David A., *George Washington's First War: His Early Military Adventures* (New York: Simon & Schuster, 2011)
Cleland, Hugh, *George Washington in the Ohio Valley* (Pittsburgh: University of Pittsburgh Press, 1955)
Colley, Linda, *Britons: Forging the Nation, 1707–1837* (London, 1992)
_____, *Captives: Britain, Empire and the World 1600–1850* (New York: Pantheon Books, 2002)
Conway, Stephen, Julie Flavell (eds.), *Britain and America go to War: The Impact of War and Warfare in Anglo-America, 1754–1815* (Gainesville: University Press Florida, 2004)
Conway, Stephen, *War, State and Society in Mid-Eighteenth-century Britain and Ireland* (Oxford: Oxford University Press, 2006)
Corbett, Julian S., *England in the Seven Years War: A Study in Combined Strategy*, Volume I (2 Vols. London: Longman's Green and Co: 1907)
Craig, Neville, B. (ed.), *Washington's First Campaign, Death of Jumonville and the taking of Fort Necessity; Also, Braddock's Defeat; The March of the Unfortunate General explained by a Distinguished Historian, traced on the ground by a Civil Engineer, and exhibited on a neat and accurate Map, prepared under his Direction* (Pittsburgh: Wright & Charlton, 1848)
Crocker, Thomas E., *Braddock's March: How the Man Sent to Seize a Continent Changed American History* (Pennsylvania: Westholme Publishing, LLC, 2011)
Cuneo, John, *Robert Rogers of the Rangers* (1952, reprint, New York: Richardson & Steirman, 1987)
Curtis, Edward E., *The Organization of the British Army in the American Revolution* (New Haven: Yale University Press, 1926; reprint, New York: AMS Press, 1969)
Darlington, Mary Carson (ed.), *History of Colonel Henry Bouquet and the Western Frontiers of Pennsylvania, 1747–1764* (Privately Printed, 1920)
Daniels, Christine, Michael V. Kennedy, *Negotiated Empires: Centres and Peripheries in the Americas, 1500–1820* (London: Routledge, 2002)
Davidson, Robert L. D., *War Comes to Pennsylvania, 1682–1756* (New York: Temple University Publications, 1957)

Delage, Denys, Jane Brierly, (trans.), *Bitter Feast: Amerindians and Europeans in Northeastern North America, 1600–1664* (Vancouver: University of British Columbia Press, 1993)
Dowd, Gregory Evans, *A Spirited Resistance: The North American Struggle for Indian Unity, 1745–1815* (Baltimore: Johns Hopkins University Press, 1992)
_____, *War under Heaven: Pontiac, the Indian Nations and the British Empire* (Maryland, 2002)
Doyle, William (ed.), *Officers, Nobles and Revolutionaries: Essays on Eighteenth-Century France* (London: Hambledon Press, 1995)
Draper, Lyman Copeland, Beleu, Ted Franklin (ed.), *The Life of Daniel Boone* (Pennsylvania: Stackpole Books, 1998)
Duffy, Christopher, *The Military Experience in the Age of Reason, 1713–1789* (New York: Barnes & Nobles Books, 1997)
Dunn, Walter, *Opening New Markets, The British Army and the Old Northwest* (Westport, CT: Praeger, 2002).
Ebersole, Gary L. *Captured by Texts: Puritan to Post-Modern Images of Indian Captivity* (Charlottesville: University Press of Virginia, 1995)
Eccles, William J., *Canadian Society during the French Regime* (Montréal: Harvest House, 1968)
_____, *The Canadian Frontier, 1534–1760* (New York: Holt, Rinehart and Winston, 1969)
_____, *The French in North America, 1500–1783* (Rev. ed. Ontario: Fitzhenry & Whiteside, 1998)
Faragher, John Mack, *Daniel Boone: the Life and Legend of an American Pioneer* (New York: Henry Holt, 1992)
Ferling, John E., *A Wilderness of Miseries: War and Warriors in Early America* (Westport, Conn: Greenwood Press, 1980)
Flexner, James Thomas, *Lord of the Mohawks: A Biography of Sir William Johnson* (Boston: Little Brown and Company, 1979)
Fortesque, Sir John, *A History of the British Army: Volume II, First Part—to the close of the Seven Years War* (London, 1899)
Fregault, Guy, Margaret M. Cameron, (trans.), *Canada: The War of Conquest* (Toronto, 1969)
Frey, Sylvia, *The British Soldier in America: A Social History of Military Life in the Revolutionary Era* (Austin, TX: University of Texas Press, 1981)
Fuller, John Frederick Charles, *British Light Infantry in the Eighteenth Century* (London: Hutchinson, 1925)
Galloway, Alan (ed.), *Colonial Wars of North America, 1512–1763* (New York, 1996)
Gann, Lewis, *Guerrillas in History* (California: Stanford University Press, 1971)

Gipson, Lawrence Henry, *The British Empire before the American Revolution*, Vol. VI, The *Great War for the Empire: The Years of Defeat, 1754–1757* (New York, 1968)

Godfrey, William G. *Pursuit of Profit and Preferment in Colonial North America: John Bradstreet's Quest* (Ontario: Wilfrid Laurier University Press, 1982)

Gould, Elijah H. *The Persistence of Empire: British Political Culture in the Age of the American Revolution* (Chapel Hill, 2000)

Greene, Jack P., J. R. Pole (eds.), *A Companion to the American Revolution* (Malden, MA: Blackwell Publishing Ltd, 2000)

Greene, Jack P., *Peripheries and Centre: Constitutional Development in the Extended Polities of the British Empire and the United States, 1607–1788* (Georgia: University of Georgia Press, 1986)

_____, *The Constitutional Origins of the American Revolution* (Cambridge: Cambridge University Press, 2011)

_____, *The Quest for Power: The Lower Houses of Assembly in the Southern Royal Colonies, 1689–1776* (North Carolina: University of North Carolina Press, 1963)

_____, *Negotiated Authorities: Essays in Colonial Political and Constitutional History* (Charlottesville, Virginia: University of Virginia Press, 1994)

Greer, Allan, *The People of New France* (Toronto: University of Toronto Press, 1997)

Grenier, John, *The Far Reaches of Empire: War in Nova Scotia, 1710–1760* (Oklahoma: University of Oklahoma Press, 2008)

_____, *The First Way of War: American War Making of the Frontier* (Cambridge: Cambridge University Press, 2005)

Grutz, Stephen G. and James H. Hutson, (eds.) *Essays on the American Revolution* (North Carolina: Chapel Hill, 1973)

Guy, Alan, *Oeconomy and Discipline: Officership and Administration in the British Army 1714–1763* (Manchester: Manchester University Press, 1985)

Hadden, James, Washington's *Expeditions (1753–1754) and Braddock's Expedition (1755) with history of Tom Fausett, the slayer of General Edward Braddock* (Second Edition, Pennsylvania, 1910)

Hanna, William S., *Benjamin Franklin and Pennsylvania Politics* (California: Stanford University Press, 1964)

Harding, Nick, *Hanover and the British Empire, 1700–1834* (Woodbridge, 2007)

Harris, Richard Cole. *The Seigneurial System in Early Canada: A Geographical Study, with a New Preface* (Wisconsin. McGill-Queen's University Press, 1984)

Hay, Douglas, Linebaugh, Peter, Rule, John G., Thomson, E.P., & Winslow, Cal, *Albion's Fatal Tree: Crime and Society in Eighteenth-century England* (New York, 1975)

Hay, D., Rogers, N., *Eighteenth-century English Society* (Oxford, 1997)

Hayter, Tom, *The Army and Crown in Mid-Georgian England* (Totowa, NJ: Rowman and Littlefield, 1978)

Henretta, James A., *Salutary Neglect: Colonial administration under the Duke of Newcastle* (Princeton, 1972)
Herbert, Archer Butler, *Braddock's Road and Three Relevant Papers*, Historic Highways of America, Volume IV (Cleveland: Arthur H. Clark Company, 1903)
Higginbotham, Don, *George Washington and the American Military Tradition* (Georgia: Georgia University Press, 1985)
Hichberger, J. W. M., *Images of the Army: The Military in British Art, 1815–1914* (Manchester: Manchester University Press, 1988),
Hinderaker, Eric, *Elusive Empires: Constructing Colonialism in the Ohio Valley, 1673–1800* (New York, 1997)
Hinderaker, Eric, Peter C. Mancall, *At the Edge of Empire: The Backcountry in British North America* (Baltimore: Johns Hopkins University Press, 2003)
Hofstra, Warren, *The Planting of New Virginia: Settlement and Landscape in the Shenandoah Valley* (Baltimore: John Hopkins University Press, 2004)
Holmes, Richard, *Redcoat: The British Soldier in the Age of Horse and Musket* (London: Harper Collins, 2001)
Horn, Bernard (ed.), *The Canadian Way of War: Serving the National Interest* (Toronto: Dundurn Press, 2006), 32.
Houlding, J. A., *Fit for Service: The Training of the British Army 1715–1795* (Oxford, 1981)
Hurt, R. Douglas, *The Ohio Frontier: Crucible of the Old Northwest, 1720–1830* (Indiana: Indiana University Press, 1996)
Inscoe, John C. (ed.), *James Edward Oglethorpe: New Perspectives on His Life and Legacy* (Savannah: Georgia Historical Society, 1997)
Jennings, Francis, *Empire of Fortune: Crowns, Colonies and Tribes in the Seven Years War in America* (New York, 1988)
_____, *The Ambiguous Iroquois Empire: The Covenant Chain Confederation of Indian Tribes with English Colonies from its beginnings to the Lancaster Treaty of 1744* (New York, 1984)
_____, *The Invasion of America: Indians, Colonialism, and the Cant of Conquest* (Chapel Hill: University of North Carolina Press, 1975)
Kent, Donald H., *The French Invasion of Western Pennsylvania* (Harrisburg: Pennsylvania Historical and Museum Commission, 1954)
Kierner, Cynthia A., *Traders and Gentlefolk: The Livingstons of New York, 1675–1790* (New York: Cornell University Press, 1992)
Kopperman, Paul E., *Braddock at the Monongahela* (Pittsburg, 1992)
Kupperman, Karen Ordahl, *Indians and English: Facing Off in Early America* (Cornell University Press, 2000)
Labaree, Leonard Woods, *Royal Government in America: A Study of the British Colonial System before 1783 2nd Edition* (New Haven: Yale University Press, 1930)

Leach, Douglas Edward, *Arms for Empire: A Military History of the British Colonies in North America, 1607–1763* (New York, 1973)
Lengel, Edward G., *General George Washington: A Military Life* (New York: Random House, 2005)
Lenman, Bruce, *Britain's Colonial Wars, 1688–1763* (Harlow, 2001)
Lewis, A. R., *The American Culture of War* (New York, 2007)
Leyland, Herbert T., *The Ohio Company: A Colonial Corporation* (Cincinnati, 1921)
MacLeod, Peter, *The Canadian Iroquois and the Seven Years War* (Toronto, 1996)
Malone, Patrick M. *The Skulking Way of War: Technology and Tactics Among the New England Indians* (Baltimore: John Hopkins University Press, 1991)
Mancall, Peter C. and James H. Merrell (eds.), *American Encounters: Natives and Newcomers from European Contact to Indian Removal*, 1500–1850 (New York: Routledge, 2000),
Mancel, Frank, *Film Study: An Analytical Bibliography* (London: Associated University Presses, 1990)
Marsh, James H., *The Canadian Encyclopaedia*, Volume IV, (Edmonton: Hurtig Publishers, 1988)
Marshall, Peter. J. *The Oxford History of the British Empire*, Vol. II: *The Eighteenth-Century* (Oxford, 1998)
Marshall, Peter J. and Glyn Williams (eds.), *The British Atlantic Empire before the American Revolution* (London, 1980)
Marston, Daniel, *The Seven Years War* (Chicago and London: Fitzroy Dearborn, 2001)
McCardell, Lee, *Ill Starred General: Braddock of the Coldstream Guards* (Pittsburgh: University of Pittsburgh Press, 1958)
McClung, Robert M., *Young George Washington and the French and Indian War, 1753–1758* (Connecticut, 2002)
McConnell, Michael, *A Country in Between: The Upper Ohio Valley and its Peoples, 1724–1774* (Nebraska: University of Nebraska Press, 1992)
_____, *Army and Empire: British Soldiers on the American Frontier*, 1758–1755 (University of Nebraska Press, 2004)
_____, *The Politics of War: Race, Class, & Conflict in Revolutionary Virginia* (North Carolina: University of North Carolina Press, 2000)
Merrell, James H., *Into the American Woods: Negotiators on the Pennsylvanian Frontier* (New York: W. W. Norton & Company, 1999)
Merritt, Richard L., *Symbols of American Community, 1735–1775* (New Haven. Yale University Press, 1966)
Middleton, Richard, *The Bells of Victory: The Pitt-Newcastle Ministry and the Conduct of the Seven Years War, 1757–1762* (Cambridge, 1985)
Middleton, Richard, Anne Lombard, *Colonial America: A History to 1763* (4th edn., John Wiley and Sons, 2011)

Moore, Bob, Henk van Nierop (eds.), *Colonial Empires Compared: Britain and the Netherlands, 1750–1850* (Hampshire: Ashgate Publishing Limited, 2003)
O'Toole, Fintan, *White Savage: William Johnson and the invention of America* (London: Faber and Faber, 2005)
Pargellis, Stanley, *Lord Loudoun in North America* (Yale, 1961)
Parker, Geoffrey, *The Military Revolution. Military Innovation and the Rise of the West, 1500–1800* (Cambridge: Cambridge University Press, 1988)
Parkman, Francis, *Montcalm and Wolfe: The French and Indian War* (Da Capo Press, 1995)
Parkman, Francis, Tebbel, John (ed.), *The Battle for North America*, (London, 2001)
Parry, J. H., *Trade and Dominion: The European Overseas Empires in the Eighteenth-Century* (New York, 1971)
Peckham, Howard H., *The Colonial Wars, 1689–1762* (Chicago: University of Chicago Press, 1964)
Penack, William P., Richter, Daniel, K., *Friends and Enemies in Penn's Woods: Indians, Colonists and the Racial Construction of Pennsylvania* (Pennsylvania: The Pennsylvania State University Press, 2004)
Perry, James M., *Arrogant Armies: Great Military Disasters and the Generals Behind them* (John Wiley and Sons Inc., 1996)
Plank Geoffrey, *An Unsettled Conquest: The British Campaign Against the Peoples of Acadia* (Pennsylvania: University of Pennsylvania Press, 2003)
_____, *Rebellion and Savagery: The Jacobite Rising of 1745 and the British Empire* (Pennsylvania: University of Pennsylvania Press, 2005)
Pole, J. R., *Political Representation in England and the Origins of the American Republic* (Stanford, 1966)
Preston, David L., *Braddock's Defeat: The Battle of the Monongahela and the Road to Revolution* (New York: Oxford University Press, 2015)
Quimby, Robert S., *The Background of Napoleonic Warfare: The Theory of Military Tactics in Eighteenth-Century France* (New York: AMS Press Inc., 1973)
Reid, John Phillip, *The Constitutional History of the American Revolution*, 4 Vols. (Madison: University of Wisconsin Press, 1986–1993)
Reid, Stuart, *Wolfe: The Career of General James Wolfe from Culloden to Quebec* (New York: Sarpedon, 2000)
Richter, Daniel, *The Ordeal of the Longhouse: Peoples of the Iroquois League in the Era of European Colonisation* (Chapel Hill: University of North Carolina Press, 1992)
Robson, Eric, *The American Revolution: In its Political and Military Aspects, 1763–1783* (New York: W.W. Norton & Company Inc., 1966)
Rogers, Alan, *Empire and Liberty: American Resistance to British Authority, 1755–1763* (Los Angeles: University of California Press, 1974)

Rogers, Clifford, J. *The Military Revolution Debate: Readings on the Transformation of Early Modern Europe* (Boulder: Westview Press, 1995)

Rogers, Colonel H. C. B. *The British Army of the Eighteenth Century* (London, 1977)

Sarson, Steven, *British America 1500–1800: Creating Colonies, Imagining an Empire* (London: Hodder Arnold, 2005)

Schumann, Matt, Schweizer, Karl W., *The Seven Years War: A Transatlantic History* (London: Routledge, 2007)

Schutz, John, *William Shirley: King's Governor of Massachusetts* (North Carolina: Chapel Hill, 1961)

Selesky, Harold, *War and Society in Colonial Connecticut* (New Haven: Yale University Press, 1990)

Shannon, Timothy J., *Colonists at the Crossroads of Empire: The Albany Congress of 1754* (New York: Cornell University Press, 2000)

Shy, John, *Toward Lexington: the role of the British Army in the American Revolution* (Princeton, NJ: Princeton University Press, 1965),

Silver, Peter, *Our Savage Neighbours: How Indian War Transformed Early America* (London: W. W. Norton & Company, 2008)

Smith, Warren Hunting (ed.) *Horace Walpole: Writer, Politician and Connoisseur: Essays on the 250th Anniversary of Walpole's Birth* (London, 1967)

Smith, William, *The History of the Late Province of New York, from its Discovery to the Appointment of Governor Colden in 1762*, Vol. II (New York Historical Society, 1830)

Spalding, Phinizy, *Oglethorpe in America* (Chicago: University of Chicago Press, 1977).

Spalding, Phinizy and Jackson, Edwin L. J., *James Edward Oglethorpe: A New Look at Georgia's Founder* (University of Georgia, 1988).

Spalding, Phinizy and Jackson, Harvey H. (eds.), *Oglethorpe in Perspective: Georgia's Founder after Two Hundred Years* (Tuscaloosa: University of Alabama Press, 1989).

Starkey, Armstrong, *European and Native American Warfare, 1675–1815* (London: University College London, 1998)

Steele, Ian K., *Betrayals: Fort William Henry & the 'Massacre'* (Oxford: Oxford University Press, 1990)

_____, *Guerrillas and Grenadiers: The Struggle for Canada, 1689–1760* (Toronto, 1974)

_____, *The English Atlantic, 1675–1740: An Exploration of Communication and Community* (Oxford, 1986)

_____, *Warpaths: Invasions of North America* (Oxford: Oxford University Press, 1994)

Steele, Ian K. and Rhoden, Nancy L. (eds.), *The Human Tradition in Colonial America* (Wilmington: Scholarly Resources Inc., 1999)

Steppler, Glenn A., *The Common Soldier in the Reign of George III, 1760–1793* (Oxford: Oxford University Press, 1985)
Swartz, Seymour I., *The French and Indian War, 1754–1763: The Imperial Struggle for North America* (Hong Kong: Simon & Schuster, 1994)
Titus, James, *The Old Dominion at War: Society, Politics, and Warfare in Late Colonial Virginia* (Columbia: University of South Carolina Press, 1991)
Thompson, E.P., *Whigs and Hunters: The Origin of the Black Act* (New York, 1975)
Tomasson, Katherine, Buist, Francis, *Battles of the '45* (London, 1978)
Torrens, William M., *History of Cabinets: From the Union with Scotland to the Acquisition of Canada and Bengal*, Volume II (London: 1894)
Ultee, Maartin (ed.), *Adapting to Conditions: War and Society in the Eighteenth Century* (Alabama: University of Alabama Press, 1986)
Van Tyne, Claude H., *The Founding of the American Republic: The Causes of the War of Independence* (Florida: Simon Publications, 1922)
Ward, Matthew C., *Breaking the Backcountry: The Seven Years War in Virginia and Pennsylvania, 1754–1765* (Pittsburgh, 2003)
Webb, Stephen Saunders, *The Governors-General: The English Army and the Definition of Empire, 1569–1681* (Chapel Hill: University of North Carolina Press, 1979)
Weigley, Russell F., *The American Way of War: A History of United States Military Strategy and Policy* (Indiana University Press, 1973)
_____, *History of the United States Army*, (Bloomington: Indiana University Press, 1984)
Weslager, C. A., *The Delaware Indians: A History* (New Brunswick: Rutgers University Press, 1972)
White, Richard, *The Middle Ground: Indians, Empires, and Republics in the Great Lakes Region, 1650–1815* (Cambridge: Cambridge University Press, 1991)
Whitworth, Rex, *Field Marshal Lord Ligonier: A Story of the British Army, 1702–1770* (Oxford: Clarendon Press, 1950)
Williams, Basil, *Carteret and Newcastle: A Contrast in Contemporaries* (Cambridge: Cambridge University Press, 1943)
Williams, Noel St. John, *Redcoats Along the Hudson: The Struggle for North America, 1754–1763* (London: Brassey's Classics, 1997)
Wilson, Kathleen, *The Island Race: Englishness, Empire and Gender in the Eighteenth Century* (London: Routledge, 2003)
Wood, George Arthur, *William Shirley: Governor of Massachusetts, 1741–1756*, Volume 1 (New York, 1920)
Wood, William, *The Great Fortress: A Chronicle of Louisbourg, 1720–1760* (Toronto: Glasgow, Brook & Company, 1920)
Wright, Wyllis Eaton, *Colonel Ephraim Williams: A Documentary Life* (Pittsfield, Massachusetts, 1970)

Yorke, Philip C., *The Life and Correspondence of Philip Yorke Earl of Hardwicke Lord High Chancellor of Great Britain* (3 vols. Chicago, University of Chicago Press: 1913)

JOURNAL ARTICLES

Abbot, W. W. (ed.), 'General Edward Braddock in Alexandria: John Carlyle to George Carlyle, 15 August 1755', *The Virginia Magazine of History and Biography*, Vol. 97, No. 2 (April, 1989), pp. 205-214

Anderson, Fred, 'Why Did Colonial New Englanders Make Bad Soldiers? Contractual Principles and Military Conduct During the Seven Years War', *The William and Mary Quarterly*, 3rd series, No. 3 (1981), pp. 395-417

Barr, Daniel P. 'Victory at Kittanning? Reevaluating the Impact of Armstrong's Raid on the Seven Years' War in Pennsylvania', *The Pennsylvania Magazine of History and Biography* Vol. 131, No. 1 (Jan., 2007), pp. 5-32

Baugh, Daniel, 'Great Britain's "Blue-Water" Policy, 1689-1815', *International History Review*, X (1988), pp. 23-58

_____, 'Withdrawing From Europe: Anglo-French Maritime Geopolitics, 1750-1800', *International History Review*, XX (1998), pp. 1-32

Browning, Reed, 'The Duke of Newcastle and the Imperial Election Plan, 1749-1754, *The Journal of British Studies*, Vol. 7, No. 1 (Nov., 1967) 22-47

Cardy, Michael, 'A French Officer among the Iroquois in the Early 18th Century', reprinted from: *North Dakota Quarterly* 55 (Summer 1987)

Clayton, T.R. 'The Duke of Newcastle, the Earl of Halifax, and the American Origins of the Seven Years War', *The Historical Journal* Vol. 24, No. 3 (Sept., 1981) pp. 471-603

Conway, Stephen, 'Continental Connections: Britain and Europe in the Eighteenth Century', *The Journal of the Historical Association*, Vol. 90, Issue 299 (July, 2005) pp. 353-374

Davis, Darnell, N. 'British Newspaper accounts of Braddock's Defeat', *The Pennsylvania Magazine of History and Biography*, Vol. 23, No. 3, (1899)

Eid, Leroy V., 'A Kind of Running Fight:' Indian Battlefield Tactics in the Late Eighteenth-century, *Western Pennsylvania Historical Magazine*, LXXI, 1998, pp. 147-171

Fleming, Thomas, 'Braddock's Defeat', *Military History Quarterly*, Vol. 3 (Autumn, 1990), pp. 84-95

Gilbert, Arthur N. 'The Regimental Courts Martial in the Eighteenth Century British Army', *Albion 8, No. 1* (Spring 1976)

Graham, Dominic, 'The Planning of the Beausejour Operation and the Approaches to War in 1755', *The New England Quarterly*, Vol. 41, No. 4 (Dec., 1968), pp. 551-556

Greene, Jack P., 'The Case of the Pistole Fee: The Report of a Hearing on the Pistole Fee Dispute before the Privy Council, June 18, 1754', *The Virginia Magazine of History and Biography*, 66, No. 4 (October, 1958), pp. 399–422
_____, 'Landon Carter and the Pistole Fee dispute', *The William and Mary Quarterly, Third Series*, Vol. 14, No 1 (Jan, 1957) pp. 66–69
Hagist, Don N., 'The Women of The British Army in America', *The Brigade Dispatch*, 24/3 (1994): 2–10; 24/4 (1994): 9–17; 25/1 (1995): 8–14, <http://www.revwar75.com/library/hagistbritwomen.htm>
Higonnet, Patrice Louis-Rene, 'The Origins of the Seven Years War', *The Journal of Modern History*, Vol. 40, No. 1 (Mar., 1968) pp. 57–90
Houston, Alan, 'Benjamin Franklin and the "Wagon Affair" of 1755', *The William and Mary Quarterly*, Third Series, Vol. 66, No. 2 (April 2009) pp.235–286
Irvine, Dallas, 'The First British Regulars in North America', *Military Affairs*, Vol. 9 (Winter, 1945), 337–354
Jennings, Francis, 'Francis Parkman: A Brahmin among Untouchables', *The William and Mary Quarterly*, 42, no.3 (1985), pp. 306–328
Jones, Clyve, 'The Duke of Newcastle's Letters on the Fall of Walpole in 1742', *The Electronic British Library Journal* (2013), art. 1, pp. 1–9 <http://www.bl.uk/eblj/2013articles/article1.html>
Ketchem, Ralph L. 'Conscience, War, and Politics in Pennsylvania, 1755–1757', *The William and Mary Quarterly*, 3rd series 20, No. 3 (1963), pp. 416–439
Kopperman, Paul E., 'The Cheapest Pay': Alcohol Abuse in the Eighteenth Century British Army', *The Journal of Military History*, 60/3 (Junes, 1996): pp. 445–70
Knowles, Nathaniel, 'The Torture of Captives by the Indians of Eastern North America', *Proceedings of the American Philosophical Society*, Vol. 82, No. 2 (Mar. 22, 1940) pp. 151–225
Lenschau, Justus M. Jr., 'Braddock's Defeat', *Military Review*, Vol. 51 (Nov. 1971), pp. 30–40
Lewis Jr., Theodore B. 'The Crown Point Campaign, 1755', *The Bulletin of the Fort Ticonderoga Museum* 12, No. 6 (1970), 13, No. 1 (1970), 13, pp. 400–426, 19–88
Mahon, John K., 'Anglo-American Methods of Indian Warfare, 1676–1794', *Mississippi Valley Historical Review*, XLV (1958) pp. 254–275
Marshall, Douglas W. 'The British Engineers in America: 1755–1783', *The Journal of the Society for Army Historical Research*, 51 (Autumn, 1973)
McCulloch, Ian, 'Within ourselves...' The Development of British Light Infantry in North America during the Seven Years War, *Canadian Military History*, Volume 7, (1998)
Meany Jr., Joseph F., 'Bateaux and Battoe Men: An American Colonial Response to the Problem of Logistics in Mountain Warfare', *New York State Military*

Museum and Veteran Research Centre: *NYS Division of Military and Naval Affairs* <http://www.dmna.ny.gov/historic/articles/bateau.htm>

Miley, Mary, 'Slave Conspiracies in Colonial Virginia', *Colonial Williamsburg Journal*, Winter 2005-2006, <http://www.history.org/foundation/journal/winter05-06/conspiracy>

Mulkearn, Louis, 'Why the Treaty of Logstown, 1752?' *The Virginia Magazine of History and Biography* Vol. 59, No. 1 (Jan. 1951), pp. 3-20

Nichols, F. T. 'The Organization of Braddock's Army', *William and Mary Quarterly*, Vol. IV (1947), pp. 125-147

Nobles, Gregory H., 'Breaking the Backcountry: New Approaches to the Early American Frontier, 1750-1800', *William & Mary Quarterly*, 3rd ser., 46 (1989), pp.642-43

Olson, Alison Gilbert, 'The British Government and Colonial Union, 1754', *The William and Maryland Quarterly*, Third Series, Vol. 17, No. 1 (Jan., 1960) 22-34

Paret, Peter, 'Colonial Experience and European Military Reform at the End of the Eighteenth Century', *Historical Research*, Vol. 37, Issue 95, (May, 1964), pp. 47-59

Pargellis, Stanley, 'Braddock's Defeat', *The American Historical Review*, Vol. 41, No. 2 (Jan., 1936) pp. 253-269

Parmenter, Jon, 'After the Mourning Wars: The Iroquois as Allies in Colonial North American Campaigns, 1676-1760', *The William and Mary Quarterly*, Third Series, Vol. 64, No. 1, pp. 39-76

Riker, Thad W. 'The Politics behind Braddock's Expedition', *The American Historical Review*, Vol. 13, No. 4 (Jul., 1908), pp. 742-752

Russell, Peter, 'Redcoats in the Wilderness: British Officers and Irregular Warfare in Europe and America, 1740-1760', The *William and Mary Quarterly*, 3rd Ser., Vol. 35 No. 4 (October, 1978) pp. 629-652

Sosin, Jack M., 'Louisburg and the Peace of Aix-la-Chapelle', *The William and Mary Quarterly, Third Series*, Vol. 14, No. 4 (October, 1957), pp.516-535

Spencer, Richard Henry, Richard Henry Spencer, 'The Carlyle House and its Associations—Braddock's Headquarters—Here the Colonial Governors met in Council, April, 1755', *The William and Mary Quarterly*, Vol. 18, No. 1 (July 1909), pp. 1-17

Steele, Ian, 'Shawnee Origins of their Seven Years War', *Ethnohistory*, 53, no.4 (2006), pp. 657-87

Steppler, Glenn, 'British Military Law, Discipline, and the Conduct of Regimental Courts Martial in the Later Eighteenth-century', *The English Historical Review*, Vol. 102, No. 405 (Oct., 1987), pp. 859-886

Tatum III, William P., 'Challenging the New Military History: The Case of Eighteenth-Century British Army Studies', *History Compass 5.1* (2007), 72-84

Thayer, Theodore, 'The Army Contracts for the Niagara Campaign, 1755–1756', *The William and Mary Quarterly*, Third Series, Vol. 14, No. 1 (January, 1957), pp. 31–46

Ward, Matthew C., 'Fighting Old Women:' Indian strategy on the Virginian and Pennsylvanian frontier, 1754–1758, *The Virginia Magazine of History and Biography* Vol. 103, No. 3 (July, 1995), pp. 297–320

Way, Peter, 'Rebellion of the Regulars: Working Soldiers and the Mutiny of 1763–1764', *William and Mary Quarterly*, 3rd ser., 57/4 (2000)

Yaple, Robert L., 'Braddock's Defeat: The Theories and a Reconsideration', *Journal of the Society for Army Historical Research*, Vol. XLVI, No. 188 (Winter 1968), pp. 194–201

WEBSITES

'Lake Champlain Maritime Museum', http://www.lcmm.org/

'McCord Museum, Montreal History Museum', http://www.mccord-museum.qc.ca/

'The Benjamin Franklin Tercentenary', http://www.benfranklin 300.org/

Index

A

Acadia. *See* Nova Scotia
Albany, 91n32, 91n40, 92n49, 151, 153, 156, 179n24, 180n33, 183n79
Albany Plan of Union, 92n49
Alexandria, 9, 152–7, 166, 227
American empire, 3, 7, 10, 21, 24, 28, 53, 59, 64, 86, 128, 152
American Revolution. *See* Revolutionary period and American War of Independence
Anglo-American, 6–8, 13, 26, 29, 31–6, 56, 64, 65, 67, 71, 97, 100, 146, 158, 171, 173, 191, 193, 194, 212, 231, 232, 234
anonymous British officer, 205, 216
Appalachian Mountains, 22
Atlantic World. *See* British Atlantic World

B

backcountry, 14, 41n5, 52, 72, 86, 91n30, 99, 117, 134, 142, 158, 161, 164, 177, 177n1, 181n45, 191, 215, 220n18, 228, 229
Batman, Robert Cholmley's, 182n57, 196, 200, 204, 210, 215, 218n2, 218n4, 220n26, 221n34, 223n52, 223n58
Battle of Lake George, 227
Battle of the Monongahela. *See* Battle of the Wilderness
Battle of the Wilderness, 205
Bellamy, George Anne, 84, 85, 95n87, 95n88, 155
Beujeu, Captain Daniel Hyacinth Mary Lidnard de, 14
Bienville, Celeron de, 36
Bland, Humphrey, 103, 137n17, 173, 184n82, 189, 191, 198, 206, 215–17, 219n16, 221n29
Board of Trade, 37, 38, 42n8, 48n54, 55, 60, 62–4, 66, 69, 78, 87n4, 92n49, 180n32, 228, 233
Boscawen, Admiral Edward, 72, 152
Boston, 15n1, 15n4, 16n15, 43n16, 43n19, 141n60, 151, 153, 155, 218n5

Braddock, Edward (II), 1, 3, 4, 6–11, 13, 15, 25, 26, 35, 36, 47n44, 51, 52, 65–7, 69, 72–4, 76, 77, 79, 80, 85–7, 92n45, 93n64, 97, 100, 101, 109, 112, 114, 118, 134, 136, 139n41, 145–77, 178n11, 179n23, 182n54, 185, 202, 209, 213, 217, 218n7, 219n16, 222n41, 224n62, 228–30, 233, 234
Braddock, Fanny, 80, 95n78
Braddock, Major General Edward
   career, 73, 74
   as a de facto Viceroy, 79
   as a Generalissimo, 10, 150
   governor of Gibraltar, 74
   orders and instructions of, 155
   relationship with colonial assemblies, 114, 146
Braddock Plan. *See also* Cumberland strategy
   central fund for, 69, 146
   prongs of, 36, 229
   weaknesses of, 145
Braddock's defeat, 3, 7, 8, 11, 13, 14, 16n12, 17n15, 18n34, 19n35, 31, 41, 95n83, 97, 98, 135, 136n2, 139n29, 145, 150, 167, 182n57, 183n74, 184n86, 186, 189, 202, 208, 213–15, 217, 218n2, 218n4, 218n7, 218n9, 219n12, 220n19, 220n26, 220n27, 221n34, 222n40, 223n49, 223n52, 223n57, 224n58, 225n65, 227–35, 236n7
British, 2, 21, 51, 97–136, 145, 187, 228
British American empire, 3, 10, 21, 24, 59, 128, 152
British Army
   cultural origins, 99, 104

   discipline, 120–6
   drafting, 108
   experiences of irregular warfare, 126–9
   Irish establishment, 108
   recruiting, 109–16
   resistance to, 104–9
   stereotypes, 101–4
   weaponry and tactics, 116–20
British Atlantic World, 13, 15, 64, 136, 145, 150, 157, 160, 217, 230, 231, 234
British Empire. *See* British American Empire
British Ministry. *See* Newcastle Ministry
Britishness, 11, 64, 70, 115, 151, 232, 233
Brown, Charlotte, 166, 182n60
Burnaby, Reverend Andrew, 23, 41n6
Burton, Lieutenant-Colonel Ralph, 198, 209–11

C
Cameron, Private Duncan, 125, 141n67, 200
Canada (New France). *See* Canadiens
Canadiens, 14, 31, 232
Chignecto Isthmus, 153
Clinton, George (Governor), 25
colonial assemblies. *See* colonial bodies politic; local legislatures; lower houses of assembly
colonial bodies politic, 3, 25, 26
colonial union, 62, 63, 91n34
Conference of Alexandria. *See* Congress of Alexandria
Congress of Alexandria, 152–7

Contrecœur, Claude-Pierre
    Pécaudy de, 174, 192, 220n21
Courer de Bois, 33
Covenant Chain, 4, 5, 15n7, 16n8,
    34, 35, 45n32, 47n42, 88n8
Croghan, George, 37, 47n44, 159,
    167, 169, 170, 175,
    183n72, 187
Croix, Francois de la, 130
Crown Point, 67, 68, 71,
    94n75, 156
Culloden (Battle), 60, 108, 118
Cumberland, Duke of, 3, 10, 51, 59,
    63–5, 70, 76, 85, 86, 90n28,
    91n36, 107, 133, 140n51, 147,
    154, 187, 213
Cumberland strategy, 6
Cuthbertson, Bennett, 102, 121,
    137n13, 140n59

D
Delaware, 34, 37, 46n39, 46n41,
    47n45, 170, 191, 193, 220n21
Delaware (tribe), 34, 37
Dinwiddie, Lieutenant-Governor
    Robert, 16n9, 38, 47n48,
    48n51, 48n54, 49n58, 49n60–
    49n63, 52, 61, 65, 87n2, 87n4,
    91n33, 91n36, 100, 109, 123,
    146, 147, 159, 165, 166, 170,
    172, 178n18, 179n22, 182n68,
    183n78
diplomacy. *See* Native American
    diplomacy
Dumas, Captain Jean-Daniel, 195,
    218n9
Dunbar, Colonel Thomas, 157, 174,
    177, 180n29, 182n63, 199, 201,
    207, 211–15, 221n32, 225n64
Duquesne, Marquis, 37

E
England, 8, 16n15, 18n32, 22, 24,
    28, 29, 38, 44n20, 49n59, 60,
    62, 90n23, 91n32, 92n43, 101,
    111, 114, 117, 121, 122, 124,
    126, 137n18, 138n25, 141n64,
    148, 149, 153, 155, 160,
    178n17, 183n79, 222n38, 234
Ensign Ward, 4
Entick, John, 159, 162, 181n41
Exceptionalism, 203

F
Forbes, General John, 111, 139n36,
    177, 230
Forks of the Ohio, 4, 37–40, 52, 78,
    158
Fort Cumberland, 164–70, 172,
    182n60, 183n71, 220n27,
    221n28, 221n34
Fort Duquesne, 3, 4, 6, 14, 35,
    47n44, 52, 67, 69, 71, 72, 78,
    79, 92n45, 94n75, 109, 111,
    139n41, 145, 147, 150, 153,
    154, 156–8, 161, 166, 168–70,
    172–7, 178n11, 178n16,
    179n25, 180n28, 184n88, 189,
    190, 192–4, 213, 218n7,
    219n16, 219n17, 222n39,
    222n44, 222n45, 224n62,
    224n63, 228, 230, 232, 234
Fort Necessity, 40, 49n66, 52, 61,
    221n38
Fort Niagara, 44n20, 67, 72, 153,
    154, 156, 227
Fort Prince George, 4, 40
Fort Saint-Frédéric
    (Fort St. Frederic). *See* Crown
    Point
Fort Ticonderoga, 103, 232

48th Regiment of Foot, 152
44th Regiment of Foot, 125
Fox, Henry, 53, 60, 67, 91n36, 93n62, 187
France (claim over the Ohio), 27–31
Franklin, Benjamin
  and Braddock, 162
  on colonial jealousies, 23
  Pennsylvania politics, 178n13
  renews hope, 162–4
Franklin, William,
French and Indian War, 1, 21–41, 58, 97, 187
Fry, Colonel Joshua, 40

G
Gage, Lieutenant-Colonel Thomas, 182n63, 187, 191, 197, 201, 209, 215, 219n17, 221n28, 221n32
George I, 70, 76
George II, 59, 70, 76, 88n7, 90n27, 213, 214
Gibraltar, 74, 78, 82, 84, 86
Gist, Christopher, 37, 176
Glenn, James (Governor), 49n59, 100
Gordon, Harry (engineer), 186, 194, 196, 210, 218n3, 223n53
governor-general (of New France), 29
governors (British colonial)
  and Braddock, 146
  relationship with assemblies; and their *domestication*, 234
Grandmaison, Thomas Auguste de, 130
Great Meadows, 6, 40, 49n62, 52
Great War for Empire, 55

H
Halifax, Earl of
  and the Braddock Plan, 65
  as President of the Board of Trade, 66, 228
Halkett, Sir Peter, 176, 180n29, 206, 207, 222n45
Hanover. *See* Hanoverian
Hanoverian, 53, 55, 70, 71, 107, 120, 133, 217
Hardwicke, Earl of, 62–4, 93n62
House of Burgesses, 39, 52, 91n33

I
Illinois, 30
Indian. *See* Native American
Indian affairs, 4, 6, 34, 66, 68, 172, 180n32
Indian diplomacy. *See* Indian affairs
Ireland, 13, 17n23, 63, 67, 78, 86, 91n39, 95n87, 99, 101, 108, 131, 132, 143n85
Iroquois Confederacy, 31, 32, 93n55, 183n77
Iroquois; Iroquois Confederacy, 31, 32, 93n55, 183n77

J
Jacobite Rebellion, 60, 117, 132, 137n18
Jesuit Order, 29
Johnson, William
  commander of Fort Saint-Frédéric expedition, 153, 156
  rivalry with William Shirley, 156
  as Superintendent of Northern Indian Affairs, 68

INDEX 263

Jumonville, Joseph Coulon,
 Sieur de, 40
Justice, mercy and terror, 123–5

K
Keppel, Admiral Augustus, 72, 93n61,
 162, 223n51

L
La Belle Riviere, 37
Lake Champlain, 28, 66, 67,
 127, 153
Langlade, Charles, 38
Lee, Charles, 73, 217, 233, 236n8
Liberty (concept), 46n41, 70, 75, 98,
 105, 112, 113, 115, 121,
 139n46, 151, 154, 229
local legislatures, 24
Logstown, 37, 47n50, 48n51,
 48n54
Loudon, John Campbell Fourth
 Earl of, 25, 229
Louisbourg, 29, 30, 56, 71, 93n60,
 103, 120, 129, 151
Louisiana, 10, 30
lower houses of assembly,
 17n19, 25, 43

M
Mackay, Captain James, 6, 40
manifest destiny, 7, 100, 109, 157,
 205
Maryland, 14, 23, 24, 49n60, 58,
 91n34, 112, 113, 139n37, 157,
 158, 166–8, 179n22, 180n29,
 182n54, 182n60, 182n61,
 184n93
Massachusetts, 24, 25, 34, 46n40,
 47n46, 67, 90n25, 91n38,

 94n75, 114, 123, 139n42,
 140n47, 155, 179n22, 180n31,
 184n90, 221n32, 225n64, 227
Miami (tribe), 34, 37, 38, 48n51,
 191, 220n21
Mingo (tribe), 34, 37, 170–2
Mississippi (river), 30
Mitchell, John, 21, 41n1, 43n16
Monkton, Robert, 4, 153, 227, 228
Monongahela (river), 37, 185, 211,
 212, 218n3
Montcalm, Louis Joseph de,
 1, 44n20, 141n74
Montreal, 28, 44n20, 71, 151, 232
Morris, Robert Hunter (deputy
 governor), 147, 149, 155, 157–60,
 163, 169, 178n7, 178n12,
 178n14, 179n21, 179n22
Mutiny Act, 100, 112, 125

N
Native American, 6, 8, 14, 33–6,
 41n2, 44n23, 44n25, 45n30,
 46n34, 66, 68, 72, 86,
 100, 127, 128, 134, 140n51,
 141n71, 141n74, 157,
 169–72, 174, 188, 193, 196,
 200, 204–6, 208, 214,
 222n39, 230
Native American diplomacy, 157
Newcastle, Duke of. *See* Thomas
 Pelham Holles
Newcastle ministry, 14, 128
New England, 8, 16n15, 28, 29,
 92n13, 114, 117, 121,
 122, 126, 148, 153, 222n38
New France
 its claim to the Ohio Valley, 27–31
 relationship with Native
  Americans, 33
 as a 'wilderness autocracy,', 28

New Military History, 136n5
New York, 6, 7, 11, 15, 16n7, 16n8, 16n11, 17n20, 17n22, 17n24, 18n25, 18n27, 18n28, 18n32, 18n34, 19n36, 23, 25, 28, 31, 36, 42n10, 42n11, 43n13, 43n17, 44n20, 47n46, 48n52, 66, 68, 72, 88n8, 89n20, 90n25, 91n32, 91n38, 93n55, 93n58, 94n75, 95n83, 126, 139, 140n55, 140n57, 141n62, 141n64, 141n66, 142n75, 142n77, 142n78, 151, 153, 155, 156, 167, 177n5, 178n8, 179n20, 179n22, 180n27, 180n28, 180n32, 181n35, 183n79, 183n81, 184n90, 213, 218n5, 218n9, 220n22, 221n32, 221n37, 225n64, 227, 228, 232, 235n1, 235n2, 235n5
North Carolina, 17n19, 43n13, 53, 87n4, 92n41, 140n46, 140n47, 143n85, 166-8, 180n31
North Carolina ranger company, 168
Nova Scotia, 7, 28, 47n46, 56, 66, 68, 71, 109, 111, 126, 153, 235n3

O
Ohio Company, 36, 37, 39, 47n48, 48n57, 159, 160
Ohio River. *See* La Belle Riviere
Ohio Valley, 2, 3, 5, 7, 14, 17n24, 21, 22, 26, 27, 31-6, 48n51, 149, 150, 153, 215, 231
Onondaga, 156
Orme, Captain Robert, 101, 114, 139n44, 167, 176, 179n25,
180n35, 187, 191, 197, 198, 224n62
Ottawa, 191

P
Patriot Whig, 53
Pays d'en Haut,, 28, 29, 45n25, 67
Pennsylvania, 15n5, 15n6, 17n15, 22-4, 36-8, 40, 41n5, 44n21, 46n39, 46n41, 52, 58, 83, 91n30, 111-13, 126, 138n26, 139n39, 141n72, 142n78, 145, 147-50, 154, 155, 157-64, 174, 177n1, 177n6, 178n7, 178n11-178n14, 179n21, 179n22, 181n40, 181n42, 181n50, 187, 191, 198, 220n17, 220n18, 220n27, 223n55, 230
Penn, Thomas (Proprietor, Pennsylvania), 147, 150, 157, 178n12
Penn, William (Proprietor, Pennsylvania), 147
Pepperell's regiment, 109
Petite Guerre,, 86, 99, 127, 129-34, 143n84, 207, 208, 232
Pickawillany, 35, 38, 48n51, 48n54
Pistole Fee dispute, 39, 48n56, 52, 87n3, 91n33
Pitt (ministry), 228
Pitt, William, 53, 55, 64, 70, 151, 231, 234
Potawatomi, 191, 220n21
psychological warfare. *See also* PSYWAR
  effects of, 205, 208
  pre-battle, 216
PSYWAR, 14, 202-13, 216

Q

Quakers. *See* Society of Friends
Quebec, 28, 45n29, 65, 71, 93n60, 101, 103, 120, 232

R

Revolutionary period and American War of Independence, 2, 3
Royal colonies, 17n19, 24, 43n13
Royal Navy, 105, 106, 228
Ryder, Dudley (Chief Justice), 149

S

Saint Pierre, Jacques Legarder de, 39
Salutary Neglect,, 15, 15n2, 17n19, 89n21, 90n26
Saxe, Marshal, 130
Scarouady, 170, 172, 175, 183n70
Scotland, 13, 86, 91n37, 99, 131, 132, 137n18, 200
Seven Years War (1756-1763). *See* Great War for Empire
Shawnee, 34, 37, 191, 220n21
Shirley's Regiment, 113
Shirley, William (governor), 6, 11, 17n20, 36, 67, 90n25, 91n38, 94n75, 113, 139n42, 153, 155, 156, 179n22, 180n31, 184n90, 213, 221n32, 225n64, 227, 228, 231
Six Nations. *See* Iroquois Confederacy
Smith, James, 193, 213, 220n22, 224n59
Society of Friends, 147
South Carolina Regiment, 6, 64
St. Clair, Sir John, 139n44, 149, 158, 163, 167, 168, 172, 176, 181n37, 181n52, 181n53, 189, 190, 198, 206, 218n7, 219n14
Stephen, Adam, 186, 188, 199, 202, 221n36
St. Lawrence (river), 28, 127
Superintendent of Northern Indian Affairs, 68

T

Tanaghrisson, 1
Thomas Pelham Holles, 38, 53
Townsend, Charles, 53, 62
traditional Whig, 55, 60
Treaty of Aix-la-Chapelle, 29, 36, 47n47, 56, 57
Trent, William, 40, 48n51, 48n54
Troupes de la Marine,, 29, 31, 39, 44n22, 174, 192, 196, 208
Troupes de Terre,, 44n22
Turtle Creek, 176, 185

V

Virginia, 16n9, 17n19, 22, 23, 36–9, 41n3, 41n5, 42n9, 42n12, 47n48, 48n56, 48n57, 49n58, 49n60, 52, 58, 63, 67, 87n2, 87n3, 91n30, 91n36, 109, 113, 123, 126, 140n49, 141n61, 141n72, 145–7, 158, 159, 162, 166–8, 173, 177n1, 177n4, 179n22, 180n28, 180n29, 181n42, 182n58, 183n78, 191, 203, 220n18, 224n62, 231

W

Walpole, Horace, 54, 55, 73, 80, 88n7, 90n27, 94n77
Walpole, Robert, 53, 55, 88n7, 90n27

Ward, Edward. *See* Ensign Ward
War of the Austrian Succession, 17n23, 74, 88n13, 107
Washington, George, 6, 17n18, 39, 40, 47n48, 48n57, 49n58, 49n66, 52, 61, 64, 82, 95n84, 98, 122, 140n49, 141n62, 141n63, 157, 167, 168, 174, 176, 180n35, 181n35, 184n84, 186, 188, 203, 211, 212, 217, 221n37, 221n38, 223n56, 230

Whig. *See* Patriot Whig; traditional Whig; Whiggish
Whiggish, 7, 116, 229
Wills Creek, 37, 125, 153, 155, 158, 159, 163–72, 223n53
Wolfe, James (British officer), 1, 45n29, 101, 102, 119, 120, 137n10, 230

The manufacturer's authorised representative in the EU is Springer Nature Customer Service Centre GmbH, Europaplatz 3, 69115 Heidelberg, Germany. If you have any concerns regarding our products, please contact ProductSafety@springernature.com

Printed and bound by CPI Group (UK) Ltd, Croydon, CR0 4YY
23/03/2026
02076736-0009